Richard Le Gallienne

**Retrospective Reviews**

A literary Log - Vol. I

Richard Le Gallienne

**Retrospective Reviews**
*A literary Log - Vol. I*

ISBN/EAN: 9783337078232

Printed in Europe, USA, Canada, Australia, Japan

Cover: Foto ©ninafisch / pixelio.de

More available books at **www.hansebooks.com**

# RETROSPECTIVE REVIEWS

## A LITERARY LOG BY

### RICHARD LE GALLIENNE

VOL. I

1891-1893

LONDON
JOHN LANE: THE BODLEY HEAD
DODD MEAD AND COMPANY
NEW YORK
1896

TO

## ERNEST PARKE

WHO FIRST GAVE ME THE OPPORTUNITY

OF EARNING MY BREAD IN THE PLEASANTEST

OF THE PROFESSIONS, THE FOLLOWING PAGES

ARE AFFECTIONATELY

DEDICATED

# PREFACE

MY original intention in making the following selection from my contributions to critical journalism during the last five years was that such selection might serve as a sort of literary diary of the time, and this service to some extent I believe it will still do. Yet it will not fulfil that intention as completely as I had hoped, for some names that have been much in men's mouths during the time, not a few deservedly, will be missed entirely from these pages. This applies particularly to certain popular novelists, whose novels either did not come my way, or my reviews of which were necessarily—and the necessity for this makes the reviewing of novels so tiresome—little more than *résumés* of the story. Thus I am denied the pleasure of decorating my headlines with such names as those of Messrs. Zangwill, Arthur Morrison, Anthony Hope, Frankfort Moore, Harold Frederic, Morley Roberts, and Coulson Kernahan, also those of Miss Harraden and Miss Ella D'Arcy.

With this exception, however, I think my book will be found representative of what I venture to believe will be most enduring in the literary output of the period it covers. The period chances to have a certain significance in that it marks a notable renaissance of poetry, the rise of a new band of poets, the most important since the Pre-Raphaelite group; and with these new poets has sprung up a new public interest in poetry. This phase of the literary history of the period my book may fairly claim to illustrate in some fulness—though I regret to find, at the last moment, that, by sheer accident, an article on Mr. A. C. Benson has been omitted. This, of course, matters more to me than to Mr.

Benson, but perhaps in a future edition I may be able to supply the deficiency. Also, owing to the fact of her not as yet having published a volume, I have been unable to make any reference to the poetry of Miss Olive Custance, the striking promise of which has been evidenced by her contributions to various magazines.

Along with papers on contemporaries I have included notes on such old poets as Herrick and Drayton; and although in their cases their appearance under certain dates may have little significance, it was necessitated by the general plan of the book, and at any rate it points to the fact that there was a revival of interest in those poets at the time.

The article on Drayton has by some mischance been printed among the 1894 instead of among the 1893 papers.

Though my book thus has a certain *raison d'être* as the gossip of history, I trust that some of its pages may be found to have a more serious critical significance as well. In this respect the value of the various papers, written under such different moods and conditions, will naturally be found to vary. I am aware that some few of my notes on distinguished writers are inadequate. The brief notes on Mr. Austin Dobson and Mr. Henry James do not, I need hardly say, pretend to express any complete view of those delicate writers. I should not have included them had I not been anxious to bring in names so typical of the time. Allowances of this nature I must rely upon the reader to make for me. I would add that I have done my best to preserve only that which should have more than less a permanent interest, either in subject-matter or treatment. Of mere journalism I trust that there will be found few traces, though I have purposely here and there allowed a passing reference to remain, as a hint of the origin of the book.

Finally, I hope that my book will fulfil the first obligation of any book whatsoever—that of being readable. I have found other books of the kind so interesting to dip about in—such a book, for example, as the too little known Nathan Drake's *Literary Hours* —that I have ventured to hope that mine may give a similar pleasure to my own generation However good or bad it may be, it does the reader the service of introducing him to many a better.

My selection has been made from articles contributed to *The Star*, *The Daily Chronicle*, *The Illustrated London News*, *The Sketch*, *The Speaker*, *The Realm*, *The Pall Mall Budget*, *The Nineteenth Century*, *The Century Guild Hobby Horse*, and *The Academy*, to the editors of which I render thanks for their permission to reprint. I desire too to express my gratitude to my sister, Mrs. James Welch, for her kindness in completing the tiresome task of arranging so large a mass of newspaper cuttings, begun for me by my dear wife; also to Mr. Fred Turner, of Brentford Free Library, for his kindness in compiling the Index.

BRENTFORD, *December* 6, 1895.

# SOME FIRST AND SECOND PRIN-CIPLES OF CRITICISM

1. Criticism is the Art of Praise.

2. A critic is a man whom God created to praise greater men than himself, but who, by a curious blindness, has never been able to find them.

3. A critic is one of those candles by which we behold the sun.

4. A critic is one who makes odious comparisons, and invidious distinctions. He is a writer of prey, the shark that gobbles up young writers, or the wasp that stings to pathetic irritation the old ones, and generally he is the cur that snaps and snarls at the heels of success. He is the goal-keeper of literature, the guardian of its vested interests, and it is

his business to keep young genius as long as possible from its birthright.

5. There are three schools of criticism : the school that praises, the school that blames, and the school that judges. The school that praises is the most important.

6. Praise is more important than judgment. It is only at agricultural societies that men dare sit in judgment upon the rose.

7. There is Epical Criticism and Lyrical Criticism. Sainte-Beuve, the Balzac of criticism, may be taken as the type of the one, Charles Lamb of the other.

8. The first thing for a critic to do—is to be thankful that there is anything to criticise.

9. The greatest critic is he who can appreciate the greatest number of beautiful things.

10. A necessary gift for the critic of poetry is—the love of it.

11. Literature is the World in Words.

12. Literary Criticism is man's sulky complaint that he was not invited to the creation.

13. The world is great, and strong, and beautiful: so must be the words. The world is little, and weak, and ugly—but so must never be the words.

14. Literature is the art of writing—not the art of telling stories or of creating character.

15. Many of the great novelists, and all the lesser ones, belong rather to drama than to literature: for as the novel sprang originally from the drama, it still remains a drama—with extended stage directions.

16. Shakespeare is the greatest English poet, not because he created Hamlet and Lear, but because he could write that speech about Perdita's flowers, and Claudio's speech on death in *Measure for Measure*.

17. Keats is the greatest English poet since Shakespeare.

18. The perfection of prose is the essay, of poetry the lyric, and the most beautiful

book is that which contains the most beautiful words.

19. Anything that is not beautiful, or that cannot be *made beautiful*, has no place in literature.

20. It is not sufficient criticism of a writer that he does not suit your taste—though it will be sufficient that he suits it.

21. In criticism you cannot be too positive. Negative criticism dies with what it slays. One critic may 'make' a good book, but fifty cannot kill it.

22. You may point out the spots on the sun, or you may foul with mud the silver face of the moon, but they will each go on shining for all that.

23. 'Personalities' are poor missiles against a Personality.

24. You may deny everything to Greatness, and spit in his face to make it sure: but that will not prevent his going to your funeral.

25. Life, they say, is more important than literature, yet, without literature—what were life?

POSTSCRIPT.

1. A critic is any undergraduate of Oxford or Cambridge.

2. William Watson, John Davidson, Francis Thompson, and W. B. Yeats, are the greatest poets since Algernon Charles Swinburne, Dante Gabriel Rossetti, William Morris, George Meredith, and Coventry Patmore, long since classic—a classic, by the way, being an old book which continues to be read by young men.

3. A gentleman is always a gentleman—even when he writes anonymous criticism.

# RETROSPECTIVE REVIEWS

NOT Shakespeare himself had more confidence in the
immortality of his verse than Robert
Herrick. He was well content to let 'his
poetry' be 'his pillar.'

*Robert Herrick: 'The Muses' Library.'*

> ' Behold this living stone
>   I rear for me,
> Ne'er to be thrown
>   Down, envious Time, by thee.
>
> Pillars let some set up,
>   If so they please :
> Here is my hope
>   And my Pyramides.'

He is constantly giving expression to this comfortable
attitude; not even 'The Nipples of Julia's Breast'—each
as 'a strawberry, half-drown'd in cream'—or her 'tem-
pestuous petticoat,' are more frequent themes. 'To his
Book,' 'To his Muse,' are constantly recurring titles,
bearing witness to that more than maternal delight
which every devoted artist finds in his work. True, that
when Charles I. gave him the living of Dean Prior, in
Devonshire, he wrote : 'Mr. Robert Herick : his farewell
unto Poetrie,' and bade a no less bitter 'Farewell to

Sack,' probably at the same time, yet we all know when the poet is sick, how the poet (like another personage) a saint will be ; and Herrick loved both sack and poetry too well to really forsake them.    No doubt he was far more glad than sorry to be ejected from his living in 1648—on the charge of disloyalty—and be once more free to join his chums in merry London, for it goes without saying that he was hail-fellow with all who loved a song and a glass—and a petticoat.    Not that Herrick never wrote what we somewhat absurdly distinguish as serious verse.    His poem, 'To his Dying Brother, Master William Herrick,' shows that he knew the tragic as well as the pathetic note of life—though there was probably little of tragic feeling in the comfortable relationship of the two brothers.    A poet always thus outsoars his theme :

> 'Life of my life, take not so soon thy flight,
> But stay the time till we have bade good-night.
> Thou hast both wind and tide with thee ; thy way
> As soon despatch'd is by the night as day. . . .
> There 's pain in parting, and a kind of hell,
> When once true lovers take their last farewell.'

And in regard to pathos, is it not really that tender, tearful quality that has made famous the best known of Herrick's verse—the Horatian sigh for youth going and gone, for the beauty that is so fair, and yet so soon past ? His cry is continually ' To the Virgins, to make much of Time,' to the daffodils to

> 'Stay, stay,
> Until the hasting day
> Has run
> But to the evensong.'

2

The passing of the glory of the world is continually filling his eyes with tears, which overflow in pearls that drop within his book. There are people—surely they must have lived in a monastery or a vacuum—who are always puzzled that the men who do these exquisite things in poetry should be sensuous, let us say sensual, in their lives; but apart from the many-sidedness of man, it is surely the sensuous man alone who is capable of these rich tearful moments. One must have lived to have lost, and Herrick lived as generously as Solomon, and his poems are a sort of Restoration Ecclesiastes, with less of the whine and a kinder heart. Yet his 'Noble Numbers,' or his 'Pious Pieces,' though at first they strike one somewhat ludicrously as coming from him, are no mere 'making it right' with the powers above—they are the result of the real religious devotion which was at the bottom of Herrick's, as of every other poet's, heart.

THAT disease of compression, which made so much of Browning's later work artistically worthless, is more than ever Mr. Meredith's master in this new novel. Some men seem to find the unknowable in *The Egoist*, but, compared with much of *One of our Conquerors*, it is simplicity itself. Mr. Meredith refuses point-blank to say a plain thing in a plain way. Indeed, he would seem to take a quite unnatural delight in wrapping simplicity in as many fantastic

*George Meredith: 'One of our Conquerors.'*

3

coverings as he can devise, just for the mere pleasure of watching the bewildered reader open one after another with growing irritation.   Of course he does not mind your being cross ; he enjoys it.   You may take him or leave him ; all's one to him.   But, unfortunately, it is not so with the reader ; he knows quite well that, however unpromising the first chapters may be, the loss will be his if he allows them to discourage him from proceeding.

Take the opening sentence of the book for example : 'A gentleman, noteworthy for a lively countenance and a waistcoat to match it, crossing London Bridge at noon on a gusty April day, was almost magically detached from his conflict with the gale by some sly strip of slipperiness, abounding in that conduit of the markets, which had more or less adroitly performed the trick upon preceding passengers, and now laid this one flat amid the shuffle of feet, peaceful for the moment as the uncomplaining who have gone to Sabrina beneath the tides.'  'Oh ! this is too bad for anything,' you exclaim, and then you tackle the next page, and then another, groping your way through many more, quite unenlightened, and unconsciously going through the successive stages of that poor sufferer sketched for us by Mr. Bernard Partridge, who wrestled with George Meredith, Esquire, and was 'thrown.'  Having borne as much as you can stand, give it up and go to the theatre. Then try again to-morrow, and you will find the fog clearing a little, and you begin to gain a glimmering of who's who and what is going forward.   Soon you scent an interesting social problem, and then at last one of

Mr. Meredith's wonderful women enters, and you have the first moment of real happiness you have known for hours. You feel comfortable after that, and, though the fogs keep continually coming down on you throughout, you know that there is a maid in the mist, and are comforted. Besides, of course, an occasional fine passage has lit up the gloom, and these, indeed, occur more often as you proceed, Mr. Meredith keeping his best wine to the last.

Now, the question arises, is it fair to tell a man's story in a review? It is Mr. Meredith's own fault that I answer in the affirmative, for how can one watch the gasping reader, lost and battling in this Meredithian Atlantic, without sending up a rocket or two to guide his course? I, therefore, venture to submit that the main features of the story are as follows: Victor Radnor, one of the great city princes, is in the prime of life and in the zenith of his ambition. But there is a shadow across his path—a certain Mrs. Burman Radnor, whom, years before, when still in his salad days, he had married, for her money presumably, she being quite double his age. Soon after their marriage, the beautiful Nataly Dreighton had entered their home as lady's companion, and left it soon after as the virtual wife of Radnor, who thus forsook the woman to whom by law he was bound. When the novel opens, Radnor and Nataly have lived before the world as man and wife long enough to have a grown-up daughter, Nesta, and though Mrs. Burman has blown upon them in one or two places where Radnor has striven to set up a country-house, the world at large knows nothing of the story. To all appearance 'the pair are a

5

married couple such as you won't find in ten households over Christendom.'

But, although Nataly was brave enough to take that great step with her lover, she shrinks from the publicity which her husband's ambition seems likely to bring down upon their lives, by his still persisting in the plan of a great country-house. With an instinct for the realities rarely found in women, she would prefer some quiet country nook; for, though she has no actual fear of the world, her sensitive refinement shrinks from the vulgar interpretations it can only put upon love like hers. Radnor persists, however, and 'Lakelands' is safely inaugurated in lavish style, in spite of Mrs. Burman. Nataly and Radnor differ in the same way on another matter, the marriage of Nesta. Radnor, like many another rebel, having become conventionalised with success, wishes the taint on her birth to be covered by an aristocratic alliance, and thus favours the suit of young Dudley Sowerby. But Nataly retains her old reverence for true love, and has always hoped that her daughter would marry Captain Dartrey Fenellan, a handsome, manly fellow of a type dear to Mr. Meredith, that type of the transition period between early manhood and middle age, uniting the unabated vigour of the one with the mature strength and wisdom of the other—handsome, athletic, yet philosophic. To this end she for once acts in opposition to Radnor, and tells young Sowerby of Nesta's birth.

At first he is shocked, but as he really loves and is no coward, in spite of his conventional training, he soon recovers and again presses his suit. But while he was wavering, Nesta, down in Brighton, had been making the acquaintance of a certain Mrs. Marsett, 'a woman,' as the phrase goes, 'with a history'; and had been learning from her of the world and its ways. Nesta's friends protested against the acquaintance, but that only made her cling the closer to the poor pariah, for whom her pity had grown into a real affection. The inherited rebellion in her blood awoke and asserted itself, and then Captain Dartrey Fenellan, being also in Brighton, and being also one upon whom from childhood she had been accustomed to look as a wise elder brother, she appealed to him. But her heart had been undergoing rapid and half unconscious changes, of which when she stood face to face with him she became confusedly aware. He, too, suddenly found a courage and a greatness in her face he had never seen there before, the look of that woman whom he had given up hoping for, having had bitter experience of the sex in an early marriage dissolved by his wife's death some few years before. Without a word of wooing each instantaneously understood the other, and the reader has one more to add to the many great love-scenes of the author.

Nataly's wish is to be fulfilled, but, such an inconstancy is woman, she no sooner suspects it than her conventional maternal fears get the better of her real nature. She has heard of Nesta's intimacy with Mrs. Marsett, and at once flies into a panic lest her daughter's destiny should be like her own. This fear leads her to join forces with Nesta's father, and Dudley Sowerby becomes for both of them the necessary safeguard. He keeps firm to his proposal, but Nesta will have none of him, and, while the issue is pending, Radnor and Nataly are summoned to the bedside of Mrs. Burman, who is near death and wishful to make peace with them before the end. All seems to be promising fair, when at a political meeting news is brought to Radnor not only of Mrs. Burman's death, but of his own Nataly's sudden illness. He hastens to her, but it is too late. The shock unsettles his reason, and we leave him in an asylum—while, after many days, Dartrey and Nesta go for their happy honeymoon to the Lake of Como.

This is, of course, the merest outline, but even from this it will be seen that Mr. Meredith's theme is the most daring he has yet attempted, and one which no living English novelist save himself could be hoped to treat with the robustness it demands. That game of 'tennis with the seventh commandment,' as Mr. Kipling phrases it, which is the stock-in-trade of the lady novelist, has, it is needless to say, nothing in common with Mr. Meredith's serious study of the problem. Once more he brings us face to face with nature for our standard, and leaves us to draw our own conclusions. He tells a vivid story of great people and great passions, and though, being an artist, he does not preach, yet we are not, of course, left in doubt as to his sympathies. What those are we have not had to wait for *One of our Conquerors* to be aware. In the battle of nature against convention Mr. Meredith has always been foremost, and in that quarter of it which concerns what he has called 'the duel between the sexes' he has in each of his novels done memorable service. Once more his women are wonderful. Nataly and Nesta are of the same flesh and blood as Diana, Sandra, Renée, and Clara, the same human and yet reverent creations.  It is indeed that power of being able to look closely and yet reverently at life which lifts Mr. Meredith so high above those mere realists who, as he once more reiterates here, think they know the world 'from having sifted and sorted a lot of our dust-bins.'

In addition to Nataly and Nesta, we have among the crowd of minor characters two studies of the weaker sisterhood, Mrs. Marsett and Mrs. Blathenoy, Dartrey Fenellan's scene with the latter being one of the most striking in the book.  Of another feminine type, Mr. Meredith gives us a sympathetic sketch in Priscilla, the Salvation lass, and by reference to her goes to the heart of the matter in this eminently sane passage : 'Look at your country, see where it shows its vitality ; you don't see elsewhere any vein in movement.  Think of that when the procession sets your teeth on edge. They 're honest foes of vice, and they move—in England !  *For gross maladies gross remedies.*'

Of the purely literary qualities of the book one need say little.  Readers of Mr. Meredith know what to expect when he takes up his pen—an epigram on every other line, an unexampled faculty for the unique word, and a cunning skill in nomenclature.  This last has hardly been sufficiently noted by his commentators. and such names as Crayes and Creckholt, Mrs. Burman, Colney Durance and Dudley Sowerby, bear the unmistakable hall-mark of the deftness which coined the magnificent Sir Willoughby Patterne of Patterne Hall. Beyond a certain point his writing is, of course, a lottery.  There are sure to be some good things, more or less accordingly as he has written in inspired or uninspired moments. This may be held to apply to any writer, but those who read him know that it applies more to Mr. Meredith than to any other, save his great poetical analogue, Browning. And impressionism of all methods is that which can only be successful at the inspired moment. Mr. Meredith does not always wait for that, and there are many pages in his new book, especially in the earlier chapters, as I have already hinted, which are simply gibbering caricatures of a style which in others he practises as magically as ever. What that style is at its best it would need a pen like his own to describe ; so keen and yet so tender, so strong and yet so supple, so delicate and yet so lusty. Few men of brain have blood enough for heart as well ; but by this token Mr. Meredith is of the race of the giants.

IN Philip Bourke Marston's *Last Harvest*, to which his *P. B. Marston :* faithful friend Mrs. Chandler Moulton con- 'A Last tributes a biographical introduction, there Harvest.' is the same magic of cadence, haunting one in lines and verses otherwise not notable, the same poignant passion, the same Shakespearean handling of flowers, and there is likewise the same paucity of meta- phor, and the same monotony of mood, such as we find in all his poetry.

Marston could not suffer as he did, and his art not suffer also. If a man be blind early, paucity of metaphor, for one thing, must follow; for metaphor, the essential power in poetry, is, of course, founded on comparison; it makes one thing speak for another, and it therefore needs a full and varied experience of the objective, outside world, of which a blind man must, necessarily, be to a large extent deprived. And as it restricts him in metaphor, so it must in subject and mood. That Marston's earlier work remains his best (his 'Christmas Vigil' and 'The Rose and the Wind') is a proof of this. When he wrote these, he had still a little sight left him, or, at any rate, his blindness had but recently come upon him. And he wrote objectively with a fine sweep of hand, which promised great things for the future. But then came his blindness, followed by crushing bereavements one upon another, and, left alone in the dark, with no outer world to distract his thoughts from sorrow, no subjects but his own over-wrought emotions, is it to be wondered at that his poems should take on the complexion of his dreary days?

More than half of his work suffers thus, work that would not have been written, even with all his suffering, had he kept his eyesight; expressions of fanciful moods of sorrow, which he would not have deemed worth the pains of his art, in the daylight. But, sitting in the dark, listening to his own tears, he very naturally gave way to them, expressing them too often in a monotonous symbolism, which is another sign of his being cut off from the world of metaphors.

'ON an evening in the latter part of May, a middle-
aged man was walking homeward from
Shaston to the village of Marlott, in the
adjoining vale of Blakemore or Black-
moor. The pair of legs that carried him
were rickety, and there was a bias in his gait which
inclined him somewhat to the left of a straight line.'

*Thomas
Hardy:*
'Tess of the
D'Urbervilles.'

When a novel begins so, who needs to be told that
we are once more in Mr. Thomas Hardy's Arcady of
Wessex, that villages with all kinds of quaint cider-
sounding names lie about us, Bulbarrow, Nettlecombe-
Tout, Dogbury, High Stoy, Bubb Down, and that here
all roads lead to Casterbridge.  The devoted student
of Mr. Hardy would also immediately recognise him
by a less pleasing token in this passage.  Who else,
except maybe Mr. Meredith, would describe the un-
steadiness in the walk home of an aged tippler as
'a bias in his gait which inclined him somewhat to
the left of a straight line'?  But this is only a trifling
example of a defect in Mr. Hardy's style which is
continually making one grind one's teeth, like 'sand
in honey.'  One cannot call it euphuism, because
euphuism tends to 'favour and to prettiness.'  It seems
rather to come from sudden moments of self-consciousness in the midst of his creative flow, as also from
the imperfect digestion of certain modern science
and philosophy which is becoming painfully obtrusive
through the apple-cheek outline of Mr. Hardy's work.
For example, a little boy talks to his sister, 'rather
for the pleasure of utterance than for audience'; a

wooer at a certain hot moment entreats the wooed :
'Will you, I ask once more, show your belief in me
by letting me encircle you with my arm?' Another
lover, trying to persuade Tess that his marrying her
cannot hurt his family, says 'it will not affect even
the periphery of their lives,' and, later on, when the
time has come to forgive, he asks, 'How can forgive-
ness meet such a grotesque prestidigitation as that?'
And when Mr. Hardy would tell us that Tess had
forgotten that children must be expected from their
union, he says that she had been 'forgetting it might
result in vitalisations that would inflict upon others,'
etc. Mr. Hardy continually delights in those long
Latin and Greek words that seem to be made of
springs rather than vowels. Think how absolutely
out of colour in Arcady are such words as 'dolori-
fuge,' 'photosphere,' 'heliolatries,' 'arborescence,' 'con-
catenation,' 'noctambulist'—where, indeed, are such
in colour?—and Mr. Hardy further uses that horrid
verb 'ecstasise.'

No doubt, these are small matters, yet the more
beautiful the rest of the work the more jarring such
defects as these. Why, one such word is as destructive
as an ounce of dynamite in any dream-world, more
especially so in Mr. Hardy's 'Sicilian vales.' Imagine
the effect were such expressions introduced into an idyll
of Theocritus, think how the flute and the pipe would
stop with a shriek before words of such terrible aspect.
They could not more potently destroy our illusion if
they were steam-whistles, and this they are constantly
doing, like the 'doctor' in the rhyme, making us dance

out of Wessex—yes, 'into France,' among other places ;
for study of French authors seems to be having a strong
influence on Mr. Hardy's work of late.    Realism as a
theory seems in danger of possessing him at times,
though happily but intermittently.    In that realism
which is not theory but a necessary artistic instinct,
Mr. Hardy has always been strong.

However, despite those dreadful words, and despite
its painful 'moral,' its noble, though somewhat obtrusive 'purpose,' *Tess of the D'Urbervilles* is one of Mr.
Hardy's best novels, second only to *The Return of the
Native*.    The beautiful simplicity of his style when, as
usual, he forgets he is writing, the permeating healthy
sweetness of his descriptions, the idyllic charm and yet
the reality of his characters, his apple-sweet women,
his old men, rich with character as old oaks, his love-
making, his fields, his sympathetic atmosphere — all
these, and many other of Mr. Hardy's best characteristics, are to be found 'in widest commonalty spread'
in *Tess*.

The motive of *Tess* is one of those simple, and
yet how cruelly tangled, sexual situations round which
'the whole creation moves,' and in which Mr. Hardy
delights to find the eternal meanings.    Mr. Hardy has
heretofore been more inclined to champion man the
faithful against woman the coquette, but in *Tess*
he very definitely espouses the cause of woman, and
devotes himself to show how often in this world—all,
alas, because the best of us is so conventionalised—
when men and women break a law 'the woman pays.'
Of course it is a special pleading, because a novel

might be as readily written to show how often a man pays too. Indeed was not *Middlemarch* such a novel? It is noticeable that most of these books against men are written by men, and that *Middlemarch* is the work of a woman. Such is the gallantry of sex, and such its ironical power.

ONE has only to look a moment at the fine portrait *James* of James Smetham, from a painting by *Smetham:* himself, which is the frontispiece to the *'Letters.'* volume of his *Letters*, to know that we are not to be introduced to a successful man. The face is a beautiful one, finely featured in that distinguished mould so rare latterly that we are beginning to associate it with miniature painting and the high cravat. Smetham, need one say, was nearer our own era than the latter, though he dates far enough back to have had his livelihood as a portrait-painter lost to him by the new invention of photography. I used the word 'successful' entirely in regard to his art, as distinct from his art-business; as when I say we feel a lack of practicality in his face, I do not use the word in that vulgar commercial sense which means a robustious activity and shrewdness in this world's affairs—qualities which, like fire and water in sententious images, are good servants but bad masters, and prone to be dangerous companions for the finer qualities of the soul. I mean that Smetham was unpractical in his art.

Not that he was unstudious ; on the contrary he was most painful in his methodical culture of himself. His sympathetic biographer, Mr. William Davies, gives us an impressive account of the thoroughness with which he not only planned, but carried out, a most comprehensive system of culture in which, of course, as in any service-able system, a specific art training was but one, though a very important part. Did he not, when under the tute-lage of Mr. Wilson, a distinguished architect of Lincoln, spend a whole year in drawing the sculpture about the cathedral? No wonder he should exclaim, 'Ah, me ! great tower of Lincoln, with the white moon shining on thee, how can I forget thee . . . !' It must have been a great time, that year of cloistral work. Then he was in the habit of making pictorial notes of all his ex-periences, filling book after book with symbolism of his thought and emotion. All this was well, it was even 'practical,' but (at any rate as regards art) it was of that unpractical practicality which characterised Shelley—the practicality of the dreamer, of the 'crank.'

One feels a certain slowness, too, about the face. It does not kindle at the eyes ; its gentle light is suffused rather than gathered into a star upon the high brow ; one feels the lack of that central, concentrating force which one generally finds in the faces of those born for the triumphant synthesis of art. The bent of Smetham's mind was analytic, he was industrious to collect, but slow to generalise. This I say without having seen a single picture of his ; but from the impression I receive of the tone of his friends' appreciation of his work, I think I am not wrong. Rossetti and Mr. Ruskin were both admirers of his work ; the latter was a close and helpful friend of his, and one of the most interesting letters describes Smetham's first visit to him in the midst of his home life, while yet a bachelor living with his parents. But somehow their praise seems to lack gusto, or to die off in the utterance, as though they said, ' Yes, beautiful, very beautiful, but . . .' I seem to miss in their praise what I miss in the face.

In the *Letters* it is different. Letters are necessarily the expressions of 'moments,' and finer moments, or a more continuous succession of them, it would be difficult to find, even in the classical letter-writers, than in these of James Smetham. It is the paradox of such natures that they should thus express themselves in the very record of their frustration. Amiel was in some respects a similar example. In confiding to his diary his hopeless inability for expressing his high thought, he expressed what is infinitely more valuable to us, himself. Failure always lets us more into the secrets of success than success itself, because success is a concrete product which has concealed its process. And that is one of the many reasons why Smetham's letters are so interesting. Had he been a ' successful ' painter he would probably never have written these letters, which tell us so much and so finely of a man who came nearer to that com-plete development of a fine spirit which is greatness, than any mere possessor of a one-sided artistic gift. In such a nature as Smetham's one often finds a far deeper sensitiveness, a keener intensity, than in the actual artist, because it is necessary that the latter should not feel too much. He must keep a balance between feeling and control. There is always a certain comparative hardness about him. But such natures as Smetham's feel too much, they continually run over. And yet the painful yearning for expression is none the less to 'ease something of that sense as if a reservoir were straining at its banks in the moonlight among Yorkshire fells'— Smetham's own fine image.

His letters are full of such poetry. For instance, in a wonderful rhapsody on *Wuthering Heights* he compares Heathcliff and Catherine to two figures, strange freaks of granite on a wild moor, which 'seem as if Michael Angelo, striding in his sleep across the wild, had been trying to realise a human nightmare which would not let him rest in his bed.' He has a criticism of 'Maud,' full of delicate perception. He says a fine thing about Keats's letters, and, indeed, little that was published between 1853 and 1877 misses some suggestive reference in his letters. A great part of them is taken up with the record of high spiritual aspiration, as became one who, in no narrow sense, was an ardent Wesleyan. Though he does not escape the tendency of that sect to rhapsodise, his intellectual opposite could not but be moved with some of his fine prayerful utterances.

MR. CHURTON COLLINS'S *Illustrations of Tennyson* is
a book, in many ways, of stimulating
*Churton*
*Collins:* significance. It raises once more several
'Illustrations artistic questions, which, treated abstractly,
of Tennyson.' one might be willing to leave unanswered,
but which, in association with so great a literary figure
as Lord Tennyson, become exceedingly sensitive.

It compels us to think out the whole question of
literary decadence. It sets us inquiring what is the
authentic pleasure we should expect from art: how
far that is dependent on learning, how far on temperament; and, as a corollary, suggests the same inquiry
in regard to artistic criticism.

If, indeed, learning must be the important qualifica-
tion for the answering of these questions, one might
well hesitate to join issue with Mr. Churton Collins:
for these *Illustrations* bear witness to an acquaintance with books, and a memory for their contents,
such as that of the Magliabecchis of old time.

But, in Mr. Collins's prodigious memory for passages
exists for me the most significant criticism of his book.
It suggests the wide difference between a commentator
and a critic : the same difference on which Mr. Collins
insists, and rightly insists, as distinguishing the 'literary'
from the 'original' poet in his manipulation of old
material. In the latter case, says Mr. Collins, what
is borrowed 'is not simply modified and adapted, but
assimilated and transformed.' Similarly, in the case
of commentator and critic : the learning of one remains
in its original form, exists as 'passages' undigested

as nails or needles, mechanically pigeon-holed, to be given out again as foot-notes; in the other it has become 'assimilated and transformed' into principles of artistic enjoyment. The ideal critic would probably be the man who remembered nothing, whose reading had all been worked up organically or rejected as waste; whereas the ideal commentator would be the man whose patient 'tick-tack' methods were never troubled by any rosy touch of feeling or vision.

Of course one is speaking of the ideal, the impossible. Without learning, or let us say memory, we should be obliged to forego the much appreciated discovery of modern criticism, the comparative method. Yet, with all proper respect to that method and to those who are sufficiently accomplished to successfully practise it, it is in reality but a makeshift, and comes of the inequality between our powers of perception and our powers of expression.

We find it impossible to express the finer shades of beauty by any final characterisation : we cannot say what this subtle quality *is*, but we can, by the aid of reading and memory, say what it *is like*, and so bring the reader some way towards what it is.

Criticism, ideally, is the perfect praise of perfect art : but, failing the perfect art, it must needs be a measurer of imperfection. And thus comes the impertinent question of degree into art, where properly it has no place.

The absolute naming of qualities, not the degree in which they are present or absent, is the function of criticism.

Of course, Mr. Collins is neither that great ideal critic, nor that little ideal commentator, but one must be pardoned for feeling that his excellencies are more those of the commentator than the critic. Mr. Collins's reading has not been sufficiently 'assimilated and transformed' into principles. His special gift would seem to be, as customary, the origin of his special defect. His pleasure in art would seem to be exactly that we would expect in an editor. He is continually laying stress on the pleasure of allusiveness in literature. It is for him, apparently, the greatest charm of Lord Tennyson's verse; and in his polemic on 'The Study of English Literature' at the Universities, he says: 'That such poems as "Lycidas" and the "Progress of Poesy," have been the delight of thousands, and will continue to be the delight of thousands, who have never opened a Greek and Latin classic, is no doubt true, but it would be absurd to contend that their pleasure would not be increased tenfold had they been scholars.'

Mr. Collins seems to aim at exactitude in expression, and when he says 'tenfold' he is not likely to mean only 'twofold.' Even so, the significance of his statement remains unaffected. The pleasure which Mr. Collins derives from a work of art comes mainly—nine-tenths, to be precise—from his ability, first to distinguish therein the separate component materials employed by the artist, and then to recall the various vicissitudes to which, in the long course of artistic usage, those materials have been subject: the pleasure that comes to him from the completed whole, the new form, the indestructible something

21

which of these idle materials has made a living, beautiful synthesis, in fact, the artist's own individual spirit—this pleasure is to Mr. Collins but as one-tenth.

Now, is the chief pleasure of a work of art to be sought in the accidental associations of its material?

The pleasure which comes of tracing such associations of phrase and word, in watching what Mr. Pater calls their 'refined usage,' is, of course, a real and exciting one, but it is one quite apart from the æsthetic, or the spiritual, impression — is, in fact, a scientific pleasure, a pleasure of the 'curiosity,' and, surely, more like one than nine-tenths of the delight we should expect from a work of art.

It is of the essence of a work of art that it is a whole. The first pleasure in it, therefore, must come from it as a whole. If it be of the essence of artistic creation that the artist should conceal his process, it is no less of the essence of æsthetic enjoyment that it should remain concealed.

It is, of course, obvious that cultured people do receive greater pleasure from Lord Tennyson's poetry than uncultured—not for the reason given by Mr. Collins, but for the reason that they receive the greatest pleasure from any poetry whatsoever, be it primitive or decadent. Such read Shakespeare and such read Tennyson for the joy of the same thing in each, the spiritual exaltation of beauty. Mr. Collins, and many others of us, talk of the 'fathers of song,' Homer, Dante, Chaucer, Shakespeare, as though they were being sold by thousands on the railway bookstalls. As a matter of fact, who reads them save the cultured? who reads any poet save the cultured? 'Cultured,' not 'learned,' remember. To be a learned man is the 'gift of fortune,' but to be cultured 'comes by nature.' Culture is mainly a matter of temperament. A man is born cultured: that is, he is born with a certain sensitive, fastidious constitution, which, of course, reading refines, but which no reading can create. Culture, moreover, is a state of the whole constitution, whereas learning is mainly the exercise of one function, that of memory. For some people learning is an unnecessary accomplishment, the acquirement of it a superstitious waste of energy. What matters it that one does not remember, or even has never read, certain great writers? Our one concern is to possess an organisation open to great and refined impressions. Great writers are but means to that end, and reading but a part of that process the product of which is culture. If we could imagine our reading of Shakespeare having done all that it can for us, what matter if we straightway forget every line? He remains in us, remains in our more refined senses, our more quickened spirit. This is, of course, at once obvious and extreme, but the obvious and extreme are both at times necessary instruments of criticism, and certainly necessary when we are told that nine-tenths of the pleasure of poetry are lost to all but 'the learned.'

That allusiveness should be Mr. Collins's chief pleasure from poetry is somewhat paradoxical, for such pleasure is one of that very decadence with which Mr. Collins seems generally to have little sympathy.

Art would seem to be interesting to him as a palimpsest is interesting, and he would appear to read one book for the sake of being reminded of others.

But what is decadence in literature? It seems largely to be confused with a decadence in the style of literature, which is not quite the same thing. Even that decadence is continually misunderstood—euphuism and quite proper organic refinements of style being continually confused with each other. Mr. Collins, and many others, continually assume that the mere exercise of conscious art in literature, the care for the unique word, the use of various literary means to literary ends, as alliteration and onomatopœia, constitute decadence. To say this is to be forced to the absurd conclusion that the nearer an instrument approaches perfection, the more it becomes adapted to the uses for which it is designed, the less its value. The only decadence in style is euphuism—and its antithesis, slang. Mr. Collins writes, too, as though the old 'original' poets sang like bird on bough the unpremeditated lay, with nothing of conscious artistic selection ; yet we know that Chaucer took as much pains over his rhymes as any latter-day poetaster, and that, indeed, the French schools, which in some respects he took as his models, were students of style to the last degree of affectation.

But decadence in literature is more than a question of style, nor is it, as some suppose, a question of theme. It is in the character of the treatment that we must seek it. In all great vital literature, the theme, great or small, is considered in all its relations near and far, and above all in relation to the sum-total of things, to the Infinite, as we phrase it; in decadent literature the relations, the due proportions, are ignored. One might say that literary decadence consists in the euphuistic expression of isolated observations. Thus disease, which is the favourite theme of *décadents*, does not in itself make for decadence: it is only when, as often, it is studied apart from its relations to health, to the great vital centre of things, that it does so. Any point of view, seriously taken, which ignores the complete view, approaches decadence.

To notice only the picturesque effect of a beggar's rags, like Gautier; the colour-scheme of a tippler's nose, like M. Huysmans; to consider one's mother merely prismatically, like Mr. Whistler—these are examples of the decadent attitude.

At the bottom, decadence is merely limited thinking, often insane thinking.

When a subject is treated proportionally, though the style bear marks of euphuism, there can be no question of decadence. To speak of decadence, therefore, in connection with such poets as Virgil and Lord Tennyson, poets of noble epic aim, of high ordered thought, poets who see life steadily and see it whole, to say nothing of the dignity of their treatment, is mere anarchy.

Let us for a moment consider the elementary characteristics of great literature. Broadly speaking, literature is a symbolic verbal expression of life. It must, to begin with, include all the primary conditions of life.

Now, through the whole of men's actions comes the interpenetrating sense of their being done beneath an illimitable sky, 'under the sun.' This sense of an all-including, overhanging Infinite is the invariable atmosphere of great literature (as, of course, of any great art): and this atmosphere is the province of the imagination.

Again, the pulse of life goes with a rhythm, which only the gods and the poets catch. Thence comes the characteristic of rhythm into literature, the poet expressing that human rhythm according to the music of his own nature.

Lastly come the various forms and other expressions of life, having their counterpart in words. Here comes in the poet's selective sense to choose the words most fitting for the forms he wishes to express—'the unique word.' But the unique word is not merely the word which is the same colour, shape, and size as the object it must stand for, but the word which will also blend with the rhythm, and heighten the imaginative atmosphere of the whole work. Too many writers consider the unique word as one fragment of a mosaic, whereas it should rather be considered as a note of music, animated with their rhythm, and transfigured with their imagination.

Now it will be seen that the whole significance of this third and final condition to literature depends mainly on the other two. As the facts of life lie all about awaiting the poet, so lie the words. Both have been used countless times before in countless combinations. Whatever originality of effect the poet is to attain will depend on the spirit he breathes through these old forms. The mere fact of his using the old words, or up to a point the old methods, cannot detract from a manifest originality of result, any more than his employment of the world-old facts for which the words stand can do so. Whatever an original poet borrows he sets anew to the music of his own nature. An original nature may borrow much, but it can never owe.

Therefore, if this view of the several elements of literature be a correct one, inferences against a poet's originality based merely on his appropriation of the words and phrases, even the ideas, of other poets are vain in the face of work which gives us the sense of a new individuality, a temperament meeting the old things through a new experience. It is thus that the cry of plagiarism is generally so absurd, for all it can point to is the use once more of common property, the mere bricks with which all men build, or at the most bits of ornament taken from former creations. The charge is never made in regard to the essentials, the vital breath of poetry.

It is thus that, to my mind, Mr. Collins's implied charges against Lord Tennyson for his assimilation of the work of other poets, are not so much unjust as merely futile—not to dwell on the fact that many of the 'illustrations' are obviously coincidences constrained to Mr. Collins's purpose.

All, it seems to me, that one has to ask as we read Lord Tennyson, or any other poet, simply is: Does this poetry give me the sense of a new personality, present as a new magic, of rhythm or what not, in the verse? If so, one need trouble no further, and we can with indifference watch the commentator, 'like a demon-mole,' burrowing his way in his little tunnels of learning beneath the text.

IT is a curious thing that that 'acute and honourable minority' which, all through Mr. Meredith's career, have been the faithful audience and zealous champions of his novels should more or less have missed his poems. Maybe it has come of a not unfounded distrust of a proseman's verse. One is always inclined to regard the latter as an amiable weakness, and to say 'Let him who is a novelist be a novelist still!' And then Mr. Meredith's admirers have been for the most part thinkers. They have welcomed him for his fearless, subtle criticism of life, rather than as an artist. It is so that Browning is mainly worshipped to this day, and that is why so many are found to make light of his ugly artistic blemishes. They have not gone to him for poetry, but thought. However it be, *Modern Love* has for the most part been missed—in common with the whole of Mr. Meredith's poems, even his wonderful earth poems, *Songs and Lyrics of the Joy of Earth*, poems with more of the Pandean inspiration, the rich smell, the spring water chastity, the central sweetness, and the shaggy indomitable vitality of earth than any other English nature poems at all. It is still more curious that while his

*George Meredith: 'Modern Love' —Second Edition.*

friends have missed them, they are the only part of his work for which his unsympathetic critics have a good word. Mr. George Moore, for example, who will have nothing of the novels, speaks in his *Confessions* in high praise of the poems. Browning, too, held the same view. And there can be no doubt that the beauty of Mr. Meredith's prose at its best is more distinctively a poetical than a prose beauty. His metaphor is too powerful and too constant, and his expression falls too much into phrases, complete in themselves, to be characteristically prose.

Mr. Swinburne, however, with the eager sympathy for other men's work which has usually distinguished him, admired *Modern Love* from the first. The *Spectator* had quarrelled with the poem because in it Mr. Meredith deals with 'a deep and painful subject on which he has no conviction to express.' Mr. Swinburne was in no mood to let such a criticism pass unchallenged in 1862, with the *Poems and Ballads* already fermenting within him. He at once wrote a fiery vindication to the *Spectator*. 'The business of verse-making,' he said, 'is hardly to express convictions ; and if some poetry, not without merit of its kind, has at times dealt in dogmatic morality, it is all the worse and all the weaker for that.' The whole letter can be read as reprinted in Mr. Lane's Bibliography of Mr. Meredith's work, but the reader can well imagine what passionate invective such an unwarrantable interdict of theme would arouse in the poet.

Mr. Meredith had been prepared for some such attack upon his subject-matter, and had prefixed as warning two lines from *The Book of Sages*—I presume, an unpublished *Pilgrim's Scrip* :

> ' This is not meat
> For little people or for fools.'

Again, in the body of the poem he had written :

> ' these things are life :
> And life, they say, is worthy of the Muse.'

Mr. Meredith has omitted the first two lines in the new edition, the second after thirty years ! Does he now feel that poetry is never, under any circumstances, ' meat for little people or for fools,' or that the general intelligence has so broadened since 1862 as to make the warning unnecessary ?

The latter is certainly the case, for there seems little to shock us at the present time in this tragedy of an unhappy marriage. True, Mr. Meredith displays the relationship in its most intimate moments ; he leaves no part of the problem unstated, though, as the *Spectator* objected, he leaves it with us still unsolved. What else could he or any poet do? Besides, surely it is a mistake to regard a poem as a problem, at least in the first instance. It is a bit of ' tragic life' seen with inspired eyes, expressed in inspired words. Its end is not to put a query, but by the sacramental use of suffering lives to transfigure mortal pain to divine meanings.

Landor, in the person of Sidney, remarks that 'the most plaintive ditty hath imparted a fuller joy, and of longer duration, to its composer, than the conquest of Persia to the Macedonian.' Its effect is precisely the same on the listener, and therein is the mystery and

sacrament of all art. It sets us above our mortal
sufferings, like the gods who, we are told, 'find' in them
'a music centred in a doleful song,' not because they
are callous, but because they know all, know the divine
event to which the pain is moving us. So is it with the
tragic treatment of suffering. Art, by revealing the
beauty beneath, touches it to the finer issues of faith.
That is what Keats meant when he wrote 'beauty is
truth.' Tragic beauty is the rainbow of promise glowing
above the mere 'tragedy.' The beauty seems to say :
'All is well beneath this suffering and wreck. Else how
could I smile ?'

It is this high significance which Mr. Meredith has
given to a pitiful modern story of small mistakes and
misunderstanding in *Modern Love* :

> ' In tragic hints here see what evermore
> Moves dark as yonder midnight ocean's force,
> Thundering like ramping hosts of warrior horse,
> To throw that faint thin line upon the shore ! '

These tragic hints are given in fifty tableaux. We
may, as Mr. Swinburne did, call them sonnets, though,
being poems each of sixteen lines, sonnets strictly
speaking they are not. But we need not resume the
unprofitable discussion that has been waged on this
head. Each poem is a vivid impression helping on the
story, a series of poignant spiritual situations. At once
in the opening poem Mr. Meredith presses the very
nerve of such a tragedy, by the fearless choice of a
situation which, night after night, would naturally con-
dense the whole 'pity of it' into one fearful point of
pain. Through the day the two unhappy ones would

have distractions, but at night! listening to each other's breathing, in the dark as in a grave together—

> 'By this he knew she wept with waking eyes:
> That, at his hand's light quiver by her head,
> The strange low sobs that shook their common bed,
> Were called into her with a sharp surprise,
> And strangled mute, like little gaping snakes,
> Dreadfully venomous to him.   She lay
> Stone still, and the long darkness flowed away
> With muffled pulses.   Then, as midnight makes
> Her giant heart of Memory and Tears
> Drink the pale drug of silence, and so beat
> Sleep's heavy measure, they from head to feet
> Were moveless, looking through their dead black years,
> By vain regret scrawled over the blank wall.
> Like sculptured effigies they might be seen
> Upon their marriage-tomb, the sword between ;
> Each wishing for the sword that severs all.'

One hears complaints of the 'obscurity' of the poem. This, however, can only apply to the story, which is a little difficult of distanglement, and perhaps at one or two points uncertain.   It cannot apply to the expression, for no modern poet has written stronger metaphorical English.   Indeed, the lines are often quite crushing in their power, striking on the ear like the twang of an iron lyre, and yet so beautiful!   Indeed, they are equal in force and beauty to the strongest passages in Browning, and the entire poem has a unity which, in poetry, Mr. Meredith has never again attained —as indeed, he has never since made quite so ambitious an attempt.   It would be unprofitable to tell the story step by step, even if it were possible.   A hint or two must suffice.   To begin with, the theme is no vulgar misalliance.   The two unhappy ones are by no means obvious people. They are each full of subtlety and refinement. Each is capable of appreciating the other's position, while at the same time each grows frenzied at the arbitrary chain that binds them. 'It is no vulgar nature I have wived,' says the husband, and he in his turn is too fine-fibred to assert his mere husband's 'rights by law established' when he comes to find that his wife has sought another lover. Old tenderness rather surges up in him :

> 'It cannot be such harm on her cool brow
> To put a kiss? Yet if I meet him there!
> But she is mine! Ah, no! I know too well
> I claim a star whose light is overcast :
> I claim a phantom-woman in the Past.
> The hour has struck, though I heard not the bell!'

It is this very super-subtlety that is the cause of their estrangement. They had been true lovers once :

> 'Lovers beneath the singing sky of May,
> They wandered once ; clear as the dew on flowers :
> But they fed not on the advancing hours :
> Their hearts held cravings for the buried day.
> Then each applied to each that fatal knife,
> Deep questioning, which probes to endless dole.
> Ah, what a dusty answer gets the soul
> When hot for certainties in this our life!'

Apparently, divergences in nature (he was a dreamer and 'plotted to be worthy of the world,' she of less serious stuff) set them turning to the 'it might have been' of the past, which brought their fatal egoism into play. Though they no longer loved each other, yet

> 'How many a thing which we cast to the ground,
> When others pick it up becomes a gem!'

Also the long association of old love has left its
tenderness behind, and when each finds that the other
is seeking in new loves what is lost, that tenderness is
fanned, so that momentarily it seems like the old love
come back :

> 'The dread that my old love may be alive
> Has seized my nursling new love by the throat.'

And so they drift on, the husband alternating between
cynicism, sensualism, and passionate tenderness.　He
seeks distraction in France with a mistress, but her
kisses are dust and ashes on his lips.　And here we
may quote one of the most powerful and terrible of all
the poems :

> 'Am I failing?　For no longer can I cast
> A glory round about this head of gold.
> Glory she wears, but springing from the mould
> Not like the consecration of the Past !
> Is my soul beggared?　Something more than earth
> I cry for still : I cannot be at peace
> In having Love upon a mortal lease.
> I cannot take the woman at her worth !
> Where is the ancient wealth wherewith I clothed
> Our human nakedness, and could endow
> With spiritual splendour a white brow
> That else had grinned at me the fact I loathed?
> A kiss is but a kiss now ! and no wave
> Of a great flood that whirls me to the sea.
> But, as you will ! we 'll sit contentedly,
> And eat our pot of honey on the grave.'

Of the wife's mind we hardly hear as much as we
would like.　It only comes to us now and again through
sympathetic flashes from the husband, who tells the
story.　However, once again near the end he finds her

in a wood with her lover. Instead of upbraiding he
merely offers her his arm:

> 'I felt the pained speech coming, and declared
> My firm belief in her, ere she could speak.
> A ghastly morning came into her cheek,
> While with a widening soul on me she stared.'

All her remaining love for him welled up at this, and
by the effort of that supreme moment his heart opened
too—they 'drank the pure daylight of honest speech,'
and an hour followed that seemed to promise real union
at last.

> 'We saw the swallows gathering in the sky,
> And in the osier-isle we heard their noise.
> We had not to look back on summer joys,
> Or forward to a summer of bright dye.
> But in the largeness of the evening earth
> Our spirits grew as we went side by side.
> The hour became her husband, and my bride.
> Love that had robbed us so, thus blessed our dearth!
> The pilgrims of the year waxed very loud
> In multitudinous chatterings, as the flood
> Full brown came from the west, and like pale blood
> Expanded to the upper crimson cloud.
> Love that had robbed us of immortal things,
> This little moment mercifully gave,
> And still I see across the twilight wave,
> The swan sail with her young beneath her wings.'

This was the poem on which Mr. Swinburne poured
out the vials of his praise, but even he could not
exaggerate its power and beauty. I quote it as in
the 1862 edition. In the new edition Mr. Meredith has
altered the last line but one to 'Where I have seen
across the twilight wave'—one of several minor emendations I have noticed.

The story ends with a characteristic rebound. The woman's love has been so aroused that she becomes quixotic.   She conceives it her duty to leave her husband free to live with his mistress, and goes from him :

> Their sense is with their senses all mixed in.
> Destroyed by subtleties these women are !
> More brain, O Lord, more brain !'

Her husband follows and brings her back, but even still she eludes him, for 'there's a strength to help the desperate weak,' and the poem ends with her suicide :

> ' Thus piteously Love closed what he begat :
> The union of this ever-diverse pair !'

ONE thing a hobby for 'first editions' may teach a man is, not to despise a verse-book for its lowly garb.

*An Undiscovered Poet:* 'Sonnets and Poems,' by 'A.'

Some *Sonnets and Poems* by 'A' are a case in point—a volume insignificant to the last degree, and who is 'A'?   Whoever he be, and he is as unknown to the writer as the babe unborn, he has in the quietude of a strong self-contained life arrived at a very considerable majority in regard to song.   I would beg the reader to read the following sonnet on 'April Day in a Market Place':

> ' Not of the country, where young April hath
>     A daisy-look, and smells of violets sweet ;
> And strews her primroses about thy path ;
>     But of the thronged and busy-footed street ;

Where the old market, 'neath the broken shade
    Of church and ancient-gabled houses, stands;
How bright she maketh *these.*  In blue array,
    And sprinkling glittering drops from her white hands,
She lives about the pave; each meeting face
    Has light and merriment by her begot;
She haunts dull courts; and in the marketplace,
    'Mongst daffodils, and small forget-me-not,
And wallflower fresh, sings clear her maiden songs,
    And loosens old dames' hearts and thoughts and tongues.'

And this of ' Woods by Moonlight ':

' How beauteous by moonlight is the wood;
    That sweet sheen falleth pure and saintly down
Flooding its dimples, where but now hath stood
    The vaunt and witness of the winter's frown;
Most eloquently doth the darkness speak
    Of some unvisioned, inner-haunting ray;
Most eloquently doth the spirit seek
    By kindred silence, kindred word to say;
There sings the nightingale—and nought else mars
    The sacred, solemn beauty of the hour;
And 'neath the outer twinkling of the stars
    The daisy hides—a strange and sleeping flower;
How white they look, that drowsy company,
    As in the moonish dew they coldly lie! '

Maybe your first criticism will be—' Shakespeare's
Sonnets !' Granted.  But every poet, before he finds
his own characteristic voice, must first sing in the voice
of his master.  The choice of the master is much.  ' A '
has set himself as apprentice to no carver of cameos, but
to the men of strong chisels and great marbles.  Besides,
whatever the Shakespearean cadence of these sonnets,
there is an individuality behind him as well, a heart that
loves, a head that thinks, a soul that dreams.  ' A ' has
done all these things deeply on his own account, and he

sings from the fulness of a full life.  You must notice a singular contained calmness about these sonnets.  There is no shade of hurry, no touch of uncertainty.  The poet knows what he wants to say, and feels that he can say it.  He is quite at his ease—'of his harmonies he is full sure.'  He might be talking ; he begins and ends so naturally, and uses such simple words, yet touches them to such fine issues.  This is one of the sacred signs of poetry.  As one reads, one finds the deep reason of this calm confidence.  'A' is one of the few happy people who is at peace with life.  He has done his thinking, and faces the universe with the quiet face of faith—a faith that apparently holds in solution the whole of modern doubt.  He has that other sacred mark of the poet, laid down by Whitman : 'in the dispute concerning God and eternity he is silent.'

> ' When here and there the violet's blue gleams out,
>     And April makes a heaven of such days,
> And quietness is everywhere about,
>     And soul sometime hath neither yeas nor nays,
>     But a dear resting in the natural good. . . .
>
> Oh, still rejoice, for Life's own witness shows,
>     Despite our sin, how dear our fate shall be ;
>     There are sweet lights about the stricken tree
> Where canker bides ;  or where the lightning goes ;
>     These are the truest prophecies. . . .
>
> Although too oft his garb be coarse and scant,
>     And foul, unto the critic-gaze doth seem,
>     Within the morning sun a man doth gleam,
> As though he were an angel radiant. . . .'

'A,' as will have been noticed in these extracts, is particularly happy in his nature pictures.  There is a freshness in them I have not met for long : there is no word for most of them but lovely.   Take this vignette of a ploughman :

> 'When larks were singing in some April-top
> Of blue amongst the clouds ; and in the glow
> The ploughman, ploughing glad, will turn and stop,
> Moved up against the sky, I sought to catch
> And set in form this living attitude
> That breathed around.'

He is especially happy in such sweet Elizabethan double words as 'April-top,' 'a daisy-look,' 'the blue-and-bright of spring'; and he has a sonnet to daffodils, which is one of the most delicious fancies in the Elizabethan manner I remember.   He is also full of those fine metaphors that bespeak imagination, such as—

> 'The countless worlds; they for an instant gleam
> As gilded motes about the ray of time.'

or a description of moonrise, 'strange as when one lieth slumbering near.'   Who 'A' may be I have not the faintest notion.   One knows of one famous 'A'—'A' of *The Strayed Reveller*, 1848.   And he proved rather a considerable poet.

'THERE are a very few men whose greatness is so
*William Wordsworth:*   conspicuous and classical that their writings have obtained a prescriptive right to
*Shorter's Selections.*   appear century after century without the formality or impertinence of introduction by other hands.   Homer, Virgil, Dante, or Shakespeare

are monumental.  They move through the ages in a long triumph, and even a preface cannot presume to walk before them.'  So wrote the prince of anthologists, Mr. F. T. Palgrave, by way of *envoi* to his pretty 1865 edition of *Shakespeare's Sonnets*. Professor Dowden would have the same deference shown to Wordsworth, and on the occasion of Mr. John Morley's complete edition of the poems, waxed very wroth because Mr. Morley's introduction had presumed to walk before them.  Mr. Shorter has the fear of that occasion before him in making the selection of the *Lyrics and Sonnets of Wordsworth*. But let not his heart be troubled.  In all humility I would submit that Professor Dowden was wrong.  It is not safe to let Wordsworth go alone.  For, if you leave him in the bulk, slag and all, of a complete edition, how are you to hope that he will receive justice at the hands of the profane or uninitiated?  And if you represent him by a selection, you are called upon to justify your principle of selection.  If you have a true care for Wordsworth's fame, there seems no doubt but that to do the great right you must do the little wrong.  In the case of Mr. Shorter, that wrong is certainly reduced to a minimum ; for he has kept to his editorial business with rigid self-denial.  He had, of course, a double reason for a preface, for had not Matthew Arnold been before him in a selection which has been acknowledged on all hands as the definitive selection, or at least that by which all succeeding selections must expect to be tested.  The Wordsworthians, of course, dispute this, and Professor Knight has represented their protest in another selection. But then Professor Knight is the Arch-Wordsworthian, and we would no more think of taking his opinion of Wordsworth on trust than we would that of the Browning Society on Browning. For it is not so much the *poetry* that such societies and schools seek in their particular master—poetry proper is not a thing to be studied or enjoyed in herds—it is the structural thought, the ethic of his work, that they meet to discuss. Such 'society' study is in fact but another form of church work; and the very fact of people thus banding together is the surest proof of their lack of the higher qualities of literary appreciation. It is, to begin with, a sin against humour, a sense of which is a necessary adjunct of all such appreciation. And it seems more than a mere coincidence that the three men selected for this latter-day form of apotheosis, should themselves be all more or less lacking in that sense— Shelley and Wordsworth signally so, and Browning certainly to some degree, else he never could have developed so grotesque a style, or written that sonnet in regard to Edward Fitzgerald. Now, that sense of humour is the quality most of all essential in an editor of Wordsworth, more, even, than the sense of beauty; for nothing stands and will stand so much in the way of a wide appreciation of Wordsworth's genius as his quite astounding lack of humour. Probably no poet has ever faced life with a solemn-owlishness so complete as Wordsworth. The great seriousness in regard to life is one thing, the householder's seriousness is another; but Wordsworth combined both in an almost unrealisable degree. This is the more unfortunate for his appreciation to-day, as the sin against humour is at present the unforgivable sin. We are, of course, cultivating the faculty out of all true proportion. We are in danger of forgetting all nobility and reverence, and our incessant sniggering is itself becoming a subject for satire.

This essential quality was, as we know, one of the most exquisite possessions of Matthew Arnold, together with his catholic culture and his instinct for seeing things, in his own phrase, steadily, and seeing them whole. It is for these reasons that, if there be one English critic whose opinion one would be willing to accept in place of one's own, that critic is Matthew Arnold. We feel safe in his hands. He is the nearest approach to authority in criticism at which we have arrived. How often we sigh for his cool utterance during the last year or two of one-sided 'temperamental' impressions! How calmly would he relegate some of the phenomena that trouble us into some comforting generalisation! The very fact of his having made a selection of Wordsworth is proof in itself, all but sufficient, of its value. Certainly, many of us would prefer to take his selection ready-made than to plod through the complete Wordsworth. The present selection reassures us in this, perhaps superstitious, faith; for Mr. Shorter has evidently gone about his task independently, and yet his selection only differs from that of Arnold's by about eighteen poems, several of which were foregone exceptions, by the fact of their being non-lyrical. These non-lyrical exceptions include 'The Brothers,' 'Michael,' 'Margaret,' and the 'Fragment from The Recluse.' But Mr. Shorter has included

'Laodameia.' Would he describe that as lyrical? Personally, I would be quite content to take my Wordsworth as thus presented, and thus forego what has always seemed to me the overpraised 'Michael.' Wordsworth's attempt to apply realism to the pastoral—and it is curious to think that he was in a naïve fashion one of the earliest exponents of realism—was a foredoomed failure. Had his sense of humour been keener it might have been possible, for along with that sense would have come a keener selective power than he possessed. He might have remained no less simple and yet have avoided the ludicrous *naïveté* into which he is continually falling, and in which he even surpasses Blake. Indeed, Wordsworth's artistic faculty was very small; more than any of our poets, he was an inspired amateur, a poet Close, educated, and allowed certain intermittent inspiration—but inspiration, of course, of the very highest order. That that was always most spontaneous in his shorter pieces, in his little ballads, in his songs and pastoral vignettes, and occasionally in his sonnets, was the text of Matthew Arnold's selection. In such poems indeed he is beyond praise; for such, as Arnold said, are 'as inevitable as Nature herself. It might seem that Nature not only gave him the matter for his poem, but wrote his poem for him.' Of course, that is just the secret of all good poetry whatsoever, but Wordsworth was rarely content that Nature should write his poems for him; he was always taking the pen from her hand and wielding it with the self-conscious air of the chosen vessel.

In no poet do I remember such a constant intrusion

of 'the poet' into the picture.  Though on the surface
so little theatrical, Wordsworth was in reality intensely
so in his office as 'poet.'  To him the Lake District was
a stage, on which, in season and out of season, he
enacted 'The Poet's Eye' to an audience of mountains,
shepherds, and tourists.  With all his sympathy for
humanity, when he thinks of those who shall come after
him among these mountains, it is not of the shepherds,
but of other spectator-poets :—

> '. . . youthful poets, who among these hills
> Will be my second self when I am gone.'

In fact, he is 'Alastor' turned Quaker and dressed
respectably.  But maybe I have dwelt too long upon
his defects, defects which, after all, merely impede the
approach to him, and do not essentially detract from his
real greatness.  When he did forget himself, then,
indeed, we take off our hats to him, for his faults are
only 'human,' but his excellencies are 'divine.'  High
as was his own estimate of his own merit, yet he builded
even better than he knew.  According to the opening
lines of ' Michael,' he loved the shepherds, the humanity
amid his mountains,

> ' Not verily
> For their own sakes, but for the fields and hills,
> Where was their occupation and abode.'

But that was only another of his misconceptions concerning himself; for Lamb, in the heart of his dear
Cockneytown, with all his love for his kind, had
not really more humanity at heart than Wordsworth
among his mists and mountains.  And that is the keynote, the justifying *raison d'être* of Mr. Shorter's

selection. 'It is desired,' says Mr. Shorter, 'to emphasise the fact that Wordsworth is not alone the poet
of Nature, that he is not alone the poet of animal life,
but that next to the three great unapproachable masters
of modern European poetry—Dante, Shakespeare, and
Goethe—he is the poet of human life.' One feels inclined
to cry 'Softly, Mr. Shorter!' midway in this sentence :
but, leaving comparison out of the question, we gladly
cry 'Hear, hear' to Mr. Shorter's main contention—
Wordsworth, not merely the poet of Nature, but of
Human Nature.

Mr. Shorter takes a practical means of emphasising
this by a new arrangement of the poems. Wordsworth,
as every one knows, evolved a classification of his own,
dividing his poems into 'Poems of Imagination,' 'Poems
of Love,' of the 'Affections,' 'Fancy,' etc.—a strange
medley of theme and method. But, to many, this
arrangement appears arbitrary, and the working of
Wordsworth's distinction between 'Imagination' and
'Fancy' is somewhat perplexing. Arnold divided the
poems according to their form, 'Poems of Ballad Form,'
'Narrative Poems,' 'Lyrical Poems,' 'Poems akin to
the Antique, and Odes,' etc., which is a plan on an
organic basis, as the form of poetry is more or less a
reflection of its mood, and is, in some degree, related to
its subject. But this has its disadvantages in separating
poems sharing closer bonds of relationship. Mr. John
Morley applied the chronological method. Though that
has its interest in a complete edition, there is, as Mr.
Shorter observes, little to be said for it when applied to
a selection. 'The greater part of Wordsworth's best

sonnets and lyrics were written within a period of ten or fifteen years, and in comparatively early life.   During this period of the life of Wordsworth, as of any young man, there were assuredly moments of action and reaction, of ebb and flow of emotion, which would make any chronological classification of comparatively little value.'

Mr. Shorter divides his selection into 'Poems of Human Life,' 'Poems of Animal Life,' and 'Poems of Nature and Nature-Worship.'   I praise this mainly, if not entirely, because, as we said, it emphasises Wordsworth's right to a position not generally allowed him as a poet of humanity: that position which, of course, Arnold made clear in his careful essay.   Wordsworth's superiority over Burns, Keats, Heine—where is it, he asked?  'It is here: he deals with more of *life* than they do; he deals with *life*, as a whole, more powerfully.'   Merely viewed as a classification, Mr. Shorter's has it drawbacks just as the others.   It is not really so scientific as Arnold's.   You have at least a uniform, if narrow, basis in his case; the basis of form.   In Mr. Shorter's case, one may say, we have the basis of theme— but then what poem ever keeps to one theme throughout? —the dominant note even is often hard to decide upon. Such a classification is apt to hinge too much on titles, and it goes without saying that a poem addressed to a dog or a daisy is just as likely to prove a 'Poem of Human Life' as any other.   This, of course, especially applies to him whose poetic profession it was to find in the meanest flower those

'Thoughts that do often lie too deep for tears.'

Does it not also seem a little quaint to find 'The Nightingale' and 'The Skylark' verses under 'Poems of *Animal* Life':—

> 'Hail to thee, blithe spirit!
> Bird thou never wert.'

However, something too much of classification. None can quite fit all round, and really none is needed: but I like Mr. Shorter's best because it implies a sound criticism. It was plucky of him to make it.

Nearly all Mr. Shorter's omissions are sonnets, and to all but one we may cry good riddance. For that one entitled 'Admonition,' and beginning 'Yes, there is holy pleasure in thine eye,' I would plead, in spite of the ludicrous note in which Wordsworth declares it to be 'intended more particularly for the perusal of those who may have happened to be enamoured of some beautiful place of retreat in the country of the lakes.' I think, too, that the sonnet to Mary Queen of Scots might have been retained for the sake of its first line, a line of gallantry so rare in W. W.—'Dear to the Loves and to the Graces vowed.' Of course there are lines here and there we would keep in the other omitted poems, but there are probably a larger proportion in the poems which Mr. Shorter has substituted. These, I am glad to say, with two or three exceptions, are not sonnets. Of those exceptions, 'There is a pleasure in poetic pains' is the most noteworthy. Of the other substitutions, 'The Thorn,' 'The Mad Mother,' 'Louise,' the verses on the death of Lamb, and the third 1802 poem to the Daisy are most important. Mr. Shorter also includes the 1805

poem to the same flower—rather undeservedly, I think.
But it is certainly hard to understand why Arnold
omitted the 1802 poem, and harder still to understand
his omission of the fine lines on Lamb. Probably it was
from fear of the 'historical' bias in poetry, against which
he rightly protested. It is true, too, that Wordsworth,
in a sort of sanctified play on Lamb's name, once more
fell into his besetting sin—

> 'From the most gentle creature nursed in fields,
> Had been derived the name he bore—a name,
> Wherever Christian altars have been raised,
> Hallow'd to meekness and to innocence. . . .'

Didn't some one say that they could never look on
Wordsworth's face without wishing to offer him a
thistle?

But listen how finely he ends :—

> 'Still, at the centre of his being, lodged
> A soul by resignation sanctified :
> And if too often, self-reproach'd, he felt
> That innocence belongs not to our kind,
> A power that never ceased to abide in him,
> Charity, 'mid the multitude of sins
> That she can cover, left not his exposed
> To an unforgiving judgment from just heaven.
> O, he was good, if e'er a good man lived ! '

THAT little clan whose appreciation of poetry is alone
*William* worth having probably made Mr. William
*Watson:* Watson's acquaintance on the original ap-
*'Poems.'* pearance of 'Wordsworth's Grave' in *The
National Review*, but long before that, a still earlier

band of his admirers had prized a volume of *Epigrams* hailing from Liverpool—a book one often used to come across in the threepenny box—for a large simplicity of thought and distinction of manner, which they could only parallel with such masters of the quatrain as Landor. Perhaps their acquaintance with Mr. Watson had begun earlier still with a poem in the dreamy Morrisian manner, *The Prince's Quest*, which Rossetti is said to have admired. The *Epigrams*, however, were Mr. Watson's first distinctive work, and in that fact we may find a significant criticism of Mr. Watson as a poet. The dominant tendency of a man usually comes out in his early work, and epigram is at once the strength and weakness of all Mr. Watson's poetry. His method is always, more or less, epigrammatic rather than lyric—even in poems where you would expect a freer treatment.

Let us take, for example, an extremely fine ode to Autumn. I will quote the first two verses—

'Thou burden of all songs the earth hath sung,
    Thou retrospect in Time's reverted eyes,
    Thou metaphor of everything that dies,
That dies ill-starred, or dies beloved and young,
    And therefore blest and wise—
O be less beautiful, or be less brief
    Thou tragic splendour, strange, and full of fear,
    In vain her pageant shall the Summer rear?
At thy mute signal, leaf by golden leaf,
    Crumbles the gorgeous year.

Ah, ghostly as remembered mirth, the tale
    Of Summer's bloom, the legend of the Spring,
    And thou, too, flutterest an impatient wing,
Thou presence yet more fugitive and frail,
    Thou most unbodied thing,

> Whose very being is thy going hence,
>   And passage and departure all thy theme;
>   Whose life doth still a splendid dying seem,
> And thou at height of thy magnificence
>   A figment and a dream.'

Now it may, of course, be my fault, but distinguished as this undoubtedly is, thoughtful, musical, and to a degree imaginative, it fails in one great quality of poetry. It does not touch us, or at least comes near doing so in two lines only, and those, as always, the simplest—

> 'O be less beautiful, or be less brief
>   Thou tragic splendour, strange, and full of fear.'

These lines have been really and deeply felt. They have the chill shudder of autumn in them. They are unconscious. We feel in them man impressed by the mystery of the seasons. But the poem as a whole gives us autumn as it appeals to man the phrase-maker. One can see the poet standing in front of the dying woods with a kind of epigrammatic camera. He has gone out with the firm intention of thinking clever things, and he comes back and says them. Nature does not confide her big metaphors to a man in this mood. She will not be patronised, even by a poet. Unless you be as the least of her children she will reveal but little. Mr. Watson, I fancy, too seldom forgets that he is a poet; if he could forget that oftener he might do great things—he would be all the greater poet for forgetting that he was a poet at all.

His method has the defect of his quality. What

he gains in precision of phrase he loses in self-consciousness. He is apt to become mechanical, and in this poem of 'Autumn' we can see the process as well as the product. Two or three large fancies—that have a way of looking like metaphors—some carefully pondered paradoxes, somewhat on Lamb's principle (as, for example, 'Antiquity! thou wondrous charm, what art thou? That being nothing, art everything!'), some real feeling, some real magic of phrase, though a magic often too easily analysable into an artful vowelisation, founded, I should say, on a very close study (I do not for a moment say imitation) of the manner of the Laureate—it is so, with no wish to be hypercritical, that I cannot help dissecting Mr. Watson's 'Autumn.' The poem, in fact, would be very much better without those very lines which Mr. Watson probably values most. At the same time, if it be rather a collection of phrases than a poem, they are very fine phrases, and there is a cadence in the poem, especially in the short last line of each verse, as of 'Autumn's' own 'hollow sighs in the sere wood.' There is, too, as I said, a distinguished air about the poem. Mr. Watson has certainly the grand style. But he must be careful lest it grow mannered and tricky. He is a little inclined to mouth it after the Elizabethan fashion, and he is too fond of polysyllabic words, such as 'dulcifluous,' and Tennysonian collocations such as—

> ' Elusive notes in wandering wafture borne
> From undiscoverable lips that blow
> An immaterial horn.'

In these two last lines, we feel too much of the 'word-mosaic artificer'—Mr. Watson's own phrase, and his own particular aversion.   Yet, oddly enough, it is his own danger.   But it is seldom he gives us an epithet so uncharacteristic as 'immaterial'; on the contrary, he has a very rare faculty for 'the unique word.' Another rare characteristic of his is the firm basis of thought which underlies his poetry.   Often it is but the fortunate paradox, the lucky hit, of the epigrammatist : the phrase and the thought just fit each other ; nothing is left outside the phrase.   But often, too, especially in 'Wordsworth's Grave,' Mr. Watson brings us the more profound suggestive thought of the poet, with deep words which, like springs on the hillside, are upwellings 'from the vital fount of things.'

Mr. Watson has also touches of that imagination of which he has given us the most suggestive definition—

> 'The Seer strayed not from earth's human pale,
>   But the mysterious face of common things
>
> He mirrored, as the moon in Rydal mere
>   Is mirrored when the breathless night hangs blue ;
> Strangely remote she seems and wondrous near,
>   And by some nameless difference born anew.'

This fine simple image tells us more of the nature of the imagination than many ponderous lucubrations on the subject.

Mr. Gosse's volume is one of real gossip. The title
*Edmund Gosse:* is not loosely applied, but does actually,
 'Gossip in   as good titles will, express the spirit of
 a Library.'  the book. Any one whose collection of
books is no mere technical apparatus, whose culture
has developed by his own instinct rather than by some
system of artificial incubation, is sure to have gathered
about him, in addition to his various classics, a fourth
estate, the poor relations of literature, who take their
place upon his shelves rather by sentiment than by
right.

This fourth estate reflects, more surely than any of
the others, his individual selective taste ; for, though
every man must have a copy of Byron or Shelley, if
only for reference, there is no unwritten law prescrib-
ing a Gerard's *Herbal*, or the *Amasia* of Mr. John
Hopkins. As the caddis-worm pleases itself entirely
as to whether it shall make its little case of bits of
reed or tiny pebble, or even glass, so in the choice
of this fourth estate the bookman knows no law but
his own whim. Mr. Dobson, doubtless, exaggerated a
little when he declared in regard to his own 'ragged
regiment '—

> '. . . . the others I never have opened,
> But those are the ones I read ' :

but certainly, those are the only books one ever thinks
of taking down for visitors.

That innocent delight, that of exhibiting one's own
particular bookish toys to our friends, is the *raison*

*d'être* of this volume.    Practically, you enter Mr. Gosse's library, and he takes down this old volume and that, and tells you why he cares about it.    He doesn't talk for the sake of imparting information, though that even he cannot help doing sometimes. All he aims at is to tell you enough about his *bouquin* to enlist your sympathy.    Criticism is defined in a well-known phrase as 'the adventures of a soul among masterpieces.'    But that the books dealt with by Mr. Gosse can rarely be described as masterpieces, his gossip might be described in the same words.    You can, if you like, consider it as so many 'studies in miniature' of so many odd volumes ; but doing so, you would miss its real significance, which abides rather in the book as a whole than in its parts.    This book is really more interesting for what it suggests of the tastes of its writer than for what it tells about any separate volume.    It is a kind of bookman's bio-graphy, as one can read it written across the shelves of any well selected library.    It is the one book which every bookman ought to write—if he is clever enough.    It is the bookman's Apologia—to his wife, an Apologia, alas, not always accepted ; but then how seldom is it so pleasantly made.    For Mr. Gosse has caught the true spirit of his theme, and rather chats than writes.

He begins by confiding his book plate, a real touch of nature.    He very properly thinks it the most charm-ing in existence.

'The outward and visible mark of the citizenship of the book-lover,' he says, 'is his book plate.    There are many good bibliophiles who abide in the trenches, and never proclaim their loyalty by a book plate. They are with us, but not of us ; they lack the courage of their opinions, they collect with timidity or carelessness, they have no heed of the morrow. Such a man is liable to great temptations. He is brought face to face with that enemy of his species, the borrower, and dares not speak with him in the gate.'

Here is a gentle touch of that affected seriousness without which a hobby is apt to grow of a very deadly boredom. Then Mr. Gosse makes the tender confidence.

'A living poet, Lord de Tabley, wrote a fascinating volume on book plates, some years ago, with copious illustrations. There is not, however, one specimen in his book which I would exchange for mine, the work and the gift of one of the most imaginative of American artists, Mr. Edwin A. Abbey. It represents a very fine gentleman of about 1610, walking in broad sunlight in a garden, reading a little book of verses. The name is coiled around him, with the motto, *Gravis cantantibus umbra.*'

But Mr. Gosse makes no appeal to the unintelligent bookman, the marine store dealer of literature, who collects old rubbish merely because it is rare, and clothes it in purple and morocco like that very ungenial old person, 'bibliotaph' is, I believe, the correct word—in Burton's 'Bookhunter,' who prided himself on the possession of the two existing copies of *Rout upon Rout: or the Rabblers Rabbled*, 'by Felix Nixon, Gent.' His opportunity came, it will be remembered, when, a scholar desiring a look at the book for a literary purpose, he was able fiendishly to refuse.

Mr. Gosse's bookman, indeed, you will have seen, is no book-lender; but still he is a very different person from this famous type. His books may belong to him by the frailest threads of association; but mere rarity of occurrence, as distinct from rarity of quality, is not his besetting charm. Mr. Gosse speaks up for the 'first edition.' (It was a profane Mr. Monkhouse, was it not, who sang of 'the first edition and the worst?')

'The excuses for collecting,' he says, 'are more than satire is ready to admit. The first edition represents the author's first thought; in it we read his words as he sent them out to the world in his first heat, with the type he chose, and with such peculiarities of form as he selected to do most justice to his creation. We often discover little individual points in a first edition, which never occur again. And if it be conceded that there is an advantage in reading a book in the form which the author originally designed for it, then all the other refinements of the collector become so many acts of respect paid to this first virgin apparition, touching and suitable homage of cleanness and fit adornment. It is only when this homage becomes mere eye-service, when a book radically unworthy of such dignity is too delicately cultivated, too richly bound, that a poor dilettantism comes in between the reader and what he reads.

'To the feudal splendours of Mr. Cobden Sanderson, a tenpenny book in a ten pound binding, I say fie.'

Mr. Gosse recalls that legend, surely the very crown of mediæval hyberbole, concerning Mentzelius, who attested to his having heard in the seclusion of his library the male book-worm flap his wings and crow like a cock in calling to his mate. Mr. Lang popularised the story in *The Library*, but I fancy that I read it first long ago in some old paper by Mr. Gosse.

There is a simple phrase, too, in this introductory chapter for which one would say grace—'A library in a garden.' 'The phrase,' says Mr. Gosse, 'seems to contain the whole felicity of man.' 'It sounds like having a castle in Spain, or a sheep walk in Arcadia.'

In turning to the books for which Mr. Gosse begs the meed of a melodious moment, one likes them the better for their real obscurity. That is, for the most part. He does not talk of what one might call the 'cant' old books; such as Burton's *Anatomy*, over which so many have sentimentalised since Lamb loved it; people who would never have discovered it for themselves, and, having bought it, never read it.

He does treat of several more or less famous books, such as Camden's *Britannia*, Gerard's *Herbal*, and *A Mirror for Magistrates*; but most of his books have a merely personal or recondite appeal. One of his best chats is entitled 'What Ann Lang read.' It has nothing to do with a gentleman of a name so similar in sound that one suspects a slyness in Mr. Gosse's title. It comes of Mr. Gosse having picked up two or three eighteenth-century novels, 'by the Ouida of the period—the great Eliza Haywood,' which novels were inscribed 'Ann Lang, her book,' Ann Lang being apparently a housemaid of the period. Another gossip on the anonymous *History of Pompey the Little : or, The Life and Adventures of a Lap-Dog*, 1751 (apparently an eighteenth-century 'Puck'), makes one anxious to read the book for one's-self.

Aurora (the fresh natural heroine, who makes the contrast to the artificiality which is the theme of satire) has returned from Bath, and assures the Count that she has had a pleasant season there.

'"You amaze me," cries the Count ; "impossible, madam! How can it be, ladies? I had letters from Lord Monkeyman and Lady Betty Scornful assuring me that, except yourselves, there were not three human creatures in the place." "But surely," retorts Aurora, "they must have been asleep, both of them, when they wrote their letters ; for the Bath was extremely full." "Full," cries the Count, interrupting her, "O madam, that is very possible, and yet there might be no company—that is none of us ; nobody that one knows."'

The writer of this, Mr. Gosse tells us, was the Rev. Francis Coventry, at the time of the satire, twenty-five years of age, and if the whole of the book is anything like this, and Mr. Gosse assures us that it is, it certainly deserves a greener memory.

Another deserved plea against oblivion is the chapter on Smart, whom, it will be remembered, Browning celebrated in his *Parleyings*. Mr. Gosse has been at the pains to discover some new details concerning his life, and altogether his account of the somewhat hardly treated poet is most sympathetic and welcome.

But I must not any longer pursue my parasitical course of gossip upon gossip, so will leave to Mr. Gosse himself your introduction to Lady Winchelsea, just hinting that Lady Winchelsea is Mr. Gosse's 'Margaret, Duchess of Newcastle.'

SCOTT'S poetry has long been out of fashion, but for *Sir Walter Scott: His Poetry.* those who have mastered that useful precept, that all schools have their value, who ask from Art a various and not merely a monotonous, restricted delight, it will always have a real place upon their shelves, seldom, probably, to be taken down, but there and unforgotten.

> 'An eye
> That hath kept watch o'er man's mortality,'

seeks for its more habitual pasture a calmer, more reflective song. Scott himself said that his poetry was rather for 'soldiers, sailors, and young people, of bold, active disposition.' And, indeed, it is essentially for young people, with the heyday still in the blood. Bounding with animal spirits, it needs animal spirits to enjoy it. Without them its 'tirra-lirra' crushes with its buoyant life.

> 'Waken, lords and ladies gay,
> On the mountain dawns the day,
> All the jolly chase is here,
> With hawk and horse and hunting spear !

> Hounds are in their couples yelling,
> Hawks are whistling, horns are knelling,
>     Merrily, merrily, mingle they,
>     Waken, lords and ladies gay.'

This breezy verse marks the dominant note of Scott's poetry. It is one great reveille. So long as the fact of the lark being up is an argument for our own early rising, Scott's song is still for us : but a time soon comes for us to learn that a merciful Providence has appointed one breakfast-hour for larks and another for ourselves, and that we are not really called upon to leave our beds because 'the mist has left the mountain grey,' or because—

> '. . . foresters have busy been
> To track the buck in thickest green '

at five in the morning. That forester was probably a myth, and the reality was Sir Walter, sitting, fresh as a daisy, at his desk, and pouring out page after page of his brimming romance. That was at the-other-end-of-the-century. Now we end the day where good innocent Sir Walter began it, and, maybe, drink to the dawn in our last absinthe.

A return to Sir Walter just now would be a most salutary reaction of taste. As Whitman says of himself, so one can say of Scott : He will be health to us, and 'filter and fibre our blood.' It is true that he was feudal and we are democratic, true that he had not in his work the *curiosa felicitas* of phrase we demand to-day, but he had instead a passion, a rhythm, of which we know little, and his heart was big with that humanity which makes aristocrat and democrat as one. Scott was so complete a man too. Like all the greatest men, he was supremely practical. His genius was but one function of his being. It was not, as with many, a tumour which sucked away the best of him for its sustenance. He kept it in its proper relation to the rest of him. It did not prevent his being a true husband, an unselfish father, an active citizen. He had none of that resigned acceptance of temperament which for many to-day is the fatal peace of science. If he saw a duty he bent his temperament to it, instead of pleading 'genius.' It was in that spirit he first studied law, for which his father had destined him; and no one can doubt that that early discipline was largely responsible for the plodding habit of his later years. Like all strong people, he used his difficulties to make himself stronger. The story of his battle with debt reads like another Iliad. Think of his setting his teeth to face that £177,000 with his own unaided pen, and in five years having reduced it to £54,000! Surely, most men would have been tempted by the £30,000 offered him by an anonymous admirer. But Scott literally preferred death to taking it.

*The Lay of the Last Minstrel* and *Marmion* mark the best period of Sir Walter's verse, and are indeed, with the exception of some ballads and lyrics, his most characteristic and inspired work. These poems stand the test of re-reading as *The Lady of the Lake* cannot. Their blithe songfulness, their manly rhythm, must surely keep them fresh for many a year. Men can hardly put them on the shelf till, having no further use for it, we have quite lost the touch of the *lyra heroica.*

WHATEVER else Severn was, he is interesting to the

*Joseph Severn:* world mainly, if not entirely, as the devoted

Life by friend of Keats. At the same time, to

William Sharp. quote Keats's own famous lines,

> '. . . . the trees
> 'That whisper round a temple become soon
> Dear as the temple's self ; '

and some, the truest lovers of Keats, who still feel an almost personal sense of gratitude to Severn, could hardly have waxed impatient had Mr. Sharp made ampler use of his more specially Severn material. For we may well ask, whether the individuality which goes to the making of great poetry is any more worthy of the biographer than that which accounts for an un-selfish devotion such as that given to Keats by Joseph Severn. Certainly the world could more easily spare such poetry than such friendship. Some are great, and some worship, and the worshipper is not unfrequently greater than the worshipped. This, of course, does not apply to Keats, for no circle of friends was ever more unanimous in its regard than his. He seems to have inspired them with nothing short of a passion. 'If I know what it is to love, I truly love John Keats,' wrote Haslam—through whom Keats and Severn first became acquainted, probably in the spring of 1816. Severn was impressed from the first moment of their meeting. 'It was his good fortune to encounter in youth,' he says, 'one of those incidents which change or make the whole course of a man's life. This was the congenial meeting with a young poet near my own age, and so gifted with a bright imagination and with such charming manners, and with such communicativeness, that I felt raised to the third heaven. Fortunately for me we soon became the greatest friends, for there was much in common between us, in addition to a mutual love of nature.' It was really to Severn—then a poor engraver's apprentice, studying art in his leisure hours—that we owe Keats's first introduction to the Elgin marbles ; and it was prompted by Severn's enthusiasm over Titian's 'Bacchus,' in the National Gallery, that Keats first went to see it, thus gaining the inspiration for his famous Bacchanal in the opening of 'Endymion.' Keats, as we know, spent many an hour afterwards dreaming in front of the Elgin marbles, and on one occasion we read that Severn came upon him 'with eyes shining so brightly, and face so lit up by visionary rapture, that he stole quietly away without intrusion.' The friends used to share their Highgate and Hampstead walks together, and Mr. Sharp has one interesting reminiscence to add to the story of the composition of the 'Ode to the Nightingale.' One night, when Keats was spending the evening with friends at the large house, then (as well as the familiar group of pine trees) known as the 'Spaniards,' he was missed. Joseph Severn, one of the company, went to look for him, and discovered him lying on the ground under the pines, and listening entranced to the song of a nightingale overhead; and either that night or the following morning he wrote his famous ode. Severn afterwards painted a picture in exact illustration of this episode. This is a beautiful reminiscence to complete the well-known story of Keats sitting under an apple-tree in Brown's Hampstead garden one morning, and returning indoors with the great ode written on scraps of paper. Severn once said of Keats that 'he was a nightingale only when he sang, at other times a wild hawk,'—one among many testimonies to that real manliness of Keats's character which critics for a time lost sight of, but which Matthew Arnold and Mr. Sidney Colvin have now once for all established. The boy-poet, sticky with nectar, and so effeminate as to be 'snuffed out by an article,' is now, we will hope, quite a myth. Two new portraits, published for the first time in this volume, are further witness to this manliness of character and demeanour on which all his friends were unanimous. Among Severn's other services, he persuaded Keats to read Milton, whom he had been disposed to neglect. The result was, of course, 'Hyperion.' It was probably also an unfortunate remark of Severn's that finally decided Keats to leave that poem, like his favourite marbles, a splendid torso. 'It might have been written by Milton,' said Severn. That was just Keats's objection to it. He did not want to write a poem 'that might have been written by John Milton, but one that was unmistakably written by no other than John Keats.'

Thus, in what at some periods seems to have been almost daily intercourse, their friendship grew, rooted in perhaps the most fruitful of all sympathies, the sympathy in art. Meanwhile Severn had been working away at his painting, and to his delight and astonishment won the gold medal of the Academy (not given for some years before) for his 'Cave of Despair.' In the painting of this he had shown the true pluck and tenacity of the artist. Not having been able to afford a model, he resorted to the grotesque alternative of painting the limbs of his figure of Despair 'from his own shivering legs, as seen in a looking-glass in the chill morning or afternoon light'; and finally he was reduced to sell his 'few treasured possessions, including his watch and his books, so that he might not lack the materials required.'

It was this manly spirit that kept him going through his long death-bed attendance upon Keats—a devotion for which he is ever canonised in the hearts of all 'Love's lovers.' Mr. Sharp has little new to add to the story, as most of Severn's letters have already been printed by Mr. Buxton Forman. But one is glad that he is able considerably to minimise Mr. Colvin's assumption that Severn went to Italy, in the first instance, as much in the interest of his art studies as for the sake of Keats. It is true there was a chance of an art studentship there, but that occurred to him as an afterthought. The manner in which he immediately took up Haslam's suggestion proves that. There had been hopes that Charles Armitage Brown would be able to accompany Keats, but those falling through, Haslam called one night on Severn and asked him, 'Will you go?' 'I'll go,' was his immediate response, though to keep his word he had a bitter quarrel with his father, who had always been so sympathetic with him in his art studies. His mother, however, approved—'my dear, angel mother,' as he affectionately calls her. A windfall of £25 just coming in for one of his miniature paintings, which were just beginning to receive recognition, was every penny he had to make his venture on ; Keats, it will be remembered, through the kindness of Messrs. Taylor and Hessey, being furnished with £100 on account of 'Endymion.' But the story is too well known to lovers of poetry to need re-telling. It is more to our purpose to say that Severn's after-life proved an ample reward for all his unselfish devotion ; and it is cheering to think that it all grew out of it. His relationship to Keats had interested the English residents in Rome, and there soon arose a demand for his paintings, the then Emperor of Russia being among his patrons. In course of time he married, and his social popularity growing with his artistic, was appointed English consul, in which capacity 'he earned the lasting gratitude of many who benefited by his large-hearted and never-failing benevolence.' So ran a circular which was issued two years after his death, with the purpose of raising funds to remove his body from a distant cemetery to its final resting-place by the side of his friend.

But for Severn his life meant but one thing—he had been 'the friend of Keats.' It is quite pathetic to notice how till the end he can hardly write a letter without some reference to his lost friend. 'It seems to me,' runs a letter to Haslam, 'that his love and gratitude have never ceased to quicken with cool dews

the springs of my life.  I owe almost everything to him,
my best friends as well as my artistic prosperity, my
general happiness as well as my best inspirations. . . .'
He goes on to say how on one occasion during his
illness Keats had turned to him, 'with a fiery life in his
eyes, painfully large, and glowing out of the hollow,
woe-wrought face,' and said, 'Severn, I bequeath to you
all the joy and prosperity I never had,' and, adds Severn,
'I do believe that the dear fellow has never ceased to
help me.'

WHAT is one really to think of Byron?  Probably, the
first step towards answering that question
*Byron :*
A Present-
Day View.
would be to read him, for, in the truest
sense, and with one or two known excep-
tions, he never seems to have been read at all.  Scott's
reading of him resulted in, perhaps, the most extraordinary literary criticism ever made—'as various in
composition as Shakespeare himself,' wrote Sir Walter,
and 'in the very grand and tremendous character of
Cain, Lord Byron has certainly matched Milton on his
own ground.'  He seems to have mesmerised the most
intelligent of his contemporaries.  But his astounding
vogue with the majority is more easily explained.  It is
needless to say that the explanation is not in his poetry.
Such a vogue could never be made by *poetry*—the
greater the poetry the less chance it would have.  We
read of the immense sales, and we exclaim, 'What a
different public from ours!'  *Perhaps* it had more care

for poetry.  But that was not the reason.  Byron was
a notorious rake, or say, lady-killer, had a romantic
reputation for beauty, an overbearing personality, and
he belonged to a class in which those characteristics
had full play and advertisement.  From the first,
therefore, he had the women on his side, and as a rule,
women are the makers of literary reputations.  Scott's
vogue was far more real and much less easy to
account for.  Now, women do often instinctively make
valuable discoveries, or perhaps they rather canvass
for them than make them.  In that, at any rate,
they are notoriously successful—they are credited
with Shakespeare in the eighteenth century, and they
have certainly done much for Browning and Mr.
Meredith.  But in the case of Lord Byron it was
certainly no subtle literary instinct that was aroused
in them;  it was simply the dazzled, worshipping
feminine.  The fact is that Lord Byron's works sold
in such numbers because all the women in England
were secretly in love with him.  He was a beautiful,
passionate, 'interesting' outlaw from society;  in fact,
the *beau idéal* of a romantic stage-hero.  He was more
than this at the heart of him, we know, but it was not
his heart, but his showy exterior, which set the Thames
on fire.  In short, it was his personal, not his poetical,
qualities which made him, and even to-day he is more
interesting as a 'figure' than a poet.  A tradition of his
beauty still lingers in the feminine blood, and plenty of
women still exist who, without having read a word of
his poetry, cherish a sneaking regret that they were born
so many years too late;  just in the same way as a

reminiscence of Lady Hamilton still haunts and teases the masculine mind. Shelley, with a passion for revolt to which Byron's was child's-play, with an ardour for 'liberty' which was lifelong and practical, if not showily quixotic, and with the similar-dissimilar sins against society, aroused no such attention. He sinned too much like a doctrinaire; Byron sinned like a 'gentleman.' To compare greater men with smaller, and thinking for the moment of the men as men, not poets, the original difference between Byron and Shelley resembled that between Shakespeare and Dante. Byron and Shakespeare 'knew how to make the best of both worlds.' Dante and Shelley were but strangers here—heaven was their home. They were as much prophets as poets, Shelley, perhaps, more prophet than poet, just as Byron was more man of the world than poet. Though not a better —certainly no worse man than Shelley—Byron was a more conventionally robust one, as assuredly he is an inferior poet.

Matthew Arnold, of course, held a very different opinion, and while one cannot go to the other extreme with Mr. Swinburne, it must be confessed that Arnold's deliverance on Byron is a sore trial to the faithful. It seems the *reductio ad absurdum* of his definition of poetry as 'a criticism of life.' Byron had more of the great human subject-matter, he contended, than either Shelley or Coleridge. In that respect he was, in our century, second only to Wordsworth, with whom it certainly seems a paradox to see him placed side by side. Wordsworth and Byron, then Keats, and then Coleridge and Shelley. That was Arnold's

famous conclusion.   It brought from Mr. Swinburne
one of his foaming hyperboles reprinted in the somewhat regrettable *Miscellanies*—ninety close pages, against
Arnold's forty well-leaded.   The truth is just the reverse, said Mr. Swinburne, Shelley and Coleridge are
first, and Byron last of all, perhaps behind Crabbe.   Mr.
Swinburne's criticism is much overloaded with all his
well-known stars and flames and thunders, strangely
bewildering after Arnold's lucid style.   Moreover, it
loses in conviction by our remembrance of the very
different opinion held by the writer in 1865, when he
had to make a selection from Byron.   His introduction
on that occasion is printed in the earlier volume of
really fine prose, the *Essays and Studies*—prose written
when Mr. Swinburne still retained some sense of
proportion and decency of expression.

On that earlier occasion Mr. Swinburne had written
of Byron's 'splendid and imperishable excellence, which
covers all his offences and outweighs all his defects :
the excellence of sincerity and strength.'   Arnold quoted
the latter phrase as the best expression of Byron's
real value, and probably pushed it too far.   He
dwelt so upon it that, as he was latterly in danger of
doing, the essential poetical qualities in which Byron
was certainly lacking seem almost to have disappeared
from his consideration.   Byron's personality, Byron's
subject-matter, seem to have blinded him to Byron's
treatment of the same.   Amid all Mr. Swinburne's
verbiage, he makes straight for that point.   Poetry,
after all, is poetry, he says, and subject to certain laws.
Granted that the greatest poetry is based upon the

broadest foundations—still the mere foundation is not
all ; the final test of poetry may be there, but the
primary test is what is built upon those foundations.
A great theme is all very well, but it must be treated
according to poetical laws before it can become poetry.
A smaller theme perfectly treated is better than a great
one imperfectly treated.　Of the essence of such treatment are, says Mr. Swinburne, 'imagination and
harmony' ; and these in any distinguished degree were
not, he would say, among Byron's gifts.　Mr. Swinburne
even, and with some show of reason, attacks the
assumption of Byron's broad humanity of theme.
Byron had but one subject, said Dr. John Nicol,
'himself.'　Still, that is not to say that his work lacks
in human nature, for that is oftenest found at the
bottom of the well of self.　Walt Whitman, for instance,
claims to know mankind, because he knows himself.

Re-reading the famous 'Giaour,' one cannot but feel
that while he has gone to an almost ludicrous extreme
of depreciation, Mr. Swinburne goes nearer the critical
truth than Arnold in this matter.　Of that dramatic
imagination which can put a scene of action visibly
before us, Byron was certainly, as Arnold claimed, the
possessor, and there are several fine examples of it in
'The Giaour' ; but of that greater imagination which
can suffuse a sentence or a mere word with a strange
sense of infinitude—such lines as—

'To be imprisoned in the viewless winds,'

one finds no trace.　There are fine bursts, which are
more than rhetoric, but which are certainly not great

poetry.   There is passion, but it is the fluency, not
the depth of passion.   There is much sentimentalism,
which Byron would have had to work out of before he
began to be a great poet.   As for the 'harmony,' Byron
himself declared it 'but a string of passages.'   What
wonder, when one considers his method of composition?
'"Lara,"' he declares, 'I wrote while undressing after
coming home from balls and masquerades, in the year
of revelry 1814.   "The Bride" was written in four,
"The Corsair" in ten days.'   Although, as Arnold says,
Byron could not have done his work in any other way,
that is not the way in which the greatest poetry is
written.

But, whatever one says about Byron's poetry, his
significance as a man is little reduced.   He was a
striking and, in many respects, a noble figure.   As one
of the earliest protesters against conventional politics
and conventional living, he has earned the gratitude of
Europe.   On the Continent, as we know, he is appreciated far more than here, but, as Mr. Swinburne points
out, such appreciation is to be received cautiously.   It is
so hard for one nation to judge another's poetry.   Had
Byron been able to put all that was in him into poetry,
he would indeed have given us great things ; but, after
all, that is but to say that had he been a greater poet,
he would have given us greater poetry.

MR. SKIPSEY must feel a proud and happy satisfaction

*Joseph Skipsey:* 'Songs and Lyrics.'

as he looks at the fine-paper *édition de luxe* of his poems which Mr. Walter Scott has issued. He must smile as he thinks of the very different conditions under which his songs first found birth. Little thought, indeed, had he of *éditions de luxe*, as he scrawled them painfully on fragments of paper in the dark narrow ways of a coal mine. All that his book means to him, all the strength, the intensity, the tenderness, of his love for it, perhaps only a woman who has reared her one child through years of struggling days, or some fellow-poet with a like story, can be expected fully to understand. But to us even such a book has a profoundly suggestive significance. Quite apart from its merits as verse, of which anon, Mr. Skipsey's book, to the serious, reflective mind, is one of those symbols of which happily the lives of our democracy afford no few examples, a symbol of all that is aspiring and indomitable in man, and in fact in life. As Whitman says of his *Leaves of Grass*—'Camerado! this is no book. Who touches this touches a man.' And yet again it is indeed, in Carlyle's solemn use of the word—'a book.'

It is so because it is the essence of a manly life 'distilled to a mere drop.' It comes straight from the central life of a man, and is not like the majority of books of every kind, the product of some isolated activity of the brain. Save as the symbol of a hard life bravely lived to finer issues, it may not be of much value.

The poems are often crude, their *naïveté* is too *naïve*—
they sometimes 'lack the quality of art.' Will you permit me just for once to say '—— art !' There is one
interest to which art must still give precedence, and
that is true life. When we have both together, all the
better. Happily, we have examples of great artists who
have been great men too.

But I must not seem to depreciate Mr. Skipsey's real
poetical gift. His poems have often touches of very
high qualities, imagination for one, deep thought continually, with perhaps a tendency to mysticism, artistic
control, if not artistic elasticity, a charming fancy, and
an earth-music all their own. What I mean is that his
book, though it has thus its own poetic charm, a charm
that often reminds one of Blake, is one of those books
that are, *par excellence*, interesting on account of the individuality they express. In the present edition Mr.
Skipsey leaves his verses to tell their own tale, as they
can well do ; but to the edition before this Dr. Spence
Watson added a brief account of their author's life,
giving details of those essential facts plainly revealed in
the poems. Thus we gather that Mr. Skipsey was not
only a coal-miner, but had been so for forty years, in
the pits of Percy Main, Northumberland, that he went
to the mines at seven, that he taught himself to write
there with a piece of chalk on the back of a little door
which it was his duty to open and shut for the passage
of wagons, and that in such arduous ways and circumstances he had acquired a culture which embraced
pretty well all of worth in the literature of the world.
Meanwhile, the lark that sings as well in prisons and

dark places as in the morning sky sang by him at his
work, and reversed for him the miracle of that fairy-
gold which always turned out to be mere coal in the
morning.   Mr. Skipsey had learned the faculty of the
other alchemy, and turned his coal into nuggets :

> ' In the coal-pit, or the factory,
>     I toil by night or day,
> And still to the music of labour
>     I lilt my heart-felt lay ;
> I lilt my heart-felt lay—
>     And the gloom of the deep, deep mine,
> Or the din of the factory, dieth away,
>     And a golden lot is mine.'

Well may such a man proudly sing :

> ' What tho', in bleak Northumbria's mines,
>     His better part of life hath flown,
> A planet's shone on him, and shines
>     To fortune's darlings seldom known ;
> And while his outer lot is grim,
>     His soul, with light and rapture fraught,
> Oft will a carol trill, or hymn
>     In deeper tones the deeper thought.'

Such a man is, indeed, independent of all we can do
or say ; he is truly 'the captain of his soul.'   Mr. Skipsey's secret, apparently, was no mere culture of an
impassivity such as Marcus Aurelius trained himself
to practise, though all who suffer have soon to learn
that too, and soon to learn, like that great philosopher,
to make their fine reflections or fine poems on the
battle-field—'among the Quadi at the Granua.'   He
seems to have been blessed with a genuine optimism
of nature, and to have been able to look on his life as

'Jinny' on her dusky lover, in this vivid and in every way charming little poem :

> 'Duskier than the clouds that lie
> 'Tween the coal-pit and the sky,
> Lo, how Willy whistles by
>   ' Right cheery from the colliree.
>
> Duskier might the laddie be,
> Save his coaxing coal-black e'e,
> Nothing dark could Jinny see
>   A-coming from the colliree.'

Mr. Skipsey's best poems all show this terse power of picture-making.  Here is one of the darker side of the collier-life :

> ' "Get up !" the caller calls, "get up !"
>   And in the dead of night,
> To win the bairns their bite and sup,
>   I rise a weary wight.
>
> My flannel dudden donn'd, thrice o'er
>   My birds are kiss'd, and then
> I with a whistle shut the door,
>   I may not ope again.'

The patient weary strain, the tragic uncertainty of the miner's life, is surely all here.  The very simplicity, almost baldness, of the verse seems to have come of the stern wrestle with the hard crust of the earth.

But such dark pictures are few in Mr. Skipsey's songs.  For the most part he looks on the bright side, on the love-making of collier lads and lasses, or he forgets all his surroundings and pursues his own moonbeam fancies.  And he can cap a conceit or turn a compliment like a courtier. Could any be prettier than this verse with a sprig of lily of the valley :

> 'It is a gem, tho' small, too rare
>     For mortal hand to pluck, and twine
> With any save an angel's hair ;
>     And that is why 'tis placed in thine.'

With all this, Dr. Spence Watson tells us that 'whilst still a working pitman he was master of his craft, and it took an exceptionally good man to match him as a heaver of coal. When, after many long years of patient toil, he won his way to an official position, he gained the respect of those above him in authority whilst retaining the confidence and affection of the men. Simple, straight, and upright, he has held his own wherever he has been placed.' In this, of course, is Mr. Skipsey most significant. He has not, like some other poets, shirked the first duties of life at the call of the muse. Certainly, sweet and powerful as many of his verses are, they had hardly been worth forsaking 'weans and wife' for—one would like to know, indeed, what poems ever have been worth that. Nor has Mr. Skipsey fallen a victim to the temptations of flattered vanity such as perhaps peculiarly beset a 'poet of the people.' Mr. Robert Buchanan has finely portrayed such a bedazzled poet in one of his *London Poems*. And yet Mr. Skipsey has not gone unlionised. The testimonial which backed his application for the custodianship of Shakespeare's House included the names of most of the men illustrious in modern literature and art, and Rossetti was especially kind to the miner poet. Mr. Skipsey has a touching reference to their friendship in one of the new poems added in the present edition.  While our minds have just been turned to the grimmer aspect of labour in the northern coalfields, it is well to have Mr. Skipsey to remind us that if the miner's life is hard, it yet produces brave men and sweet women, and that it too has its share of sunshine and song.  ' Perhaps, if we could see things as they really are,' said Dr. Spence Watson, ' Joseph Skipsey is the best product of the north-country coalfields since George Stephenson held his safety-lamp in the blower at Killingworth pit.'

THAT tireless huntsman of Tennysonian parallels, Mr.
*Lord Tennyson : 'The Foresters.'* Churton Collins, has, doubtless, already noted for a new edition of his *Illustrations* one more coincidence in the fact that Ben Jonson in his latter days also turned to the story of Robin Hood.  So has Lord Tennyson in *The Foresters*.  The opening of Ben Jonson's prologue is singularly appropriate, with one alteration of happy significance, to Lord Tennyson to-day.

> ' He that hath feasted you these forty years,
> And fitted fables for your finer ears . . .

begins Ben Jonson.  Lord Tennyson, however, can say sixty !—sixty-two in fact, reckoning from the *Poems, chiefly Lyrical*, in 1830.  In one other happy particular also the Jonsonian parallel does not apply.  Poor Jonson had at that time hissed his ' Come leave the loathed stage ' into the faces of an ungrateful public. Lord Tennyson still sits high and honoured amongst us

—a Merlin whom the Vivien of Time has robbed not of his charm.

Ben Jonson, too, in writing *The Sad Shepherd*, had his eye not so much on Robin Hood and Maid Marian as on Æglamour, a sorrowful swain who had lost his love, and went, therefore, wandering across Sherwood, mourning her in such exquisite verse as—

> 'Here she was wont to go! and here! and here!
> Just where those daisies, pinks, and violets grow:
> The world may find the spring by following her.'

There is some pretty love-play between Robin Hood and Maid Marian; but they are evidently happily married, with their romance behind them, settled down in Sherwood as successful outlaws. Possibly the witch Maulkin suggested to Lord Tennyson the inclusion of 'an old woman,' reputed witch, among his *dramatis personæ*, though the part played by her does not in the most trifling degree resemble that played by Jonson's, whose pastoral, half English and half classical, as was his wont, we may now, so far as Robin Hood is concerned, dismiss from our minds.

Dr. Garnett, in his preface to the recent re-issue of Peacock's delightful *Maid Marian*, fears that there can be little doubt but that Robin Hood was a myth. 'The name originally belonged to a mythical forest elf,' says his learned authority. An old ballad admits that there was even then some difficulty about the manner of Robin's birth :

> 'There's mony ane sings o' grass, o' grass,
> And mony ane sings o' corn;
> And mony ane sings o' Robin Hood
> Kens little whar' he was born;'

but it still leaves him his humanity, if it be humanity illegitimate.   Friar Tuck, too, must go, we are told, go pack with Friar Rush.

However, 'a mythical forest elf' is not much use in drama, save, may-be, as an 'attendant sprite'; and in dealing with his story Lord Tennyson not only restores Robin his humanity, but also his earldom, thus following the main stream of tradition which makes him Robert Earl of Huntington, outlawed for shooting the king's deer.   The other characters in *The Foresters* are the old familiar ones, including Sir Richard Lea, who has one fair daughter, Marian, a dauntless girl in love with Robin Hood.   Sir Richard has as little control over her as his prototype, Baron Fitzwater, has over Matilda, in Peacock.   Bidden to Robin's birthday in the greenwood, she says she means to go :

SIR RICHARD : 'Not if I barred thee up in thy chamber, like a bird in a cage.'

MARIAN : 'Then would I drop from the casement, like a spider.'

SIR RICHARD : 'But I would hoist the drawbridge, like thy master.'

MARIAN : 'And I would swim the moat like an otter.'

SIR RICHARD : 'But I would set my men-at-arms to oppose thee like the Lord of the Castle.'

MARIAN : 'And I would break through them all like the King of England.'

It is just so father and daughter play at draughts in Peacock, though in the dropping of the spider Lord Tennyson has, with his usual felicity, found a more exquisite image than any of Peacock's.   Of course, escape by such desperate fertility of expedient was not Peacock's invention, dating back at least to the transformations of Loki, in the Edda.

The other familiar characters also troop in as under other greenwood trees, Friar Tuck, Will Scarlet, Much, the Sheriff of Nottingham, the Abbot who holds Sir Richard Lea's lands in pawn, while the figure of the cunning, lascivious King John haunts the whole plot, and King Richard comes in, as in *Ivanhoe*, to pronounce the benediction.

Some critics have thought it worth while to compare unfavourably *The Foresters* with *Ivanhoe*. But that, I think, is to weigh it in the wrong scales. Full-blooded romance or poignant drama were not, apparently, Lord Tennyson's aims. Besides, the latter at least was hardly possible. Where, in the blithe, merry story, where men sing songs and crack jests one minute, and just as merrily crack skulls the next, where is there opportunity for dramatic intensity? There is hardly room even for characterisation, the *dramatis personæ* have been such well-known types this many a year. Peacock had the art to recognise these, and at the same time his own, limitations, when he turned the story into a sort of prose masque, filling it as full of songs as a wood with birds, and at the same time adding a touch of burlesque, lest we should be in danger of thinking his characters meant anything so serious as real romance.

If Englishmen must have their comparisons, let them make them with *Maid Marian* in this case, not with *Ivanhoe* and *As You Like it*. For *The Foresters*, like *Maid Marian*, is really a masquerade. The figures are really all actors, who for a time have donned the Lincoln green and 'fleet the time carelessly' in the greenwood, in a sort of dangerous picnic.    It is a mistake to weigh *The Foresters* as 'a drama.'    Lord Tennyson does not describe it so.    It is, in fact, a pastoral, on the model of an Elizabethan masque—a dainty piece of convention, in which the characters are types, and the manner prescribed.    To morning papers asking in robustious bass 'of its power as an acting drama,' we may reply, Yes, it is actable, as a pastoral play is actable.    It will not harrow up your soul, freeze your young blood, but it will give you a pleasant woodland entertainment, such as a certain noble lady used to give to her friends —a pleasing English landscape, with graceful figures moving across it, and sweet little bird-like songs in the air.

As in reading one of the Elizabethan masques one's eye always seeks out first the welcome italics, so do we first run through *The Foresters*, picking out the little daisies of song.    There are many of them, and one at least as exquisite as any Lord Tennyson has written, this invitation to sleep :

> 'To sleep ! to sleep ! the long bright day is done,
> And darkness rises from the fallen sun.
> To sleep ! to sleep !
> Whate'er thy joys, they vanish with the day ;
> Whate'er thy griefs, in sleep they fade away.
> To sleep ! to sleep !
> Sleep, mournful heart, and let the past be past !
> Sleep, happy soul ! all life will sleep at last.
> To sleep ! to sleep !'

This type of song, on one or two notes, of which there are several examples scattered through *The*

*Idylls of the King*, is peculiarly the property of Lord Tennyson. Birdlike is for once the scientific adjective to apply to it, for the recurrence of the refrain and the changes on one or two simple ideas seem to suggest the very manner of some birds—I will not venture to say which. A call, a call, and then a warble; a call, a call, and then another warble. So, it seems to me, go both the birds and Lord Tennyson's song.

In a song beginning,

> 'There is no land like England,
>     Where'er the light of day be;
> There are no hearts like English hearts,
>     Such hearts of oak as they be,'

Lord Tennyson once more exemplifies his well-known poetical thrift, for the song originally appeared so long ago as the 1830 *Poems, chiefly Lyrical*, and was, with another patriotic song, selected for especial scorn by 'Christopher North.' Lord Tennyson has made no changes in the body of the song, the two verses being reproduced, word for word, as in 1830; but he has entirely changed the chorus, which was originally in two parts, and ran as follows:

> *Chorus*—'For the French the Pope may shrive 'em,
>     For the devil a whit we heed 'em;
>     As for the French, God speed 'em
>       Unto their heart's desire,
>     And the merry devil drive 'em
>     Through the water and the fire.

> *Full Chorus*—'Our glory is our freedom,
>     We lord it o'er the sea;
>     We are the sons of freedom,
>     We are free.'

It is certainly impossible to plead either against Crusty Christopher or oblivion for these lines, though he might have employed comments a little more civil than 'miserable indeed' or 'that is drivel.' Lord Tennyson has now substituted a chorus more in the spirit of the greenwood.

A plot of italics, from which one expected most, proves somewhat disappointing. But, then, it was no little temerarious for even Lord Tennyson to give us another Titania, though he has before now shown himself the modern Fletcher. Robin lies asleep in the wood and dreams of Mab and of the fairy king. The fairies do not appreciate the outlaws. One by one they come to the queen with complaints—of carriage-frogs crushed, sward and bracken laid waste, daisies done to death—the conventional fairy imagery—and finally suggest the removal of the court to some more secluded spot. Titania consents, and, after promising the dreaming Robin happiness with Marian, she gives the order to march, in a line which at least has all the old Tennysonian dexterity of suiting the rhythm to the action :

'Up with you, all of you, off with you, out of it, over the wood
     and away ! '

Surely this is the very grasshopper flitter of the fairies.

The same dexterity is shown in the romping ring-a-roses metre of the concluding song, with which the outlaws hail the return of Richard :

'Now the King is home again, and never more to roam again,
Now the King is home again, the king will have his own again,
Home again, home again, and each will have his own again,
All the birds in merry Sherwood sing and sing him home again.'

Of the body of the play, one must admit that it

lacks vitality, it kindles all too rarely, and we miss the gusto of the mediæval knock-about comedy. The wit combats are apt to be somewhat of sham-fights, all too easily settled with Shakespearean word-play. But when it does kindle, we get unmistakable passages such as that in which Marian protests her faithful love for Robin. The reader will find several such passages to mark and hive, and one or two more songs besides, such as the charming little ballad of 'Master and Man.' But I fancy that the play as a whole will act better than it reads, its very verbal frugality being one of the rare characteristics of good acting plays. Room is left for the actors, for acting, not merely for elocution. Lord Tennyson, of course, intended his play for the stage, and doubtless that is why he has been somewhat less a Chrysostom than usual.

A RE-ISSUE of Caldwell Roscoe's poems leaves one
*William Caldwell Roscoe: Poems.* with the impression that Roscoe is a poet best represented in an anthology. He was a poet. His song was of the true fount, but it was very slender. In single sonnets, in many a detached passage, he gives us satisfying delight ; but his poetry is not full enough in body to hold one in the bulk. Its colour is too elusive, its fragrance too volatile. It seems the poetry of a man whose blood ran a little too thin, whose refinement was a little too refined, whose gentleness

was a little too gentle.  A voice 'low and sweet' is
an excellent thing in a poet as well as in woman, but
it can be pitched so low that it is hard to catch
its *timbre*.   It was so with William Caldwell Roscoe,
though it is noticeable that, in his descent from literary
parentage, he marks a distinct advance in poetical
power.  Indeed, the Roscoe family afford a rare instance
of literary power being cumulative from one generation
to the next.  Usually, as one well knows, this is
by no means the case.   William Roscoe, ardently
commemorated by Washington Irving, wrote that
sonnet on leaving his books which breathes so real
a sorrow that it will long keep his memory green.
In William Stanley Roscoe the voice grew stronger,
though to no such degree as we next hear it in the
sonnets of his son.

These were first collected by his son-in-law, Mr.
William Hutton, who prefaced them with a memoir
and criticism of great interest.   Mr. Hutton, if I remember aright, laid special stress on Roscoe's critical
essays, which he at the same time also collected.
These, indeed, show a critical gift of the calm Arnoldian
order, and possess a real distinction of treatment.
They would bear reprinting entire much better than
the poems, of which a small selection would do Roscoe
greater justice.

Miss Roscoe hesitated, she tells us, whether to print
the two plays of *Eliduke* and *Violenzia* entire, or to
represent them by selections.   She has chosen the
former course.  Perhaps it was the best, for plays, of
all forms of writing, are ill-represented by selection.

At the same time *Violenzia*, the maturer of the two
dramas, would have been more than sufficient; for
though in that Roscoe shows a real dramatic hold
of his hero, Earl Ethel, yet the drama in his hands
was more a Shakesperean convention than an instinctive vehicle of expression. All through the phrasing
is almost painfully Shakesperean, though often forcible
and beautiful :

> ' Look, how the heavy-foliaged elm-trees stand,
> Like clustered pictures in the western sky ;
> And there a fainter blue doth still betray
> Where bright Apollo had his bedding-place.
> High overhead the angels light their lamps,
> And with rich gifts and precious influence
> Walk the night-wandering winds.   Look up, my Ethel,
> When on the glances of the upturned eye
> The plumèd thoughts take travel, and ascend
> Through the unfathomable purple mansions,
> Threading the golden fires, and ever climbing
> As if 'twere homewards winging—at such time
> The native soul, distrammelled of dim earth,
> Doth know herself immortal, and sits light
> Upon her temporal perch.'

Roscoe's best-known sonnet is probably that beginning :

> ' Like a musician that with flying finger
> Startles the voice of some new instrument.'

I will quote one less familiar, of no less beauty—an
Amiel-like sigh of frustration :

> ' The bubble of the silver-springing waves,
> Castalian music, and that flattering sound,
> Low rustling of the loved Apollian leaves,
> With which my youthful hair was to be crowned,
> Grow dimmer in my ears ; while Beauty grieves
> Over her votary, less frequent found,

And, not untouched by storms, my life-boat heaves
Through the splashed ocean-water, outward bound.
And as the leaning mariner, his hand
Clasped on his ear, strives trembling to reclaim
Some loved lost echo from the fleeting strand,
So lean I back to the poetic land ;
And in my heart a sound, a voice, a name
Hangs, as above the lamp hangs the expiring flame.'

It is the paradox of such natures to best express themselves in the very sigh in which they mourn the
impossibility of expression.

OF all books in the world the *Vita Nuova* is, in Omar

*Dante and his Circle:* **Rossetti's Translations.** Khayyam's phrase, 'youth's sweet-scented manuscript.' Youth, all dream and passion, dream as terribly fair as the almond bloom against a morning sky, passion ardent as a sunrise. Indeed if we were to compare the literature of the world to a wood of various trees, the *Vita Nuova* would be the almond-tree — the almond-tree of youth. In every characteristic it is the very em-bodiment of youth. Not only in its passion and its dream, but in the self-consciousness with which one sees Dante deliberately fanning both with constant care ; the artifice with which he delighted to fret little golden 'chambers of imagery' for the honey, and deli-cate lachrymatories for the sorrow, of his love. The intense life in words so characteristic of the poet, and especially the young poet, the ecstasy, the consolation of them, never found a more perfect illustration than in the *Vita Nuova*—the book 'which first of all he made when young.' Is there any stranger paradox than that to sing of sorrow should bring so great a joy? Yet it is hardly cynical to say that to such a nature an elegy is no small compensation for a loss. By the time a poet has finished singing, his tears will usually be dry. It still happens with him as in the old mythology, out of the tomb of every grief springs up a flower, which though he read, 'Ai! Ai!' on its petals is no less to him a joy for ever. As some men fly to wine in sorrow, the poet flies to verse. Dante is said to have sought both and other consolations after the death of Beatrice, but he thus speaks of his deliberate turning to verse :

'When mine eyes had wept for some while, until they were so weary with weeping that I could no longer through them give ease to my sorrow, I bethought me that a few mournful words might stand me instead of tears. And therefore I proposed to make a poem, that weeping I might speak therein of her for whom so much sorrow had destroyed my spirit ; and I then began "The eyes that weep."'

But before copying out his poem Dante prefixes one of those curious elaborate analyses of its contents which is one of the quaintest and most significant characteristics of the *Vita Nuova* :

' *That this poem* (he beautifully begins) *may seem to remain the more widowed at its close, I will divide it before writing it ; and this method I will observe henceforward. I say that this poor little poem has three parts. The first is a prelude. In the second, I speak of her. In the third, I speak pitifully to the poem.*'

This is, indeed, as Polonius would say, 'the very ecstasy of love,' but if, amid all its charming convention, we miss the real pitiful sob underneath, we do wrong both to Dante and to youth :

> ' Who speaks thereof, and feels not the tears warm
> Upon his face, must have become so vile
> As to be dead to all sweet sympathies.'

These are lines from the poem which then follows, addressed to girl-sympathisers of his, whom he reminds

> ' How it was pleasant, ere she went afar,
>     To talk of her with you, kind damozels,
>     I talk with no one else,
> But only with such hearts as women's are.
>     And I will say,—still sobbing as speech fails,—
> That she hath gone to Heaven suddenly,
> And hath left Love below, to mourn with me.
>
> Beatrice is gone up into high Heaven,
>     The kingdom where the angels are at peace ;
>         And lives with them : and to her friends is dead.
> Not by the frost of winter was she driven
>     Away, like others ; nor by summer heats ;
>         But through a perfect gentleness, instead.'

In fact, she was, as a lover should always suppose, too good for this world, and God had taken her to Himself. This beautiful illusion is, of course, characteristic, like the rest, of youth. Some commentators have spent much vitality in arguing that Beatrice was intended by Dante as a personification of divine beauty, but such can have known nothing of the mystical temper of youth, which in its time has set some very commonplace maidens among the stars. The *Vita Nuova* gains in significance if we regard Beatrice rather as the same kind of giggling young miss

as our own first-love, now haloed beyond all recognition
of her relatives—and we have data for such a view in the
book itself. Very soon Dante had probably idolised her
out of all her personal character, and as he mingled
more and more with actuality, in the form of marriage
and his various political activities, she ascended higher
and grew brighter in his imagination, as the type of that
angel first-love to which we all look back, which we
know never really did or never can exist in this world,
but which, perhaps, we still go on hoping to meet, as
Dante his Beatrice, in Paradise. Not Beatrice Portinari, daughter of a magnate of Florence, but that
mystical Beatrice, 'even she who was called Beatrice
by many who knew not wherefore.' Those commentators who claim an allegorical significance for Beatrice are thus half right. It was not Beatrice Portinari
for whom Dante kept a lifelong troth, no earthly individual woman, for that he notoriously did not keep.
His friend Guido Cavalcanti 'rebukes' him in one of
his sonnets 'for his way of life after the death of
Beatrice'; Beatrice herself reproaches him for it in the
*Purgatorio*; that, indeed, was the cause of his vision
of the Inferno, as she implies :

> 'So low he fell, that all appliances
>      For his salvation were already short,
>      Save showing him the people of perdition.'

In the same poem he admits :

>      'The things that present were
> With their false pleasure turned aside my steps,
> Soon as your countenance concealed itself,'

and even in the *Vita Nuova* itself he confesses that

what he would call his 'susceptibility' was such that he was in danger of falling in love with one of those very 'ladies who had intelligence in love,' so well had she comforted him for the death of Beatrice. His 'eyes began,' he says, 'to be gladdened overmuch by her company, through which thing many times I had much unrest, and rebuked myself as a base person.' Yes, Dante was true to Beatrice, as a man is true to his first love! She became to him, in the beautiful phrase of a modern writer, 'that angel who is the type of all women.' But to imagine that Dante was true to Beatrice the school-girl is surely to dehumanise him, and to turn his noble idealism into a mere sentimentalism.

Rossetti's translations of the *Vita Nuova*, and of the circle of poets before and associated with Dante, have long been acknowledged as among the finest ever made. Perhaps Fitzgerald's Omar Khayyam is the only other parallel instance of perfection, at least in recent years. And Fitzgerald is a real analogue in that—as Mr. W. M. Rossetti well expresses it in the preface to a new edition—the translator has entered so keenly into the spirit of his originals, and 'has reinforced them with so manifest a poetic tone and savour proper to himself, that the versions have taken rank as a sort of cross between translated and original work.' Rossetti's translations thus, as Mr. W. M. Rossetti further says, in addition to their value as translation, 'serve likewise as a kind of prologue to Rossetti's personality among English poets.' It is, of course, a commonplace how much Dante Rossetti's poetry owed in character to his being steeped in Italian influences.

Besides, he had Dante in his blood, his father being a well-known Dante commentator, though with the misguided enthusiasm of a 'crank.' He preached one of those theories so depressing to the artistically-minded, viz., that Dante's work had a hidden political significance; that it was, in fact, not so much a great poem as the cipher of state intrigues, just as Shakespeare's plays have been proved to be ciphers of the philosopher's stone, and heaven knows what else.

The Dante enthusiasm, however, came out quite pure of such theory in the next generation, and certainly no enthusiasm for a poet was ever more fruitful of true service to his fame than Dante Gabriel Rossetti's for Dante. Of course the secret of his translations being so good was in the fact that he was a poet himself. Shelley's translation of Calderon and Coleridge's of *Wallenstein* are good for the same reason. Translation to be successful must be literally a second birth of the original through the mind of the translator, and poetry can only thus be born again through the mind of a poet. A translator, so to say, makes within himself a saturated solution of the poem to be translated, and then allows it to crystallise out again as near the original form as possible. He must not, as Rossetti said in his admirable preface, suffer himself to be bullied by the bugbear of 'literality.'

'The life-blood of rhythmical translation is this commandment—that a good poem shall not be turned into a bad one. The only true motive for putting poetry into a fresh language must be to endow a fresh nation, as far as possible, with one more possession of beauty. Poetry not being an exact science, literality of rendering is altogether secondary to this chief law.

I say *literality*,—not fidelity, which is by no means the same thing.'

Nothing more helpful could be written on the art of translating. Rossetti followed his own precept with so remarkable a success that his translations have all the bloom and fragrance of originals. Very often in the case of the smaller poets there can be no doubt that they have gained by filtering through a richer temperament. There can hardly be another volume on our shelves which is such a quintessence of poet's poetry as this of *Dante and his Circle*. Space does not permit me to deal with the sixty odd poets who make up or precede that circle, not even with the great and gallant Guido Cavalcanti, whom Dante speaks of continually in the *Vita Nuova* as his chief friend, but I may quote this anonymous ballata, 'Of True and False Singing,' as medicinable at the present time :

> 'A little wild bird sometimes at my ear
>     Sings his own verses very clear :
> Others sing louder that I do not hear.
> For singing loudly is not singing well ;
>     But ever by the song that's soft and low
> The master-singer's voice is plain to tell.
>     Few have it and yet all are masters now,
> And each of them can trill out what he calls
> His ballads, canzonets, and madrigals.
> The world with masters is so covered o'er,
> There is no room for pupils any more.'

A TURN for epigram and paradox evidently runs in Dr.
Garnett's family. One of the versions

*Richard Garnett:* included in this *Chaplet from the Greek*
'A Chaplet,' *Anthology* proves it to have been among
etc. the gifts of the late Rev. Richard Garnett,
and those who possess the somewhat scarce 'Paradox
Club' will know that Dr. Garnett has also transmitted a
portion of his inheritance to his son. The volume, of
which this dainty volume is substantially a reprint, has
for some time been a 'very desirable' rarity. Published
by Messrs. Macmillan in 1869, under the title of *Idylls
and Epigrams*, chiefly from the Greek anthology, it
has up till now existed in an *editio princeps*, though
a majority of the translations included in Mrs. Marriott
Watson's selection from the Greek anthology were taken
from Dr. Garnett's volume. Dr. Garnett's union of
eighteenth-century terseness, with somewhat of modern
intensity, admirably adapted him for the translation
of those wonderful poems where passion and epigram
exist in so odd and yet so happy a marriage. As an
example of the perfection of terseness, take this translation of the famous anonymous hyperbole :

> 'I send thee myrrh, not that thou may'st be
> By it perfumed, but it perfumed by thee.'

Compare it with Miss Strettell's rendering—admirable,
but how much less forcible :

> 'I send to thee sweet myrrh, thereby favouring it not thee,
> Since even the perfume by thy touch yet more perfumed may be.'

Ben Jonson adapted the same fancy in his 'Song to Celia':

> 'I sent thee late a rosy wreath,
>   Not so much honouring thee
> As giving it a hope that there
>   It could not withered be;
> But thou thereon didst only breathe
>   And sent'st it back to me:
> Since when it grows, and smells, I swear,
>   Not of itself, but thee.'

Dr. Garnett's new title is a little misleading. The word 'chiefly' is still needed in connection with 'the Greek anthology,' for several of Dr. Garnett's own epigrams are, as before, included. These, however, are so much in the spirit of the rest—in many cases being adapted from Greek originals, and are, besides, all identifiable in the table of authors—that the generalisation hardly matters.

The charming opening dedication and invocation, which form a sort of clasp to the box of 'sweets compacted,' are Dr. Garnett's own, and there are none neater in the book:

I.

> 'Hither, dear Muse, I pray, and with thee bear
> A madrigal for Melitè the fair,
> Evil with good repaying; for 'tis she
> Who tempts me to oblivion of thee.

II.

> The Muse invoked, whom next shall I address
> To grant my strain both merit and success?
> May Phœbus melody, may Pallas sense,
> And Bacchus geniality dispense;

By Graces grace, passion by Venus be
Bestowed, the love of nature, Pan, by thee ;
And last, without which all were not enough,
Vouchsafe, most potent Æolus, a puff.'

Here are two or three more of Dr. Garnett's own epigrams, the first a really beautiful *pensée*, and the second reminding one of Omar Khayyam in its grim anti-deistic irony :

' Simplicity is best, 'tis true,
    But not in every mortal's power !
If thou, O maid, canst live on dew,
    'Tis proof thou art indeed a flower.'

' Most ancient Saturn, Deity sublime
Of endless and inexorable Time,
I tempt thee not with gifts to be my friend,
For nought can thee appease, or aught offend ;
Nor needs it any sacrifice to bring
To thee, who of thyself tak'st every thing.'

And this, founded on an anecdote of Tom Paine :

' Sturdy Tom Paine, biographers relate,
Once with his friends engaged in warm debate.
Said they, " Minorities are always right ; "
Said he, " The truth is just the opposite."
Finding them stubborn, " Frankly now," asked he,
" In this opinion do ye all agree—
All, every one, without exception ?"   When
They thus affirmed unanimously, " Then
Correct," he said, " my sentiment must be,
For I myself am the minority." '

Dr. Garnett is not the first who has thus associated his own wit and grace with that of the poets of the anthology. The Rev. Robert Bland and the ' others' engaged with him on the *Collections from the Greek Anthology* for John Murray, in 1813, used, it may be remembered, to engage in illustrative wit combats of their own in their somewhat copious notes, John Herman Merivale being one of the four.

THE sword of the Lord and of Henley! Once the sword *W. E. Henley:* was mightier than the pen, then went forth 'The Song of an epigram and 'the pen' was 'mightier the Sword.' than the sword.' Mr. Henley combines both eras in a deadly weapon we may name the Sword-Pen. Yet, after all, with all its lightnings there remains more of the pen than the sword about what, remembering Sigurd, we may call 'The wrath of Henley.' The comparative harmlessness of the pen, for example: the innocuousness of those hard words which proverbially break no bones, for

> '. . . when the great juggler makes as to swallow,
> It's just the sword-trick.'

And indeed there is something of a trick, something of a cant, about this new gospel which so emphatically brings not peace but a sword, this sword-evangel begot of Jingoism by a Berserker. It is, in fact, not so much a gospel as a pose—our modern substitute for a gospel. If it were not so, we should hear less of it. The true sons of the sword are men of few words, and those they let their swords speak for them. They do not speak for their swords. They use them when the time comes, and then put them by as the time passes. Mr. Henley's *Song of the Sword* is a fine bit of dithyrambics in a sort of out-of-breath 'Beowulf' metre, but it is impossible to admire it without asking, why all this excitement as of a new prophecy? Does England really need any flame-headed Scottish Titan to teach it courage? Is it so rotten with ease as some fire-eaters would have us believe? Has the *libertatis sacra fames* left us? and is the Laureate's valorous counter-jumper merely a poet's phrase?

It seems necessary to remind the apostles of this 'new manliness' that the true masculine is at least as much a matter of brain as of brawn. Indeed, they might be women, these prophets, so keen is their gusto for thews and sinews. They might be animals, so resolutely would they seem to prefer to speak of an 'honest' primitive lust rather than of 'love.' This bathing in the Demiurgus cup of things is all very well, but, after all, as thus preached, it is but the health-bath of the emasculate, the puritanism of the neurotic; while to insist on the merely primitive is to ignore the laws of life, those laws by which

> ' From flesh unto spirit man grows
> Even here on the sod under sun.'

Mr. Henley apparently anticipates such criticism in a satirical poem beginning :

> ' As like the Woman as you can '—
>   (*Thus the New Adam was beguiled*)—
> So shall you touch the Perfect Man '—
>   (*God in the Garden heard and smiled*).
> Your father perished with his day :
>   A clot of passions fierce and blind
> He fought, he slew, he hacked his way :
>   Your muscles, Child, must be of mind.'

No, it was only Mr. Henley who was in the garden,
and to anticipate criticism is by no means the same as
to answer it.   Lord Tennyson's finely expressed ideal of
'the marriage of true minds' in 'The Princess,' which
I presume must bear the brunt of Mr. Henley's satire,
will none the less remain the rational ideal; and if
Mr. Henley regards the Laureate as a carpet-knight,
what has he to say to Mr. George Meredith?   No one
has more vigorously preached the necessity of our being
'rooted in good gross earth' than Mr. Meredith, and
yet his ideal of true manhood and womanhood is precisely that of Lord Tennyson's.   'Get you'—he says in
'The Ballad of Fair Ladies in Revolt'—

> '. . . . something of our purity,
> And we will of your strength : we ask no more.'

And again, in 'The Tragic Comedians,' 'You meet now
and then men who have the woman in them without
being womanised ; these are the pick of men ; and the
choicest women are those who yield not a feather of
their womanliness for some amount of manlike strength.'
In fact, it would seem as though Mr. Henley had made
up his mind to head a rally of the abused male against
the great captain of womankind, and the situation
resolves itself into Henley *v*. Meredith.   (*God in the
Garden heard and smiled.*)
It is a pity that Mr. Henley takes this so aggressively
masculine stand, because it considerably mars our
appreciation of the true manliness of his poems.   One
is continually suspicious of the creed, and all the various
marks of virility seem to be pointing a moral to a weak-

kneed generation. Just feel these muscles! Listen to this voice—right from the chest! In fact, as the music-hall song used to run, Mr. Henley is, before all things, 'the solid man.'

However, we must endeavour to forget all this, and, as Mr. Henley is a very genuine poet, that is, after all, soon done. 'The Song of the Sword' (appropriately dedicated to Mr. Kipling) is by no means the best thing in the book. Yet, it is a fine piece of dithyrambic, in the hurtling Norse rhythm, a mystical hymn elevating the sword of steel into a symbol of the sword of the spirit, otherwise the central creative 'will' in things, 'the will of God':

> 'I am the Will of God:
> I am the Sword.'

Here are one or two quotations:

> *The Sword*
> *Singing—*
> *The voice of the Sword from the heart of the Sword*
> *Clanging imperious*
> *Forth from Time's battlements*
> *His ancient and triumphing Song. . . .*

> Glittering and keen
> As the song of the winter stars,
> Ho! then, the sound
> Of my voice, the implacable
> Angel of Destiny!—
> I am the Sword.

> Heroes, my children,
> Follow, O follow me,
> Follow, exulting
> In the great light that breaks
> From the sacred companionship:

> Thrust through the fatuous,
> Thrust through the fungous brood
> Spawned in my shadow
> And gross with my gift ! '

Mr. Henley, in fact, like many a one before him, realises life as a fight. Strength comes but with continual wrestling. To quote Mr. Meredith once more, ' Contention is the vital force.' Fight the good fight.

But better than Mr. Henley's continuously showing fight—better because more needed perhaps—is his hearty reiteration of his belief in life. Page after page does he

> ' Thunder the brave,
> Irresistible message :—
> " Life is worth living
> Through every grain of it
> From the foundations
> To the last edge
> Of the corner stone, death."'

And again :

> ' Life—life—let there be life !
> Better a thousand times the roaring hours
> When wave and wind,
> Like the Arch-Murderer in flight
> From the Avenger at his heel,
> Storm through the desolate fastnesses
> And wild waste places of the world !
>
> Life—give me life until the end,
> That at the very top of being,
> The battle-spirit shouting in my blood,
> Out of the reddest hell of the fight
> I may be snatched and flung
> Into the everlasting lull,
> The immortal, incommunicable dream.'

a gusto there is in all these lines ! The passion

of the verse, page after page, is almost terrible.   It
flares like some intense, splendid light, that we feel
must surely burn itself out at any moment.   Indeed the
gusto of the book is almost delirious, as of one madly
seeking in action escape from his thoughts.   The quite
ecstatic joy in mere living becomes almost pathetic. Mr.
Henley on a spring day is phosphorus in oxygen.
Read number four of the ' London Voluntaries,' on the
whole perhaps the best poem in the volume.   Better
still, read number two, the wonderful impression of the
Strand in a golden October afternoon :

> ' Down through the ancient Strand
>   The Spirit of October, mild and boon
>   And sauntering, takes his way
>   This golden end of afternoon,
>   As though the corn stood yellow in all the land
>   And the ripe apples dropped to the harvest-moon ' ;

the transfiguring sun—

> ' Making a thousand harnesses to shine
>   As with new ore from some enchanted mine,
>   And every horse's coat so full of sheen
>   He looks new-tailored, and every 'bus feels clean. . . .

> the high majesty of Paul's
>   Uplifts a voice of living light, and calls—

> Calls to his millions to behold and see
>   How goodly this his London Town can be !
>   For earth and sky and air
>   Are golden everywhere,
>   And golden  with a cloud so suave and fine
>   The looking on it lifts the heart like wine.
>   Trafalgar Square
>   ('The fountains volleying golden glaze)
>   Gleams like an angel-market . . .
>   The glistening signs, the rejoicing roofs and spires'—

In fact—

    ' 'Tis El Dorado—El Dorado plain,
    The Golden City !'

Even still better is the weird picture of a London dawn, as seen from a hansom rattling home in the small hours.   Mr. Henley's fine gift of picture-making in two or three firm strokes, his instinct for 'the unique word,' and likewise his uncanny phantasy, were never better displayed than in this poem, number one of the 'London Voluntaries':

    ' Still, still the streets, between their carcanets
    Of linking gold, are avenues of sleep :
    But see how gable ends and parapets
    In gradual beauty and significance
    Emerge !   And did you hear
    That little twitter-and-cheep,
    Breaking inordinately loud and clear
    On this still, spectral, exquisite atmosphere?
    'Tis a first nest at matins !   And behold
    A rakehell cat—how furtive and acold !
    A spent witch homing from some infamous dance—
    Obscene, quick-trotting, see her tip and fade
    Through shadowy railings into a pit of shade !'

Was ever anything more perfect than that cat?   Mr. Henley has also a fine phantasy of 'the Wind Fiend, the abominable,' the influenza-wind, whom he pictures

    ' A craftsman at his bench, he settles down
    To the grim job of throttling London Town.'

Similar 'hospital' moods are to be found in two fine bits of indigestion, numbers two and seven of the *Rhymes and Rhythms.*   In one the moon is pictured as a bedraggled, tinselled courtesan, decoying victims for her paramour the sea :

> 'She aloft
> As in the shining streets,
> He as in ambush at some fetid stair.'

And—

> 'Stationed out yonder in the isle,
> The tall Policeman,
> Flashing his bull's-eye' . . .

In the other the poet, tormented by thoughts of those 'deeds undone' which

> 'Rankle, and snarl, and hunger for their due
> Till there seems naught so despicable as you
> In all the grin o' the sun,'

compares himself to an old shoe which 'the sea spurns and the land abhors' upon 'the beach of Time.'

There are more fine pictures and phrases than songs in the volume, but here is a verse from one of the noblest songs ever sung in the name of England :

> 'Ever the faith endures,
>     England, my England :—
> Take and break us : we are yours,
>     England, my own !
> Life is good, and joy runs high
> Between English earth and sky :
> Death is death ; but we shall die
>     To the Song on your bugles blown,
>         England—
> To the stars on your bugles blown ! '

THOUGH superior persons may sneer, I mean well

*Rudyard*    when I say that Mr. Kipling's *Barrack-*
*Kipling:*    *Room Ballads,* the best of them, are the
'Barrack-    finest things of the kind since Macaulay's
Room
Ballads.'    *Lays.* Mr. Kipling will at least take this as
a compliment, I fancy : and, at any rate, he has not been
above taking a hint here and there from Macaulay
in his rhythm. It is in their rhythm that his Ballads
are especially striking, their hearty, exhilarating march,
irresistible as the 'Marseillaise.' Such a ballad as
'Mandalay' simply takes one by storm. There is no
arguing with such an Orphic metre. You take up
your staff ₍and march along, as the rats marched
along to the river Weser, and the little lame boy to
the Venusberg.

'By the old Moulmein Pagoda, lookin' eastward to the sea,
There's a Burma girl a-settin', and I know she thinks o' me ;
For the wind is in the palm-trees, and the temple-bells they say:
"Come you back, you British soldier; come you back to
    Mandalay!"
    Come you back to Mandalay,
    Where the old Flotilla lay :
    Can't you 'ear their paddles chunkin' from Rangoon to
      Mandalay?
    On the road to Mandalay,
    Where the flyin'-fishes play,
    An' the dawn comes up like thunder outer China 'crost the
      Bay !

'Er petticoat was yaller an' 'er little cap was green,
An' 'er name was Supi-yaw-lat—jes' the same as Theebaw's
    Queen,
An' I seed her first a-smokin' of a whackin' white cheroot,
An' a-wastin' Christian kisses on an 'eathen idol's foot:

Bloomin' idol made o' mud—
Wot they called the Great Gawd Budd—
Plucky lot she cared for idols when I kissed 'er where she
    stud !
On the road to Mandalay. . . .'

Apart from its intoxicating rhythm, ' Mandalay' has
another of the sacred signs of fine poetry—its wonderful use of the commonest material.   Its magic is made
of the very refuse of language.   It reminds one of the
magic of certain paintings, say a portrait by Mr. Sargent,
which close at hand looks all slaps and dashes of paint,
like an untidy palette ;  but as we move farther and
farther away, the vision comes out of the chaos, and
soon we forget all about the brush-marks in the beauty.
Similarly, with the best of these *Barrack-Room Ballads*,
the poor Cockneyisms are transfigured out of recognition by the imagination working at white heat, and a
rhythm that might set rocks to dance music.   And
could love-poetry be tenderer than the latter half of the
second verse quoted :

' An' a-wastin' Christian kisses on an 'eathen idol's foot . . .
        Plucky lot she cared for idols when I kissed 'er where
        she stud ! '

Never is the miracle of art more fully brought home to
us than when such coarse material is thus touched to
finer issues.   There is a piquant beauty, coming, of
course, of the meeting of extremes in form and material,
about a modelling in clay that perhaps hardly survives
in the marble.
    But this observation suggests another.   It reminds
us that clay is perishable, and that such literary clay
as the Cockney of Mr. Kipling, and the Yankee of Mr.

Bret Harte must perish earlier than the more classical forms of language, and with it the strong and moving forms with which they have each impressed it. Of course, 'immortality,' 'on a world with a core of fire and a crust of fossils,' is but a relative term, whatever language a poet may employ. But because one thousand years are but as yesterday to Saturn, they are no less a pretty considerable 'immortality' to us, and though by writing in classical forms of speech a poet may give a more permanent expression to the creative power of beauty that is in him, it is impossible not to sigh for those essays in clay which apparently reveal a power of hand no less masterly than that revealed in the more durable marbles. Of course, we are told that it is easier to do finely in clay than in marble, but then art is not to be judged by the difficulty or the facility of its production, but simply by its result. Possibly there is some quality in the clay work, independent of original force and beauty, that dazzles our judgment.

That Mr. Kipling's 'plain English' poems (stirring as is the 'Ballad of East and West,' and the spirited 'Flag of England') do not, in imaginative power, come up to those in Cockney, may or may not be indicative of the truth of the above conjecture. From these must be excepted 'Tomlinson' and the fine 'Ballad of the Bolivar.' Some of the lines in the latter are among the most forcible Mr. Kipling has ever written :

> 'Trailing like a wounded duck, working out her soul ;
> Clanging like a smithy shop after every roll ;
> Just a funnel and a mast lurching through the spray—
> So we threshed the Bolivar, out across the Bay !
>
> .　　.　　.　　.　　.　　.　　.　　.

Heard the seas, like drunken men, pounding at her strake ;

. . . . . . . .

Watched the compass chase its tail, like a cat at play—

. . . . . . . .

Just a pack o' rotten plates puttied up with tar,
In we came, an' time enough, 'cross Bilbao Bar.
Overloaded, undermanned, meant to founder, we
Euchred God Almighty's storm, bluffed the Eternal Sea !'

There is an imaginative grip in these lines, quoted at random, from which we may almost expect anything.

But let us return to the *Barrack-Room Ballads.* The best of these, after 'Mandalay,' are undoubtedly those we have already known, 'Danny Deever' and 'Tommy' :

'I went into a public-'ouse to get a pint o' beer,
  The publican 'e up an' sez, "We serve no red-coats here."
The girls be'ind the bar they laughed an' giggled fit to die,
I outs into the street again an' to myself sez I :
        "O it's Tommy this, an' Tommy that, an' Tommy, go
          away" ;
        But it's "Thank you, Mister Atkins," when the band
          begins to play,
        The band begins to play, my boys, the band begins to
          play,
        O it's "Thank you, Mister Atkins," when the band
          begins to play.'

And 'Fuzzy-Wuzzy' :

'  'E rushes at the smoke when we let drive,
    An', before we know, 'e's 'ackin' at our 'ead ;
  'E's all 'ot sand an' ginger when alive,
    An' 'e's generally shammin' when 'e's dead.
  'E's a daisy, 'e's a ducky, 'e's a lamb !
    'E's a injia-rubber idiot on the spree,
  'E's the on'y thing that doesn't give a damn
    For a Regiment o' British Infantree !
        So 'ere's *to* you, Fuzzy-Wuzzy, at your 'ome in
          the Soudan ;
        You're a pore benighted 'eathen but a first-class
          fightin' man ;

An' 'ere's *to* you, Fuzzy-Wuzzy, with your 'ayrick
'ead of 'air—
You big black boundin' beggar—for you broke
a British square !'

The others strike one as too technical. They are, doubtless, no less typical of army life, but they need 'T. A.'—
Mr. Kipling's dedicatee, Mr. Thomas Atkins—to appreciate them. Mr. Kipling has not succeeded, save in
odd lines and verses, in elevating them into the universal, as he assuredly has done in the ballads quoted.
One quality significant of imagination, one pauses to
note, his power of onomatopœia—and I would beg leave
to apply the word to sight as to sound. When he has not
a word to express the peculiar effect he wants to get,
he invents one, which is simply the thing itself. For
example :

'Elephants a-pilin' teak
In the sludgy, *squdgy* creek.'

' As the shape of a corpse *dimmers* up through deep water.'

Of course, Mr. Kipling has already exemplified that in
his prose. Did he not invent that awful 'pobby' ghost,
that fell upon you from the trees, and 'remained.'

It remains to speak of 'Tomlinson.' Here are the
fine opening lines :

'Now Tomlinson gave up the ghost in his house in Berkeley
Square,
And a Spirit came to his bedside and gripped him by the hair—
A Spirit gripped him by the hair and carried him far away,
Till he heard as the roar of a rain-fed ford the roar of the Milky
Way:
Till he heard the roar of the Milky Way die down and drone
and cease,
And they came to the Gate within the Wall where Peter holds
the keys.

> '' Stand up, stand up now, Tomlinson, and answer loud and high
> The good that ye did for the sake of men or ever ye came to
>     die—
> The good that ye did for the sake of men in little earth so lone !"
> And the naked soul of Tomlinson grew white as a rain-washed
>     bone.'

The imagery of every new strong poet reveals to us once again how the simple analogies still lie all about, as when man first began to see them. But return we to Tomlinson, in whose fate Mr. Kipling vigorously satirises the modern man, who never lives at all in himself, but at second-hand through books and 'art.' Asked in heaven concerning good deeds, he can only refer to what Mr. Pater would call his 'sensations and ideas' :

> ' "' This I have read in a book," he said, "and that was told
>     to me,
> And this I have thought that another man thought of a Prince
>     in Muscovy "——
> The good souls flocked like homing doves, and bade him clear
>     the path,
> And Peter twirled the jangling keys in weariness and wrath.
> " Ye have read, ye have heard, ye have thought," he said, "and
>     the tale is yet to run :
> By the worth of the body that once ye had, give answer—what
>     ha' ye done?"'

But with all his 'sensations,' poor Tomlinson had *done* nothing; so Peter sends him down to hell, where the same trouble awaits him, for his evil had been no less timorous than his good deeds. They, too, had been 'in the imagination,' merely read of in books. The devil, though 'all o'er-sib to Adam's breed,' is in no mind to waste 'good pit-coal' on such a weak-backed, character-

less creature, so he sends the soul of Tomlinson to be
'winnowed,' and returning, the demons say :

> 'The soul that he got from God he has bartered clean away.
> We have threshed a stook of print and book, and winnowed a
> chattering wind
> And many a soul wherefrom he stole, but his we cannot find.'

So the doom of Tomlinson is to be sent back to his
body on the earth, that he may develop either some real
good deeds or some hearty sins of his own.    Quotation
does poor justice to this fine bit of satire, in which
sublimities and absurdities jostle each other in so odd
a fashion.    But it is a success in that daring allegorical
vein, which Mr. Kipling essays in another stinging
satire against the 'Art' people, 'The Conundrum of
the Workshops,' of which the first verse will indicate
the delightful treatment :

> 'When the flush of a new-born sun fell first on Eden's green and
> gold,
> Our father Adam sat under the Tree and scratched with a stick
> in the mould ;
> And the first rude sketch that the world had seen was joy to his
> mighty heart,
> Till the Devil whispered behind the leaves, " It 's pretty, but is
> it Art?"'

In trying the same allegorical method for a solemn
celebration of his dead friend Mr. Wolcott Balestier,
Mr. Kipling fails, and reveals the danger, and perhaps the limitation, of such rough allegory.    The big
hyperboles with which he tries to bridge space and
time suggest a too palpable stretching of the octave.
The large colloquialisms in which he presents the
heavenly powers utterly fail in dignity.

However, if but a fourth of Mr. Kipling's volume is of his best, that best is of signal fulfilment, and those who have prophesied that his verse will be finer than his prose, must see of the travail of their souls and be satisfied.

MR. STEVENSON has three or four distinct reputations.

*R.L.Stevenson:* 'Across the Plains,' etc. Even his reputation as a story-teller is subdivided. For the majority his is the Promethean fire reluming the torch of Old Romance. For such he wrote *Treasure Island* and *Kidnapped.* To others, a chance expenditure of a shilling on a railway journey—a shilling that might just as easily have been credited to Captain Hawley Smart—made them and Mr. Stevenson acquainted.

In the light of later days, such readers have doubtless come to regard *The Strange Case of Dr. Jekyll and Mr. Hyde* as a prophecy of the Whitechapel murders. In fact, I know that for certain members of Mr. Mansfield's audience, at one of his representations of Hyde, 'Jack the Ripper' was the one possible explanation—in spite of some most painstaking psychology on the play-bill. Then we step up to *The New Arabian Nights*, thus approaching the still fairer fame of the *Travels with a Donkey in the Cevennes, An Inland Voyage*, and *Virginibus Puerisque*. It is curious to notice how, as the number of editions diminish, 'the murmur of the loved Apollian leaves

grows on the ear.    Mr. Stevenson's final fame will be
that of an essayist, nearest and dearest fame of the
prose writer.    Nearest and dearest, because the largest
amount of selfish pleasure enters into the writing of
essays, approaching, as it does, as nearly as possible to
writing merely for writing's sake—as the lyric-poet just
sings for singing's sake : the joy in the mere exercise
of a faculty.    In the essay no architecture has to be
considered, with a half-heart that would fain be at the
floriation of niche and capital.    Such is, one supposes,
the greater work, certainly it is bigger ; though the
essayist cannot but feel the essential and somewhat
jeering limitation of the greatest monuments of art
—monuments which attain their air of majestic com-
pletion simply by a roof which shuts out the stars.    The
essayist is essentially a son of Shem, and his method is
the wayward travel of a gipsy.    He builds not, but he
pitches his tent, lights his fire of sticks, and invites you
to smoke a pipe with him over their crackling.    While
he dreamily chats, now here, now there, of his discursive
way of life, the sun has gone down and you begin to
feel the sweet influences of Pleiades.

At least, so it is with Mr. Stevenson, the Stevenson
we care for most.    And it seems certain that it is so
he would be remembered of us : for this new volume
of essays abounds in continued allusions to the joyous
practice of the literary craft, plainly confiding to us that
the pleasure of the reader and the writer in their
'Stevenson' is mutual.    One of the great charms of
Fontainebleau for Mr. Stevenson appears to have been
its sympathetic environment for the young student of

'style,' for that end and aim of existence was in the air, not only in the ardent chatter of young artists, but in the very dignity and grace of the woods themselves. Only in such a place and in such company, of his fellow-craftsmen, may the young artist hope to be understood, hope to preserve his temperament unspoiled of Polonius.

'For art is, first of all and last of all, a trade. The love of words and not a desire to publish new discoveries, the love of form and not a novel reading of historical events, mark the vocation of the writer and the painter. The arabesque, properly speaking, and even in literature, is the first fancy of the artist; he first plays with his material as a child plays with a kaleidoscope; and he is already in a second stage when he begins to use his pretty counters for the end of representation. In that, he must pause long and toil faithfully; that is his apprenticeship; and it is only the few who will really grow beyond it, and go forward, fully equipped, to do the business of real art—to give life to abstractions and significance and charm to facts. In the meanwhile, let him dwell much among his fellow-craftsmen. They alone can take a serious interest in the childish tasks and pitiful successes of these years. They alone can behold with equanimity this fingering of the dumb keyboard, this polishing of empty sentences, this dull and literal painting of dull and insignificant subjects. Outsiders will spur him on. They will say, "Why do you not write a great book? paint a great picture?" If his guardian angel fail him, they may even persuade him to the attempt, and, ten to one, his hand is coarsened and his style falsified for life.'

'The business of real art—to give life to abstractions and significance and charm to facts.' The latter half of this simple and suggestive statement is especially applicable to Mr. Stevenson's own work, particularly in the case of such books as the *Travels with a Donkey*, and *An Inland Voyage*. Nothing could be more commonplace than the adventures which supply the

theme, nothing less so than Mr. Stevenson's account of
them.    Looking ahead, sometimes, the road seems
straight and uninteresting enough.    Nothing in sight
promises anything.    So we are often inclined to feel
when, slowly but surely, some well-worn fact, which
we had ignored as quite unpromising, begins opening
out beneath the eye of Mr. Stevenson's meditative
imagination like a morning flower.    He sees everything
as if it had never been looked on before.    Nothing has,
so to say, gone cold for him.    For him there is no such
thing as merely hard fact.    Each fact is a sensitive
centre of infinite interests.    And he makes us aware
of this with a simplicity so natural that we are apt to
forget that his record is anything more than a record
of actual fact, that it is, as Mr. Pater would say, 'the
transcript of the sense of fact rather than the fact'
itself.    The expression which his themes thus take on
is not that of mystery or wizardry, as in Coleridge or
Miss Christina Rossetti ; it is rather, to use a phrase
of Mr. Stevenson's own, that of a 'solemn freshness,'
born, I should say, of a constant habit—a co-operation
between the philosophic and the poetic instincts—of
relating particulars to generals.

Travelling 'Across the Plains' to San Francisco, in a
dreary emigrant train, Mr. Stevenson turns to look on a
fellow-passenger, a Chinaman, and straightway his mind
is applying to that 'dhirty Mongolian' its various re-
agents of deduction and dream :

' When either of us turned his thoughts to home and childhood,
what a strange dissimilarity must there not have been in these
pictures of the mind—when I beheld that old, grey, castled city, high

throned above the Firth, with the flag of Britain flying, and the red-coat sentry pacing over all ; and the man in the next car to me would conjure up some junks and a pagoda and a fort of porcelain, and call it, with the same affection, home.'

Of his other fellow-travellers he makes this acute observation, just a little acid with the memory of their somewhat undesirable company :

'They were mostly lumpish fellows, silent and noisy, a common combination ; somewhat sad, I should say, with an extraordinary poor taste in humour, and little interest in their fellow-creatures beyond that of cheap and merely external curiosity. If they heard a man's name and business, they seemed to think they had the heart of that mystery ; but they were as eager to know that much as they were indifferent to the rest.'

This humour, always so quiet and exquisite, just perceptibly brightening the eye, no more, communes with itself all through that dreary journey. And well is it to have so gentle and common-sense a companion. There is nothing like a sense of humour to help one with one's temper in times of trial. Once only does Mr. Stevenson break loose—and that only in his narrative. It was in North Platte, at supper one evening :

'One man asked another to pass the milk-jug. This other was well dressed and of what we should call a respectable appearance ; a darkish man, high spoken, eating as though he had some usage of society ; but he turned upon the first speaker with extraordinary vehemence of tone —

'"There's a waiter here !" he cried.

'"I only asked you to pass the milk," explained the first.

'Here is the retort verbatim—

'"Pass! Hell! I'm not paid for that business ; the waiter's paid for it. You should use civility at table, and, by God, I'll show you how !"

' The other man very wisely made no answer, and the bully went on with his supper as though nothing had occurred. It pleases me to think that some day soon he will meet with one of his own kidney ; and that perhaps both may fall.'

But, though seldom aroused thus, Mr. Stevenson often kindles to the surprises of the country lying along the route, expressing himself in those sudden unexpected turns of phrase and analogy in which he has always been so happy. Nearing Sacramento, after a dreary monotony of mountains, 'Suddenly,' he writes :

—' we shot into an open ; and before we were swallowed into the next length of wooden tunnel, I had one glimpse of a huge pine-forested ravine upon my left, a foaming river, and a sky already coloured with the fires of dawn. I am usually very calm over the displays of nature ; but you will scarce believe how my heart leaped at this. It was like meeting one's wife. I had come home again—home from unsightly deserts to the green and habitable corners of the earth.'

*It was like meeting one's wife!* The comparison comes on one with just the very unexpectedness that belonged to the moment described. One dreamed of it as little as Mr. Stevenson of the green ravine.

Another such delicious unexpected thing occurs in the Epilogue to *An Inland Voyage.*

' The Arethusa,' thanks to that suspicious vagabondish appearance at which Mr. Stevenson loves to poke fun, has been thrown into the village lock-up at Chatillon-sur-Loing, as a spy. He had left his comrade, ' The Cigarette,' some few miles behind him. Such, it will be remembered, was their plan of obviating those social difficulties of walking-tours, of which Mr. Stevenson wrote in *Virginibus Puerisque*. Before incarceration, he humorously warns the commissary to be sure to arrest 'The Cigarette.' Consequently—and here is the delicious phrase I set out to quote—'at the town entry, the gendarme culled him like a wayside flower'! The whole episode is of Mr. Stevenson's best, and a welcome addition, indeed, to a book far too short.

The papers of which I have spoken are, as we have seen, in the fashion of *The Inland Voyage*, not so much essays as the inspired log of trivial voyaging. They are all on the move, object succeeds object as seen from a railway train. Of the essay, pure and simple, where the talk pursues its wayward round about a given theme, there are three or four examples in the present volume worthy to rank with anything in *Virginibus Puerisque*. Of these, 'The Lantern-Bearers' and 'Pulvis et Umbra' are the most striking.

Mr. Stevenson has never touched a home-spun theme to finer issues than in 'The Lantern-Bearers.' His power, referred to above, of transfiguring facts into symbols, is here seen in its triumph. The strange passion of small boys for a bull's-eye lantern is the humble text for a large and literally illuminative discourse on that poetry more difficult than anything in Browning—other people's poetry ; and on the true realism, which 'always and everywhere is that of the poets.' He describes how, when autumn nights began to set in, half-a-dozen of the 'fellows' used to meet on the links, equipped with bull's-eye lanterns fastened to their waists, but carefully swathed in buttoned greatcoats. 'When two of these asses met, there would be

an anxious " Have you got your lantern ?" and a gratified
" Yes !" That was the shibboleth.' Why they carried
them they hardly knew. True, they would now and
again crouch inside some hollow of the links, and,
revealing the blazing eye in their centres, 'delight
themselves with inappropriate talk.' But—

'the essence of this bliss was to walk by yourself in the black
night ; the slide shut, the top-coat buttoned ; not a ray escaping,
whether to conduct your footsteps or to make your glory public : a
mere pillar of darkness in the dark ; and all the while, deep down
in the privacy of your fool's heart, to know you had a bull's-eye at
your belt, and to exult and sing over the knowledge.'

Realism would describe these youngsters as little boys

' very cold, spat upon by flurries of rain, and drearily surrounded,
all of which they were ; and their talk as silly and indecent,
which it certainly was . . . but ask themselves, and they are in
the heaven of a recondite pleasure, the ground of which is an
ill-smelling lantern.'

Thus in depicting life at large, 'To miss the joy,' that
is, the lantern—'is to miss all.' 'To find out where
joy resides, and give it a voice far beyond singing,'
that is at once the true poetry and the true realism.

In 'Pulvis et Umbra,' Mr. Stevenson starts in one of
those strange fantastic moods of low spirits, when, like
Hamlet, we ask ourselves, 'What is this quintessence
of dust?'; when the familiar countenance of life
changes to an unmeaning fantastic visage, just as
sometimes, in reading, a familiar English word will
take on a more gibberish aspect than the remotest
Welsh, and won't come right again. In such a mood
Mr. Stevenson ponders on the truth that man was
made of the dust of the earth. He takes it literally.

He sees dust full of strange fertility, swelling up and taking shape, becoming flowers and beasts and men— man 'grown upon with hair like grass,' 'fitted with eyes that move and glitter in his face, a thing to set children screaming.' He sees all these various lives living on the murder of each other—a circumstance which in his dream seems more quaint than terrible. Then the aspect of this 'monstrous spectre,' man, 'the disease of the agglutinated dust,' begins to wear a kindly, though still more comical aspect. This mere sport of winds, this fortuitous concord of atoms, actually imagines that such a chance-child as he owes duties to an unseen something and to his neighbour ; he has a conscience, cherishes a 'duty.' Not only man, but 'the whole creation, groans in mortal frailty, strives with unconquerable constancy.' And, with the hearty laugh that comes of the contemplation of this odd spectacle, the sickly, spectral vision takes a better meaning—

> 'Surely not in vain
> My substance from the common earth was ta'en.'

The strong reminiscence of the style of Sir Thomas Browne in 'Pulvis et Umbra' is appropriate to the quaint vision which is its theme, and is blent with Mr. Stevenson's own individual style no less successfully than Lamb used to blend the same rich old colours in his own wonderful writing. In these two essays, and in similar essays in *Virginibus Puerisque*, Mr. Stevenson reminds us of the old prose masters by reason of another quality than their Latinism. He has the same high solemnity of accent, stirring one's heart

by groups of simple words, wherein one seeks in vain
for the secret of the magic. We have no writer of
nobler English than Mr. Stevenson at present among
us. Occasionally, one admits, the art peeps out a
little, but it serves to remind us that we are in the
hands of a writer who will not willingly give us less
than his highest.

And then the all-pervading manliness, blowing like
the breath of pine-woods through all Mr. Stevenson
writes, the real feeling of camaraderie set up between
him and his reader, and the still untroubled sanity of
his simple philosophy of life. These are the root-
qualities beneath all his charm of expression. Mr.
Sidney Colvin, who has seen the book through the
press, expresses the fear, in a prefatory letter to Mr.
Stevenson, that the tone of the later essays (those of
which I have been writing) may be found 'less
inspiriting' than Mr. Stevenson's wont. Surely Mr.
Colvin is needlessly disquieted. It is true that one
feels in them the struggle of faith with experience,
but it is a struggle in which faith is no less victorious,
if just a little wearied, than of old.

One of the most significant of the essays is entitled
'Letter to a Young Gentleman who proposes to embrace
the Career of Art.' It is a manly protest against that
literary commercialism which has recently been somewhat blatant. In an atmosphere, so to say, darkened
with the sky-signs of the Society of Authors, it is indeed
refreshing to find so eminent (and paying) a man of letters
considering his art in so untradesmanlike a spirit. It
reminds one of old prints of Oliver Cromwell refusing

the Crown. If literature is ill-paid, says Mr. Stevenson, 'the wonder is that it should be paid at all. Other men pay, and pay dearly, for pleasures less desirable.'

'The direct returns—the wages of the trade—are small, but the indirect—the wages of the life—are incalculably great. No other business offers a man his daily bread upon such joyful terms.'

Literature, like virtue, is its own reward. A view in which, undoubtedly, there is a large measure of truth ; for, when the writer grumbles about poor pay, he must not forget that he did his work not to please the public, but himself. In fact, the practice of art—like the practice of prayer—is simply the indulgence of one of the higher appetites. But, in a sort of fakir zeal for cutting himself with knives, Mr. Stevenson goes on to deduce from the pleasure in the production of literature the essential unmanliness of literature as a profession.

'To live by a pleasure is not a high calling ; it involves patronage, however veiled ; it numbers the artist, however ambitious, along with dancing girls and billiard markers. The French have a romantic evasion for one employment, and call its practitioners the Daughters of Joy. The artist is of the same family, he is of the Sons of Joy, chose his trade to please himself, gains his livelihood by pleasing others, and has parted with something of the sterner dignity of man.'

Is not 'a romantic evasion' delicious? In blunter English the artist is a spiritual prostitute. At the first blush, the position has the attractiveness of all half-truths. But, really, it is perhaps hardly true at all. For the essence of prostitution is not in the pleasure, but in the sale ; and Mr. Stevenson admits that the artist, when he does his real things, that is, when he *is* an artist, works first to please himself, sings, writes, paints, because he must, and would do so were there never a buyer in the world. The idea of sale is but a second thought. In some cases, doubtless, it becomes a second nature. But by that time the man has ceased to be an artist, and is out of the question. Take such a case as Montaigne's. No writing relies more for its charm on its personal revelation than his, and yet we know that he proposed to himself 'no other than a familiar and private end.' Whether or not his vanity really had an eye to publication does not matter. Certainly he did not write to sell himself. In fact the artist, consciously or unconsciously, is always a Narcissus, and he writes books and paints pictures as so many mirrors of his own darling individuality; to give to others, but chiefly to himself, the delight of 'the taste of himself.' If either is of the Children of Joy, the writer or the reader, it is surely the reader; his is the barren pleasure, certainly not the writer's—often no little prolific. Yet one can quite understand the fascination which this 'Daughter of Joy' theory has for Mr. Stevenson as a man of letters. It is the fascination of suicide.

Let us consider a moment that question of 'a more manly way of life,' for on this question of manliness a good deal of cant is abroad. Whether, properly speaking, the question of comparative degree enters into the quality or not, I am not sure. Personally I feel that there can be no question of 'more' or 'most' manly. A calling is either manly or unmanly, and there we leave it. It is true that thews and sinews and the open air may enter more into one than the other, but it yet remains to be proven that such are the essential components of manliness. One may surely, like Whitman, be 'enamoured of growing out-of-doors,' without stigmatising as mannikins those who must grow within doors. The business of the 'soldier and the explorer' would seem to be Mr. Stevenson's ideal of a manly way of life. They have, he says, 'moments of worthier excitement' even than the artist's, ' but they are purchased by cruel hardships and periods of tedium that beggar language.' What about those other hardships which Carlyle declared made the history of letters more sickening than the Newgate Calendar? And as for those moments of worthier excitement, has the man of letters no nobler excitement in the pursuit of his craft than the small peddling, technical triumphs of phrase on which Mr. Stevenson alone insists? What of the seasons, not few, of his highest work, when quite literally *laborare est orare* — when Mr. Stevenson wrote the ' Lantern-Bearers,' for example? To make the comparison between the soldier and writer equal, you must put them both either on a technical or an ideal basis. Mr. Stevenson would appear to put the writer on the technical and the soldier on the ideal basis, unless those ' moments of worthier excitement' refer to some particularly neat sabre-stroke or particularly happy shot with his Martini. And I can't help thinking that the worthiness of the soldier's excitement depends a good deal on his conception of why he is fighting. The mere passion of fighting for fighting's sake, the mere lust of slaying 'Fuzzy-Wuzzy,' may be more manly than the splendid idealism, the enthusiasm of humanity, the brave battle with adverse fates, which often has given us the classics of literature, but if it be so—well, hurrah for petticoats !

Then, as to the pleasure given by the writer to the reader.   Does the comparison with the dancing girl and the billiard marker cover the field?   Surely it but applies to the skirts of it—especially, it may be thought, as regards the dancing girl.   But Mr. Stevenson, it will be remarked, is generalising, not particularising—and certainly not distinguishing.   'Pleasure' surely means anything, and nothing is gained by pretending that there is any serious analogy between the pleasure of the ballet and billiards, and the pleasure derived from fine literature.   If, too, the question of the 'barrenness' of the pleasure of art, which has become a catch-word since 'The Kreutzer Sonata,' be raised—is an emotion necessarily barren because it does not per-suade us to go right away and break the sixth and seventh Commandments?   ''Twas the manner of primitive man,' we know ; but really we have other ways of utilising our emotion.   And if march-music does not lend valour to our arm, it may to our thought—which is better.   Besides, if this theory of barrenness hold, we must never look at a sunset, a flower, a woman, or any object which inspires in us those thoughts that do often lie too deep for—blows.

Finally, there is this fundamental weakness in the theory : it ignores the necessity of evolution.   It was as inevitable that there should be men of letters as that there should be cavemen.   Here they are in the process of the suns, and why not make the best of them? After all, they have done a good deal for us. Manly or not, they have often made us better men.

Let us clear our souls of cant—even of this cant of manliness—and remember that the manliness of an occupation is not in its being outdoor or indoor, or in the amount of physical strength we put into it. It is impossible to insist too much on the distinction between what is merely male and what is manly. This, of course, is platitude unashamed; but he who combats sophistry must not be afraid of platitude. Sophistry, too, proves often but inverted platitude. In the present instance, for example, what is more obvious than that art, like every other human activity, has its prostitutes? There is the platitude. Mr. Stevenson simply ignores the limits of its application, and says that all artists are Sons and Daughters of Joy. And so we get the sophism.

To differ with so accomplished, so classical, an anthologist as Professor F. T. Palgrave must seem ungrateful, as it is certainly rash. The more ungrateful, as this very selection from Keats, in its original Golden Treasury issue, has so often proved a 'companion for the fortunate moments of travel or the country.' That is a quotation from the little preface, delightful as is Mr. Palgrave's wont. Let us quote the opening passage :—

*John Keats: Palgrave's Selections.*

'Copiousness in exquisite detail, perpetual freshness of phrase, characterise all the poetry of Keats, and in the work of his earlier days are generally more conspicuous than unity of interest or perfection of form—qualities which (as, perhaps, with Shakespeare), his imaginative wealth of mind,—*aurea facilitas*,—prevented him from acquiring until the first youth was over. Keats is hence a poet especially fit to be read, as the bee tastes the flower, a little at a time, and in those pleasant places which he loves and describes so well :—He is a companion for the fortunate moments of travel or the country :—the

> latis otia fundis,
> speluncæ vivique lacus,

are his natural landscape, the stage and the scenery in presence of which he, in the fullest measure, adds happiness to happiness.'

One would seek far to find a passage of criticism so terse and yet so full, so sure in its touch, so exquisite in its expression. The little sheaf of notes at the end of the volume is distinguished by the same qualities. Professor Palgrave had, too, an interesting idea to guide him in his text—the exact reproduction, so far as possible, of the rare original texts. Not merely 'as a little tribute of affectionate honour' to the poet, but because being, as we know, very fastidious, even to the mint and cumin of his art, Keats 'certainly revised his three little volumes (not reprinted till long after his death) with great care, following certain rules of his own, as every finely-gifted poet will, in order to express and aid his rhythm by his punctuation and arrangement.'

So far so good. If Professor Palgrave had restricted himself to this reprint, though it had been a pity, one could have had nothing to say. He would have been consistent. His edition would have been complete so far, and there would have been no question of a selection. This comes in by his inclusion of several 'posthuma.' 'My scheme being to reprint the poetry which bore the sanction of the poet's *imprimatur*,' continues Professor Palgrave, 'it may be asked on what principle a few pieces, left in manuscript (but the absence of which most readers, I think, would have regretted), have been here diffidently added? No rigid law can be laid down, perhaps, upon this difficult problem, except that it is treason to the dead to publish (unless for purposes of historical truth) anything discreditable to the living man. The rule which ordinarily seems to me the safest and best—to insert only what is altogether, or fairly, on a level with the poet's best work—I have here endeavoured to follow.' Of course, that is an obvious golden rule, and the question the reader rather asks is—How has Professor Palgrave applied it? Having once gone past his first idea of a reprint, one inevitably expects that all the best of Keats will be included in the selection. But when we come to look into this, we indeed 'sigh the lack of many a thing' we 'sought.' Perhaps, after the opening line of 'Endymion,' there is no line of Keats better known, as there is certainly none finer, than the second of these two lines :

> ' —bards who died content on pleasant sward,
> *Leaving great verse unto a little clan.*'

Can a man claim to know Keats who is ignorant of that line? Yet if he relied on Professor Palgrave, as from that gentleman's wide and just fame as an anthologist he might conceivably do, he would certainly go through life without knowing it, not to speak of his also

missing the hardly less famous, and no less beautiful,
conclusion of the same fragment.  As the whole of it
is contained in a dozen lines, I propose to quote it
entire :

> ' Mother of Hermes ! and still youthful Maia !
>      May I sing to thee
> As thou wast hymned on the shores of Baiæ ?
>      Or may I woo thee
> In earlier Sicilian ?  Or thy smiles
> Seek as they once were sought, in Grecian isles,
> By bards who died content on pleasant sward,
> Leaving great verse unto a little clan ?
> O, give me their old vigour, and unheard
> Save of the quiet primrose, and the span
>      Of heaven and few ears,
> Rounded by thee, my song should die away
>      Content as theirs,
> Rich in the simple worship of a day.'

On what conceivable principle of selection can Professor
Palgrave have omitted these fine lines ?  Surely where
any two or three pieces of Keats are gathered together,
there should these be in the midst of them.  It cannot
surely be because they form but one verse of a con-
templated ode, a fragment.  On that principle we had
better humour Mr. Frederic Harrison and send the
Elgin marbles back to Greece, because they are but
torsos.  Besides, this 'fragment' is really complete in
itself—complete, anyhow, as a hand or a head surviving
a complete marble is complete.  And talking of the
Elgin marbles, another poem we seek for in vain is the
sonnet, ' On seeing the Elgin Marbles for the first time,'
the first five lines of which (quite apart from the historic
interest of the sonnet) are singularly fine, and another
of Keats's best known things :

> 'My spirit is too weak—mortality
>   Weighs heavily on me like unwilling sleep,
>   And each imagined pinnacle and steep
> Of godlike hardship, tells me I must die
> Like a sick eagle looking at the sky.'

Lines one, two, and five are surely masterly. Then, again, the sonnet beginning, 'Why did I laugh to-night?' though poor on the whole, is redeemed by its four concluding lines—lines again among the famous :

> 'Yet would I on this very midnight cease,
>   And the world's gaudy ensigns see in shreds ;
> Verse, Fame, and Beauty are intense indeed,
> But Death intenser—Death is Life's high meed.'

Poor, nay miserable, as were the poems Keats wrote on his visit to Scotland, yet 'Staffa,' with its fine fancy of the great cave having become the home of Lycidas, should, we think, find a place in any adequate selection of the poet :

> 'Not Aladdin magian
>   Ever such a work began ; . . .
> This was architectured thus
> By the great Oceanus !—
> Here his mighty waters play
> Hollow organs all the day.' . . .

And not a word of 'The Eve of St. Mark,' that interesting bit of pre-pre-Raphaelitism, nor of this charming little fairy song :

> 'Shed no tear ! oh shed no tear !
> The flower will bloom another year.
> Weep no more ! oh weep no more !
> Young buds sleep in the root's white core.

131

> Dry your eyes! oh dry your eyes!
> For I was taught in Paradise
> To ease my breast of melodies—
>                     Shed no tear.'

And is it possible that either Mr. Palgrave or the readers of Golden Treasury editions are so prudish as to object to the honest amorousness of 'The Devon Maid'?  There can be no other reason for its omission, for it is one of the healthiest, heartiest little songs of the kind out of Burns :

> 'Where be you going, you Devon maid?
>     And what have you there in the basket?
> Ye tight little fairy, just fresh from the dairy,
>     Will you give me some cream if I ask it?
>
> I love your meads, and I love your flowers,
>     And I love your junkets mainly,
> But 'hind the door I love kisses more,
>     O look not so disdainly.
>
> I love your hills, and I love your dales,
>     And I love your flocks a-bleating—
> But O, on the heather to lie together,
>     With both our hearts a-beating!
>
> I 'll put your basket all safe in a nook,
>     Your shawl I 'll hang up on the willow,
> And we will sigh in the daisy's eye,
>     And kiss on a grass-green pillow.'

This little poem is especially valuable as perhaps being the only instance in Keats of the rollicking 'Bobbie Burns' manner of gallantry.  As a rule, his loves were more of the yearning æsthetic order.  True, he has also a disreputable rhyme on 'Sharing Eve's Apple,' yet, witty as that is, one cannot blame Professor Palgrave for its omission.  But the slight to 'the Devon Maid' it is impossible to overlook. There are one or two other things one would like in a perfect selection, for old sake's sake at least—that sonnet written in 'The Flower and the Leaf,' and beginning, 'This pleasant tale is like a little copse'; that other beginning, 'The day is gone, and all its sweets are gone!' and an otherwise bad sonnet on the sonnet containing the now proverbial phrase, 'Misers of sound and syllable.' But these I do not press. I insist but on the poems from which I have quoted. And I have quoted familiar things at length simply to emphasise the value of the omissions; scanning them again as thus gleaned together, and not forgetting the unquoted 'Eve of St. Mark,' which covers four pages—why, they make quite an exquisite little sheaf. And they are, let it be observed, no mere aftermath : they are of the poet's best—already nimble on the lips of fame. Surely it is a pity that Professor Palgrave has omitted them from an edition which is otherwise so admirably done. Had Keats been a voluminous poet, even one or two of the omissions had been still impossible to understand ; but, as he was just the reverse, the only tenable explanation would have been in the carelessness of a binder who had missed out one of the 'sixteens.' To be so near perfection, and yet so oddly to miss it ! Well, the one thing to do is to write in the omitted poems in one's best monkish hand. Then the edition will be the most perfect Keats to be had.

YOU will sometimes hear it said that the author of *Obiter Dicta* is an overrated man. I hope you always beg to differ when the statement occurs. It is true that the phenomenon of a little volume of literary essays going into edition after edition, arriving, indeed, at no less than a 'popular' edition, seemed an uncanny thing for England. Yet, after all, it was just that kind of unexpected which is continually happening amongst us. Some people, at a loss to account for it, suggest that there was a mistake somewhere. The public, maybe, mistook the book for a volume of short stories, or a handful of sermons in stones. Or, may we admit that the public is not at all times such an ass as the humourist would insist? True, it is continually going mad over some worthless sensation, but it has its lucid intervals, and in one of these it bought *Obiter Dicta*.

*Augustine Birrell: 'Res Judicatæ.'*

I hope *Res Judicatæ* may also prove to have come thus in the nick of time, for it is a volume of criticism worth infinitely more than some precious and affected volumes of the time. Its value, as in the case of *Obiter Dicta*, is that it is 'of the centre.' It is in lineal descent from Addison, for it reverses the process of modern criticism, starting from its subject, rather than from its author. It is refreshingly concrete. In an admirable note on Sainte-Beuve, Mr. Birrell says, 'Sainte-Beuve was always willing to write like another man. Joubert was not. And yet, strange paradox! there will be always more men able to write in the strained style of Joubert than in the natural style of Sainte-Beuve. It is

easier to be odd, intense, overwise, enigmatic, than to be
sensible, simple, and to see the plain truth about things.'
Strange, too, that the man who is content to write like
other men is just the one whose style will prove most
characteristic in the end.   For 'such a power hath
white simplicity.'   Oddly enough, it is eccentricity that
is always the same, that always ends its career in an
ignominious classification.   ·

I don't know whether it happens to you, but I always
find that when a book has real stuff in it, it sets my
mind once more at work upon old projects of culture, or
other achievement, which, time after time, have burned
so ardently, and time after time have sunk down into
a waiting quiescence as of an idle blacksmith's forge.
We will read, let us say, Mr. Symonds' big *History of
the Renaissance*, we will really make a start on Italian, or
make a determined sally upon Mr. Bullen's eight-volume
Middleton ; or we will write a volume of literary essays,
which shall be as nearly as good as *Res Judicatæ* as is
possible.   So we always think when we read Matthew
Arnold, or Mr. Robert Louis Stevenson, and we think it,
too, whenever we read a fine novel.   We feel our own
novel leaping inside us ; but, alas ! those premonitions
of parturition result not even in a mouse.   Such stimula-
tion is a sure sign that the book we have been reading
possesses real vitality.

Let us try and disengage Mr. Birrell's characteristics.
Beneath all, he has a sustaining constitution of English
Puritanism, not, of course, seventeenth century or
Spurgeon Puritanism, but Puritanism up to date.   Those
who heard Mr. Birrell's father preach, or who only knew

by sight his 'natty' distinguished figure, will understand his son all the better for it. The remembrance of him in the pulpit illuminates the style and tastes of the author of *Obiter Dicta*. He reminded one, at least from a distant pew, of Charles Lamb. There was a similar eighteenth-century distinction about his neat, sprightly, and studiously well-bred personality. It comes out in especial relief in anecdotes which contrast him with the burly individuality of Hugh Stowell Brown. The elder Mr. Birrell had, too, a quaint, quiet humour, which his son has also inherited and deepened. Perhaps this odd blend of Puritanism and humour, neither obtrusive, are the extremes within which are included Mr. Birrell's other characteristics. He is a welcome example of the truth that a man need not stop being (quietly) in earnest because he is a (quiet) humourist—or *vice versâ*. Mr. Birrell's humour, albeit he has a reputation for it, is not 'professional'; like Cardinal Newman's —according to Mr. Birrell's truly 'judicious' essay upon the Cardinal—it 'always takes us unaware.' For instance, speaking of the alleged futility of Cardinal Newman's work, Mr. Birrell writes, earnestly and regretfully enough, ' It is very puzzling and difficult, and,' he adds, as though he never meant us to laugh at all, 'drives some men to collect butterflies and beetles.' I know not if the comparison be pleasing, but Mr. Birrell's humour reminds me—that is, in the manner of it—of Max O'Rell's. It seems to come as a sort of laconic afterthought. It is the sedate, sly humour of the law and the Church. The jest does not always come off, as in his note on George Borrow, where, in regard to Borrow's

unfairness to Scott, Mr. Birrell says that, after all, seeing
our need of Borrow, 'It is just possible to thank heaven
(feebly) that it was no worse.  He might have robbed a
church!'  The alternative, I am afraid, leaves one cold.

In regard to fairness, Mr. Birrell is singularly fair.
He has his bias, of course.  He is a 'lover of all things
that are quiet and gentle and true in life and literature,'
in contrast to whatsoever things are noisy and sensational and narrowly 'modern'; but even in dealing
with the latter he would seem to try, so far as mortal
may, to 'look at the heart.'  He is able to speak of
'Wesley's great missionary tours in Devon and Cornwall, and the wild remote parts of Lancashire,' as
lacking 'no single element of sublimity,' in the body of
a very sympathetic essay on Cardinal Newman.  He
loves, too, to vindicate such old-fashioned, even ridiculed,
reputations as Cowper's or Richardson's; and he has
one other comfortable characteristic: he does not
assume, in a lofty way, that the reader knows everything.  He does not blush to say that he likes his
poetry to have thought as well as poetry, that
he likes it to be 'useful' as well as beautiful, as in
the case of Matthew Arnold; that the much-sneered-at
British appetite for sermons is no bad thing, after all;
and he is in various ways a reassurance to our smarting
nationality.  He does not deny that we are often
Philistine enough, but, as he is not afraid to champion
certain of our 'standard works,' he does not shrink from
defending some of our 'sterling qualities' and tastes.
And while he does this with one hand, he can also
soundly box our ears with the other: 'No foreigner

needs to ask the nationality of the man who treads on his corns, smiles at his religion, and does not want to know anything about his aspirations.' Yes, Britannia's heart yearns to such a one, for is he not her own well-beloved son?

Is there any writer with whom one is so continually
*Andrew Lang:* falling out and continually making it up
'Grass of     again as Mr. Lang? To-day he alienates
Parnassus.'   us by his middle-aged cynicism, to-morrow
he redeems it by some honest manly sympathy, and so he plays at see-saw with our affections. A short time ago he was poking fun at a batch of young Parnassians, and now we find him, young of heart, republishing his own verses—a 2s. 6d. reissue of the *Grass of Parnassus*, uniform with the recent reissue of his essays. Nor is it a mere reprint. *Grass of Parnassus: First and Last Rhymes*, is the full title, and the volume, in addition to the original 'grass,' includes a few of the translations from the rare *Ballads and Lyrics of Old France*, as well as about thirty new pieces, some few of which are collected from the magazines. Mr. Lang is also boyish enough to tell us, he 'cannot resist the pleasure of mentioning' it, 'that the versions from the Greek Anthology were prompted by the encouraging kindness of the late Mr. James Russell Lowell.' What deft and altogether charming versions they are we have long known. In lightness of touch they are, perhaps, only equalled by Mr. Lang's other translations from the

old French poets. As a whole this volume is very typical of Mr. Lang's poetical gift, in its varied application. How oddly the moods change between golf and the *tædium vitæ* ; but on the whole Mr. Lang's muse is a melancholy one, as 'wild with all regret' as the Greek Anthology. A new introductory poem, in which Mr. Lang makes believe to bid 'Vale' to his muse, strikes the minor note of the volume :

> 'Once the Muse was fair,
>     Once : when we were young,
> Gay and debonair,
> Or with pensive air,
>     So she came, she sung.'

Is it not rather, Mr. Lang continues, the poet not the muse, who has grown old :

> ''Tis not she, but we,
>     That are weary now ;
> Well, howe'er it be,
> Her we shall not see,
>     Broken is the bough.'

Yet life would seem to have one firm anchorage even for Mr. Lang—that of an old friendship. Old books, old wine, old friends, says the adage. Two of these joys, at least, we know, remain faithful to Mr. Lang. He has often sung of his books, here are a few of his lines to an old friend, whom he addresses as 'E. M. S.' :—

> 'Change, Care, nor Time, while life endure,
> Shall spoil our ancient friendship sure,
> The love which flows from sacred springs,
> In " old unhappy far-off things."
>   From sympathies in grief and joy,
>   Through all the years of man and boy.

> Therefore, to you, the rhymes I strung
> When even this "brindled" head was young
> I bring, and later rhymes I bring
> That flit upon as weak a wing,
> But still for you, for yours, they sing!'

After all, Mr. Lang is more fortunate than some of us. One old friend is no inconsiderable asset in this bankruptcy of life. And, for all his pessimism, Mr. Lang is always the brightest and most entertaining of writers. Homer may nod, but his translator never.

A RE-READING of Andrew Marvell had just set me *Norman Gale:* sighing for simple, quiet, garden-loving 'A Country men; and here, as luck would have it, I Muse.' took up the latest new book of verse, and read thus :

> 'Why should I fret myself to find out nought?
> Dispute can blight the soul's eternal corn,
> And choke its richness with the tares of thought.
>
> I am content to know that God is great,
> And Lord of fish and fowl, of air and sea—
> Some little points are misty.   Let them wait.
>
> I well can wait when upland, wood and dell
> Are full of speckled thrushes great with song,
> And foxgloves chime each purple velvet bell.
>
> Our village is encircled by sweet sound
> Of bee and bird and lily-loving brook:
> Hence, Unbelief, for this is holy ground!
>
> At early dawn I stand upon the sod
> And let the lark rain this upon my soul—
> The smaller in man's sight the nearer God. . . .

At eventide I lean across a gate,
And, knowing life must set as does the sun,
Muse on the angels in the Happy State.

Ah, let me live among the birds and bloom
Of hazel copses and enchanted woods
Till death shall toll me to the common tomb. . . .

My song is all of birds and pleasant homes,
For on such themes my heart delights to dwell
And sing in sunshine till the shadow comes.

I sing of daisies and the coloured plot
Where dandelions climb the thistle's knee—
I take what is nor pine for what is not.

I am for finches and the rosy lass
Who leads me where the moss is thick, and where
Sweet strawberry-balls of scarlet gleam in grass.

And this I know, that when I leave my birds,
The lichened walls, the heartsease and the heath
I shall not wholly fail of kindly words.

And while I journey to the distant Day
That first shall dawn upon the eastern hills,
Perchance some thrush will sing me on my way.

The Great Republic lies towards the East,
And Daybreak comes when Christ with tender face
Welcomes the poor in spirit—who were least.'

Those who care, in addition to loving the old poetry, to keep an eye on whatever young promise is stirring, have been aware for some time of a shy anonymous bard, who, through Mr. George E. Over, of Rugby, has issued two or three very dainty volumes, in editions limited to no more than eighty copies, the two volumes known to us being *Meadowsweet* and *Violets*. There was something very sweet and generally arresting about the personality they suggested, and, a pretty sure sign,

bibliophiles bought copies, paying as much as two
guineas for one of the tiny volumes, done up in a card-
board box like a valentine.   Well, this poet, hardly less
shy than Mr. Bridges, proves to be Mr. Norman R. Gale,
and the little volume of verse, entitled *A Country Muse,*
which he has just published, is a selection from the
privately-printed volumes aforesaid.   It is, however, a
selection which is no means satisfying.   One note that
was especially characteristic of the unnamed author of
*Violets* was a robust frankness in his love-songs, a union
of warmth and chasteness, which we have missed since
the days, lamented by one of Andrew Marvell's talking
horses, of 'Old Bess in the ruff.'   To give an example,
I quote one of the unselected poems, a bit of gallantry
on the part of 'Strephon to Chloris':

> 'Chloris, unbend that gathered brow!
>     'Twas but a straying touch or twain
> That followed on this slope of snow,
>     The azure runnel of a vein!
> Come, sweet, be neither saint nor shrew—
>     The heart behind the hand was true.'

The theme here is surely touched with a reverent, if a
daring hand.   I shall venture on another, also un-
reprinted :

> 'O to think, O to think as I see her stand there
> With the rose that I plucked in her glorious hair,
>     In the robe that I love,
>     So demure and so neat,
> I am lord of her lips and her eyes and her feet!
>
> O to think, O to think when the last hedge is leapt,
> When the blood is awakened that dreamingly slept,
>     I shall make her heart throb
>     In its cradle of lace,
> As the lord of her hair and her breast and her face!

O to think, O to think when our wedding bells ring,
When our love's at the summer but life's at the spring,
    I shall guard her asleep
    As my hound guards her glove,
Being lord of her life and her heart and her love!'[1]

A new poet is always best left to speak for himself.
I have, therefore, let quotation take the place of
criticism, and when quotation and the intelligent
reader come together, where is the need of criticism?
Being plain as a pikestaff that Mr. Gale is a poet not
merely of promise, but of achievement—and of achievement in a manner of poetry almost obsolete with us
at present, a manner in the best tradition of English
poetry at its strongest and sweetest, English love,
English pastures—can we make it plainer by comment?
A modern writer has finely said that some flowers
have roots deep as oaks; Mr. Gale's poems are such,
deep-rooted in the simplicity of nature; they have the
fragrance, the spontaneity, and the strength of all
earth-born things.

DARLEY, like Lamb, was a divine stammerer. But,
*George Darley:* whereas Lamb's stutter was a social thing,
  'Sylvia.'    often giving additional piquancy to his
talk, Darley's made him much of a social outlaw,
self-conscious and misanthropical. He enjoyed, however, the proverbial compensation of the stammerer,
the gift of song. A lyric gift of most delicate airiness,
and the fancy of a fairy; his contemporaries recognised

[1] These Poems have been reprinted since the above was written.

these gifts in him.    Lord Tennyson even offered to
defray the expenses of his publishing, and Browning confessed to Darley's influence in his own early
work.    Yet Darley has received less of his due even
than Beddoes and Wells, who with him and others
made a little constellation of poet's poets about the
forties, and have, for the general reader at least, been
eclipsed by the robuster genius of such contemporaries
as Lamb, Wordsworth, and Coleridge.    Outside Miss
Mitford's *Recollections* there has been little written of
Darley, and Miss Mitford was somewhat inaccurate.
She did, however, give one or two enticing' quotations from *Nepenthe*, a poem even less known than
*Sylvia*, and, in fact, of much less value.    There is a
touch of 'Kubla Khan' wizardry about such a verse
as this :

> 'Over a bloomy land untrod
>     By heavier foot than bird or bee
> Lays on the grassy-bosomed sod,
>     I passed one day in reverie :
> High on his unpartitioned throne
> The heaven's hot tyrant sat alone,
> And like the fabled king of old,
> Was turning all he touched to gold.'

Darley was an Irishman, the son of a Wicklow
squire.    He was born in 1795, and was educated
at Trinity College, Dublin, where, owing mainly to
nervousness resulting from the impediment in his
speech, he was somewhat late in graduating.    The
same infirmity robbing him of a scholarship for which
he was competing with every chance of success, he
left Dublin in disgust, turning to London to seek his

fortune in literature. In 1822 he published his first
volume, *The Errors of Ecstasie*, which introduced him
into the literary circles of the time. But his impediment soon began to prove a hindrance to him, and
he grew shy of going about. He was, however, not
long in getting on to the staff of some of the best
periodicals, including the *London Magazine*, where he
wrote under the pseudonym of 'John Lacy.' His first
contributions were a series of criticisms on 'Dramatists
of the Day,' in which he excepted only Joanna Baillie
and Beddoes from general condemnation. At the death
of the *London Magazine*, Darley, together with Charles
Lamb, Hood, and 'Barry Cornwall,' went over to the
then young *Athenæum*, where he still continued to
write severe dramatic criticism, and to which he contributed some striking letters on Italian art, written
during a holiday in Italy. As he grew older he grew
still more shy of society, and a sense that he was not
valued at his true worth seems to have made him
jealous of his more famous contemporaries. According to Miss Mitford, he thought little of Wordsworth
and Scott, and, indeed, of any poet except Shakespeare or Milton. How pathetically hungry for praise
and how intolerant of unfavourable criticism he was
his letters abundantly illustrate. In thanking Miss
Mitford for appreciation of *Nepenthe*, he writes : 'Seven
long years did I live on a charitable saying of Coleridge, that he sometimes liked to take up *Sylvia.*'

It is not necessary here to follow Darley through all
his literary undertakings. Those who care to do so are
referred to Mr. John H. Ingram's interesting biographical

introduction to his dainty reprint of *Sylvia*. Darley died in 1846, aged fifty-one.   His petulant epitaph is characteristic of his solitary, comfortless life :

> 'Mortal, pass on !—leave me my desolate home,
>   I ask of thee no sigh—I scorn thy tear !
> To this small spot let no intruder come,
>   The winds and rains of heaven alone shall mourn me here !

We usually resign ourselves to the acceptance of a certain measure of prose in our poetry.   It is, perhaps, a necessary sustaining element in the greatest, but in such poetry as Darley's it is certainly out of place — poetry 'of imagination all compact'; sheer fantasy and ever-bubbling song ; a revel of pure pleasure ; flowers and bees, and the sound of falling water ; nothing to do but listen, nothing to understand but music ; mere deliciousness of phrase and fancy. Darley was steeped in the Elizabethans, and the *genre* of *Sylvia* is that of *The Midsummer Night's Dream*. His faery verse is, perhaps, the most charming out of Shakespeare.   He has, too, the Shakespearean touch in his treatment of flowers.   One quotation will afford a double illustration.   Nephon, a sort of Puck, enters with his lap full of flowers :

> '*Nephon* : Lady and gentlemen fays, come buy !
> No pedlar has such a rich packet as I.
>
>      Who wants a gown
>        Of purple fold,
>      Embroidered down
>        The seams with gold ?
>          See here !—a Tulip richly laced
>          To please a royal fairy's taste !

Who wants a cap
　Of crimson grand?
By great good hap
　I 've one on hand:
　　Look, sir !—a Cock's-comb, flowering red,
　　Tis just the thing, sir, for your head !

Who wants a frock
　Of vestal hue?
Or snowy smock?—
　Fair maid, do you?
　　O me !—a Ladysmock so white !
　　Your bosom's self is not more bright !

Who wants to sport
　A slender limb?
I 've every sort
　Of hose for him:
　　Both scarlet, striped, and yellow ones:
　　This Woodbine makes such pantaloons !

Who wants—(hush ! hush !)
　A box of paint?
'Twill give a blush,
　Yet leave no taint:
　　This Rose with natural rouge is fill'd,
　　From its own dewy leaves distill'd.

Then lady and gentlemen fays, come buy !
You never will meet such a merchant as I.'

This is but one of many songs no less perfect in
which *Sylvia* is rich. Much of Darley's most beautiful writing is to be found in the octosyllabic proems
to each act and scene in which he sets his pastoral
stage. Here is a beautiful impression of English
pastoral scenery, 'knee-deep in June':

'Green haunts, and deep enquiring lanes,
　Wind through the trunks their grassy trains . . .
　Millions of blossoms, fruits and gems,
　Bend with rich weight the massy stems;

147

Millions of restless dizzy things,
With ruby tufts, and rainbow wings,
Speckle the eye-refreshing shades,
Burn through the air, or swim the glades :
As if the tremulous leaves were tongues,
Millions of voices, sounds, and songs,
Breathe from the aching trees that sigh,
Near sick of their own melody.'

In his description of the fiend-king's home, Darley shows that his eye was not merely for the delicious. There is something of sombre awe about his grim picture of that 'Ruder than Cyclops' mountain home':

'Lightning has scorch'd and blasted all
Within this dark cavernous hall ;
Through every cranny screams a blast
As it would cleave the rocks at last ;
Loud rapping hail spins where it strikes,
And rain runs off the roof in dykes ;
And crackling flame, and feathery sleet,
Hiss in dire contest as they meet ;
Tempests are heard to yell around,
And inward thunders lift the ground.'

We get somewhat too much of Shakespearean clowning, but that is only because it is possible to have too much of a good thing. *Sylvia* needs the predestined reader, but for such a one who happens not to have come across it, as may easily have happened even to a well-read man, the book will come like an unexpected remnant of youth, another of those happy isles 'which bards in fealty to Apollo hold.'

ALTHOUGH I have kept a sharp look-out for Mr. Lloyd Osbourne, I have not found him—seldom

*R. L. Steven-son and Lloyd Osbourne: 'The Wrecker.'* indeed suspected his presence. Once or twice it has occurred to me, is this an Osbourne chapter? And then would come an unmistakable Stevensonian word, a word, maybe, which had travelled all the way from Sir Thomas Browne, to find unwonted setting in a salt narrative of the high seas. Doubtless, Mr. Osbourne's share in *The Wrecker* is subterranean, or submarine, he has worked with Mr. Stevenson on the plot, and thrown in out-of-the-way experience of ships and shipmen. But I fancy Mr. Stevenson has done all the writing.

For curiously, as the book is a collaboration, Mr. Stevenson's individual style is, perhaps, more stamped upon *The Wrecker* than upon any other of his stories of adventure. Indeed, it is in this, and the reason of it, that the book is somewhat unique among Mr. Stevenson's writings. He seems to have been bent on making his extremes meet in one volume. The mere title, of course, proclaims the *Treasure Island* Stevenson, the boy's Stevenson, his head still on fire with the romance of buried treasure, pirates, and the Spanish Main. The ingenuity of the plot, together with some whimsicalities of characterisation, unmistakably recall the baffling mysteries and the fantasy of *The New Arabian Nights*; while, for many a rich page, it might seem incongruously, we have the best Stevenson of all, the man's Stevenson, him of *Virginibus Puerisque*. An epilogue addressed to Mr. Stevenson's friend, Mr. Will H. Low, already associated with the Stevensonian muse in the *Underwoods*, tells us that this choice blend has been of design.

Yarning together, in one of their Samoan nights, on the sale of wrecks, and the occasional romance thereof, the authors saw opportunities, they tell us, of wonderful 'detective' complications of story. 'What a tangle it would make,' suggested one, 'if the wrong crew were aboard. But how to get the wrong crew there?' Mr. Stevenson happily felt with some of us in regard to the detective type of story. In such a story, he well says : 'The mind of the reader, always bent to pick up clues, receives no impression of reality or life, rather of an airless, elaborate mechanism ; and the book remains enthralling, but insignificant, like a game of chess, not a work of human art.' That is just the reason, doubt-less, for that feeling of humiliated self-respect with which we put down a Wilkie Collins story. We have indulged a weak inquisitiveness, suffered ourselves to be dragged, breathless, through a maze of doubts and fears, just for the sake of coming out of it—no richer, but rather poorer (by nervous loss) than when we entered. We have met nobody worth meeting, no sentence worth remembering, and the sieve does not sooner forget the water than we do the whole business. Mr. Stevenson's aim in *The Wrecker* has been to make such excitement more legitimate, to give us people with faces we can remember, and writing to mark and turn to again. Moreover, the mysterious plot does, as he puts it, the more 'inhere in life,' by its being the history of real men rather than romantic lay figures. Such stories, as a

rule, are the improbable narratives of impossible people ;
however improbable the story of *The Wrecker*, its
authors have determined that its actors shall, at least,
be flesh and blood, and so the more convincing.   So far
as I am aware, this blend of the novel of manners and
the pure 'adventure' romance is new.   However that
be, it is surely successful.   The oddly-assorted elements
mingle with quite unexpected harmony, and the book is
as much a whole as though it had been entirely carved
from a piece of old man-of-war.

Loudon Dodd is the son of a Yankee stock-broking
millionaire.   He is put to a school which is little more
than a mimic stock-exchange, and of which we have
a charmingly whimsical description.   Each boy begins
his education with a certain amount of the school
'stock,' wherewith to speculate, and the day is spent,
for the most part, in playing at bulling and bearing : as
in Wall Street fortunes are made and lost in a day, and
he who is Jay Gould in the morning is glad of a clerk-
ship in the afternoon.   Dodd is bitten with that love of
art which is still more infatuating than Mr. Kipling's
'delicious East.'   He persuades his father to send him
to Paris, to start study as a sculptor.   This gives Mr.
Stevenson the opportunity for some charming sketches
of Parisian artist life, to fill out the picture of Fontainebleau in his recent essays.   We even get just one
enchanting glimpse of 'that extinct mammal, the
grisette.'   But Dodd's destiny was to be an amateur
rather than an artist.   His father suddenly loses all in
a speculation, and dies.   Dodd's allowances cease, and
he is left penniless, and Paris, says Mr. Stevenson, is

a bad place to starve in.   However, he has one quaint
friend—Jim Pinkerton, an American lad of spirit, who
studies art with a Yankee superstition for 'culture,'
though without a gleam of talent, and supports himself
on a 'Paris letter' to a San Francisco paper.   Dodd
has won his eternal friendship, curiously, by telling him
that he cannot paint 'a damn.'   Pinkerton 'was not
therefore sad,' but sensibly leaves what he cannot do,
for what he can.   His real passion is for the romance of
commercial speculation.   So he returns west in search
of it, begging Dodd to come and share his luck.   But
Dodd still prefers the dinner of herbs where art is, and
stays behind steadily to starve.   However, it is of no
use, at last he is persuaded, and he joins Pinkerton
'across the sapphire sea.'   Pinkerton is already flourish-
ing in San Francisco, keeping a dozen speculations
going at once, the corner stone being 'Thirteen Star
Golden State Brandy, Warranted Entire.'   He soon
finds Dodd something to do, as the popular manager of
'Pinkerton's Hebdomadary Picnics,' with their 'Monster
Olio of Attractions—Sun, Ozone, and Music!'   On this
amusing sketch of Yankee sensational commerce I
must not dwell.   Among Mr. Pinkerton's miscellaneous
ventures were occasional purchases of wrecks.   It is in
this way that we come·upon the story of 'The Flying
Scud.'   She has run aground in the South Seas, and her
remains are to be sold by auction.   Pinkerton bids,
expecting, as he is in the ring, to buy her for a hundred
or two dollars.   To his surprise he finds an unknown
person bidding against him, and suspicion arising that
the bidder represents the captain, he at once jumps to

the conclusion that there must be more valuable cargo aboard than is dreamed of in the manifest—smuggled opium, for instance! On this mere guess, he at last buys at a ruinous figure. Then he hears that all the ship's crew have left San Francisco, evidently speeding to the wreck. He loses no time in chartering a schooner, in which Dodd sails as his supercargo. The wreck is reached, but there is no sign of its crew—and next to no opium! But a photograph is found on board, purporting to represent the crew of the ' Flying Scud,' with the name written over each man—and not one man in the group agrees with the crew as seen in San Francisco. So you see Mr. Stevenson has succeeded in getting 'the wrong crew aboard.' How he got them there I think it is only fair both to him and the reader to let you find out for yourself.          •

Before, however, leaving *The Wrecker*, I must not neglect to quote one of those *Virginibus Puerisque* passages of which I spoke, a passage in which Mr. Stevenson once more speaks of the 'more manly way of life,' and his own passion for the South Seas :

' In my early days,' he says, in the person of Dodd, ' I was a man the most wedded to his idols of my generation.  I was a dweller under roofs ; the gull of that which we call civilisation ; a superstitious votary of the plastic arts ; a cit, and a prop of restaurants. . . . That was a home word of Pinkerton's deserving to be writ in letters of gold on the portico of every school of art : " What I can't see is why you should want to do nothing else." The dull man is made, not by the nature, but by the degree of his immersion in a single business.  And all the more if that be sedentary, uneventful, and ingloriously safe.  More than one half of him will then remain unexercised and undeveloped ; the rest will be distended and deformed by over-nutrition, over-cerebration,

and the heat of rooms.   And I have often marvelled at the impu-
dence of gentlemen who describe and pass judgment on the life of
man in almost perfect ignorance of all its necessary elements and
natural careers.   Those who dwell in clubs and studios, may paint
excellent pictures or write enchanting novels.   There is one thing
that they should not do, they should pass no judgment on man's
destiny, for it is a thing with which they are unacquainted.   Their
own life is an excrescence of the moment, doomed, in the vicissi-
tude of history, to pass and disappear.   The eternal life of man,
spent under sun and rain and in rude physical effort, lies upon one
side, scarce changed since the beginning.   I would I could have
carried along with me to Midway Island all the writers and the
prating artists of my time. . . .'

But supposing Mr. Stevenson were to do so, would
they not simply set up their easels and writing desks
and go on painting and writing?   What does Mr.
Stevenson do in Samoa?   Apparently he writes novels.
Long may it be ere he takes up a more 'natural' career.
One tires a little of this iteration of the simple and the
physical as the only 'natural.'   It is as natural to be
a man of letters as to be a cannibal :

> ' For the dear God who loveth us
> He made and loveth all,'

including even the minor poet.

As wealth draws the poor relation from his hole, so
*William* fame attracts the remainder from the pub-
*Watson :* lisher's cellar.   Twelve years, maybe, it
' The Prince's has waited massed upon the shelves, but
Quest.'
now at last is heard a sound as of the breaking-up of
an Arctic winter; it is being taken down in big

bundles and baled off to another publisher's, to be dressed up in a nice new title-page, and thus, 'with new-spangled ore,' at last it 'flames in the forehead' of the *Athenæum.*

But all remainders are not so honest as Mr. William Watson's remainder of *The Prince's Quest and other Poems.* They pretend they are new editions, and some people believe them. In a note, however, to this poem of Mr. Watson's, 'which first of all he made when young,' it is confessed that, with the notable exception of Rossetti's appreciation, it attracted but little attention on its publication twelve years ago. Those interested in Mr. Watson have long known, from those famous notes to Mr. Sharp's *Sonnets of This Century*, that *The Prince's Quest* was admired by Rossetti. Mr. Sharp refers to his possession of Rossetti's copy of it, made interesting by 'several markings and marginalia.' Mr. Sharp quotes a few lines which were marked as specially excellent. It will thus be doubly interesting to quote them here :

> 'About him was a ruinous fair place,
> Which Time, who still delighteth to abase
> The highest, and throw down what men do build,
> With splendid prideful barrenness had filled,
> And dust of immemorial dreams, and breath
> Of silence, which is next of kin to death.
> A weedy wilderness it seemed, that was
> In days forepast a garden, but the grass
> Grew now where once the flowers, and hard by
> A many-throated fountain had run dry,
> Which erst all day a web of rainbows wove
> Out of the body of the sun, its love.
> And but a furlong's space beyond, there towered
> In midmost of that silent realm deflowered,

A palace, builded of black marble, whence
The shadow of a swart magnificence
Falling, upon the outer space begot
A dream of darkness where the night was not.'

One can understand the special appeal of this passage
to Rossetti, being, as he was, painter as well as poet.
It is, for a dream, singularly concrete.  It might serve,
recalling a favourite title of Marvell's, for 'instructions
to a painter.'   Indeed, Mr. Watson has evidently the
painter's eye.   One feels this quality of objectivity
in striking promise in this early volume.   The forms,
especially the profiles, of everything are seen and
drawn with rare firmness.  Colour is not so evident,
but that one might expect in an eye for profile.
A Sunset ' provides an example of this :

'The incendiary sun
Dropped from the womb o' the vapour, rolled
'Mongst huddled towers and temples, 'twixt them set
Infinite ardour of candescent gold,
        Encompassed minaret
        And terrace and marmoreal spire
With conflagration : roof enfurnaced, yet
Unmolten—columns and cupolas flanked with fire. . .'

Fine, but a silhouette rather than a picture.  You will
notice how even already Mr. Watson loves to fill his
mouth with good fat vowels—to play with beautiful
centipedes like 'marmoreal,' and how he loves the
grand Marlowe sweep of line as in 'the shadow of a
swart magnificence.'  Unlike his later style, as at
first sight *The Prince's Quest* is, it yet has those strongly
marked characteristics of his later work, those and
that objectivity just referred to.

In the (just a little grandiose) publisher's note prefixed to the volume, we are told that Rossetti combated
the opinion of some reviewer that *The Prince's Quest*
owed dues to Mr. William Morris. 'He goes right
back,' says Rossetti, 'to Keats, with a little modifica-
tion.' After all, it is no very serious matter. It is
taken for granted that every young poet is derivative
of his elders, and so that Mr. Watson show some signs
of wearing his rue with a difference, what are the odds
whether the creditor be Keats or Mr. William Morris.
Both are good men to steal from, their 'bounty is as
boundless as the sea.' As a matter of opinion, and
ignorant of what Rossetti had to say on the matter,
we think that the reviewer referred to, so long as he
made the statement with a due sense of its unimportance,
was right. Of course, if he talked about plagiarism
he was silly; but I think there can be no doubt
that, differ as it may in expression when looked into,
the *genre* of *The Prince's Quest* is that of *The Earthly
Paradise* rather than any model in Keats. Of course,
the whole æsthetic school is practically a rib out of
the side of Keats, deriving from him, with this difference, that it inherits his sweetness and sensuousness,
but little of that picture-making power which is so
striking a quality of Keats's best work. This quality I
have remarked in Mr. Watson, and, therefore, in regard
to the stronger parts of his poem, the little isles of
tightly-packed verse, he may be said to hail from Keats
—though even on that side I should prefer to say
Tennyson—but the main stream of his narrative has certainly a Morrisian flow. The theme, too, is just a Morris

theme ; indeed it has a certain resemblance to 'The Man Who Never Laughed Again' in *The Earthly Paradise*.

A prince in dreams is taken to a fair city, and beholding a lovely queen is told that she waits for his coming. Then, waking, the vision impresses him as a prophecy; and, haunted by the face, he seeks the fair city through the world, cheered by intermediate dream-messages. It is noticeable that in this earlier volume Mr. Watson shows a lyric gift hardly in evidence since. Here are two charming verses, first and last, from the lullaby with which the Prince sings himself to sleep :

> ' O sleep, thou hollow sea, thou soundless sea,
>    Dull-breaking on the shores of haunted lands,
> Lo, I am thine : do what thou wilt to me.
>
>      .        .        .        .
>
> So may I see in dreams her tresses fair,
>    Down-falling, as a wave of sunlight rests
> On some white cloud, about her shoulders bare,
>    Nigh to the snowdrifts twain which are her breasts.'

And very beautiful is the long lyric which celebrates the happy ending of the quest : the very song seems to sink its head to rest :

> ' As flowers desire the kisses of the rain,
> She his, and many a year desired in vain :
> She waits no more who waited long enow.
> Nor listeth he to wander any more
> Who went as go the winds from sea to shore,
> From shore to sea, who went as the winds go.
> The winds do seek a place of rest ; the flowers
> Look for the rain ; but in a while the showers
> Come, and the winds lie down, their wandering o'er.'

The reader will notice that in lines five and six Mr.

Watson is playing with words, as Mr. Stevenson says the young artist should, as the savage plays with his coloured beads—'fingering the dumb key-board,' Mr. Stevenson admirably expresses it. There is a good deal of that in the volume, and a good deal of that jugglery with two or three ideas which marks the epigrammatist. 'A Song of Three Singers' is an exceedingly clever instance of both :

> ' Wave and wind and willow-tree
> Speak a speech that no man knoweth ;
> Tree that sigheth, wind that bloweth,
> Wave that floweth to the sea :
> Wave and wind and willow-tree.'

Can't you picture yourself at the Pavilion, and see the glass balls going up and round and round from the hands of the cunning juggler? The mere words, perhaps, are as little significant as the glass balls, but the skill! It was so Poe used to play with words; indeed, the rhyming of this poem is very much after his fashion, the feeling, too, just a little hard, the words being recognised as mere counters for the exercise of skill. Lord Tennyson, the poet from whom I think Mr. Watson has learnt most, is also fond of thus ringing the changes on one or two notes, but his notes have a mellowness not felt here.

IT is not always easy to be just to 'bibliolatry.' Like

*On Book-Collectors.*
every other form of worship, it is liable to suffer from its professors. For instance, you come across some busy Philistinish person who collects your own exquisite author, and you look at him and know how little such a man can know of those precious, unique qualities which make even the very binding sacred. You can well understand those who have fallen under the spell of his qualities, been stirred and charmed and roused to answering moods by them, wishing to 'collect,' to make a little tutelary deity of him, one of their *Lares Bibliothecæ*, with a shrine built of first editions; but that a man who has not only never read him, but has no possible affinities with him, should, in ape-like fashion, also 'collect' him—there's the respect that gives the true believer, the true worship, to the scoffer. Yet how common are such people : men without a spark of poetry in them who collect early Elizabethans, others without a gleam of humour who collect Dickens ; men for whom you have always to discover the best passages in their own particular authors—that is, if you are allowed, for their copies may be 'unopened,' in a double sense. Odd, is it not, that a man should come to prize that which was made to be opened merely because of its remaining shut? The more we consider the bookman in his lower forms, the mere curiosity hunter, and his cousin the mere commentator, the more do we see the aptness of the term 'bookworm'; for are they not the maggots which breed in the perishable parts of

great fames? They are the marine store-dealers of literature, hoarding up the rags and tags, the non-essentials, the littlenesses, of great people. Of the greatness, that which alone matters, they have no hint. They can show you a complete set of Fielding's wigs, but they have no opinion on *Tom Jones*. They know all the servant-girl gossip about Shelley and Harriet, though they have never read a line of *Prometheus Unbound*. But the true collectors are not so. They too may read little, but they are men of fine antennæ, and know their affinities in books by some delicate sensitiveness of impression, a sense for the spiritual aroma of a book, which in half-an-hour will learn more of the essence of an author than can be learned by another man in a month, or, in fact, a lifetime. For, of course, nothing is properly understood except through affinity. And on this account the true collector often suffers with the false : for both are seen to read but little, though, as a rule, the true collector does more reading in secret than he is credited with. Besides, he might, if he pleased, make some such defence as this : 'You don't,' he might say, 'insist on the collector of old china continually eating and drinking from his fragile pieces, nor do you maintain that a man should not keep a couple of old swords over his mantelshelf unless he occasionally flesh them on his neighbours ; why, then, would you restrict me to the merely ele-mentary use of my books? True books were made to be read, but they were made for other, and to me daintier, uses. They were made beautiful in print and page and binding to delight my eye as with a picture, they were made to fondle, to carry under one's arm, to go to sleep over. Like all human possessions, the older ones are rich in the associations of human handling, the alluvium of the stream of time : in short, beauty and sentiment, and all the subsidiary characteristics which lie like a fine glaze over the mere first uses of things.' In these the book-collector has as much right to dwell as any other connoisseur, but there is one thing he should never forget, that it is all in play, though here Mr. Lang reminds us that most other activities in life are play too :

> ' Prince, all the things that tease and please—
>     Fame, hope, wealth, kisses, cheers, and tears—
>   What are they but such toys as these—
>     Aldines, Bodonis, Elzevirs?'

We begin with foreign coins, and end in accumulating coins of the realm. Where is the difference ? One is a boy's game, and the other is a man's ; but both are games.

MR. LANG has wittily said that 'there are literary
*Anatole* reputations in France and England which
*France:* seem, like the fairies, to be unable to cross
'La Vie
Littéraire.' running water.' M. France, modest man
though he be, is evidently not of these. Already he is well known here as, if not the inventor, at least the most distinguished exponent of the personal, the auto-biographical, or the impressionist, form of criticism. It was he who formulated it in the now almost proverbial

dictum that the good critic simply relates the adventures of his soul among masterpieces. Were he quite frank, continued M. France, he would at the outset announce that he proposed speaking of himself — *à propos* of Shakespeare, Racine, Pascal, or Goethe. *C'est une assez belle occasion.*

In a charming preface to his fourth volume of *La Vie Littéraire*, he discourses further on the same text, the fallacy of the judicial, the impossibility of finality, in æsthetic criticism. It is a castle in the air, he says. Base it, if you will, upon ethics. Where are your ethics? We have not even a science of sociology; nay, not even a science of biology. We think we have. But, according to M. France, the achievements of science existed only in the brain of Auguste Comte. When we have a science of biology, that is to say, in some few million years, we may, perhaps, after many more centuries, construct a science of sociology, and then, and then only, may we begin to talk of a science of æsthetics.

Or, say you base it upon the universal opinion. Certain books there are which the world has agreed upon as classics. To this M. France enjoins, with mournful truth : 'The books which all the world admires are those which nobody examines.' Certain real appreciators of them have started the fashion, and the world, in its apish spirit of imitation, follows it. This was fairly obvious. We have only to think what the average Englishman's bluster about Shakespeare amounts to. He takes him on trust, without examination, as he does his other superstitions, as his father and grandfather did before him. M. France gives one or two amusing illustrations of the value of such universal opinion.  One especially goes home to us.  Ossian, he says, when he was believed to be a genuine ancient seemed equal to Homer.  Now that we know he was only Macpherson, we despise him.  It was the same, too, with the Shakespearean forgeries of W. H. Ireland.  Few have the capacity for judging anything absolutely on its own merits, or even with sincerity to their own impressions.

To be sincere to one's own impressions.  How easy it seems, how hard it really is !  To make up one's mind as to what one really feels, the impression itself, rather than the expression of it, is the great difficulty.  One may sometimes have thought that these professors of the *moi* in criticism have adopted their method in mere indolence, or from the incapacity to be judicial.  No opinion could be more unjust, for one has only to try to find out how hard, even in a brief criticism, it is to keep fast hold of one's *moi*, 'à garder notre *moi* comme un trésor . . . et, fût-on seulement une vaine ombre, ne vendre cette ombre ni à Dieu, ni au diable, ni aux femmes.'  This is a quotation from M. France's charming paper on M. Maurice Barrès, the high priest of 'La religion du moi, le culte de la personne intime, la contemplation de soi-même, le *divin égotisme*,' to whom M. France prettily says the world is the grain of opium which he smokes in his little silver pipe, the curling smoke therefrom being his dreams.

But, after all, when one thinks of it, there is nothing fundamentally new about this gospel of the *moi* in criticism.  It is only the formulation of it that is new.

Every critic who has ever written, however he might be shrouded in the sinaitic anonymity of *The Quarterly* or *The Edinburgh* could really only speak for himself, however he might pretend to be speaking for 'the soul of the wide world.' Even if he stole his opinions, or trimmed them in deference to prevailing fashion, such theft and such trimming would, after all, be only characteristic of his miserable *moi*. And the really great critics, the critics whose opinions have, oddly enough, come to be in some measure impersonal, wrote as much from their own personal standpoint as ever M. France or M. Lemaitre—Hazlitt, and Lamb, for instance, and even Matthew Arnold, for all his magisterial air. What is new, I repeat, about the impressionist criticism is its formulation. It is, indeed, but one more expression of the democratic spirit. Its battle is not so much against personal authority as abstract authority— such *ex cathedrâ* authority as that of *The Quarterly Review* for example. It attacks the divine right of criticism, as the same spirit has overthrown the divine right of kings.

'To thine own self be true,' by all means—supposing you have a self worth being true to. Like so many such purely dramatic admonitions, this of Polonius is constantly misapplied. It was meant for Laertes, and it is applied to the whole world—applied loosely to people who had better be true to anybody but themselves. How one is bored, especially in criticism, by people being so conscientiously true to their dull, conceited selves! There is a certain safety against such in the acknowledged personal criticism. They are soon found out.  They are not sheltered under the wing of great newspapers.  They are personally liable for their own dulness.  An incompetent actor is not protected by the reputation of his theatre; why should a dull writer be saved by the reputation of his paper?  Let every writer stand or fall on his own signature.  With that incredible superstition peculiar to us, one often hears people say that criticism would not come with such authority if it were all signed.  Well, who cares?  Who wants an oracular authority that refuses to reveal its credentials?  Besides, as I have said, that real authority which means the guidance of superior brain will really be strengthened.  We shall know our men and measure their authority accordingly.  Of course, we shall not follow them blindly, but when disposed to differ with them we shall think twice or thrice before doing so.  It is their subject, they have shown themselves so often wise guides, that it will probably be worth our while to listen to them.

Thus is M. France authoritative in spite of himself.  His catholicity is so great, he includes so much, unites so many extremes, has so good a heart, and yet so cool a head.  Abreast of all that is most modern he has also the ballast of an old-fashioned wisdom and scholarship.  He is a regular development, with roots in the past, no mere forced fruit of the new era.  He reads his Bourget *avidement*, but when he has finished he turns to his *Imitation of Christ*, at the page where it opens of itself, and, paradoxically enough, finds a motto for his causerie.  'Ah, if M. Bourget's hero, if the young poet René Vinci had read each morning, in his room on the Rue Coëtlogon, chapter viii. of the *Imitation*. . . .' ! With all his charm Bourget leaves a taste of dust and ashes in the mouth. That is why M. France turns to his *Imitation*, but it is with no affected saintliness. ' We by no means love only those who save us,' he says somewhere. ' On the contrary, we dread being robbed of the pleasure of being lost. The best of us are like Rachel, who would not be comforted.'

Not the least of his charms are his constant amiability and modesty. In an affectionate testimony to the worth of his old friend and publisher, M. Calmann Lévy, lately deceased, he alludes quite touchingly to the encouragement he had himself received from the great publisher. It was he only who had conquered his idleness and timidity, he says. He won't hear of his being a critic, he is only a *conteur de lettres*. ' Il y a des contes de fées. S'il y a aussi des contes de lettres, c'en sont là plutôt.' Then he has so many impressions, and all so sympathetic. Now it is an old historian, some great respectable pillar of the Academy of whose manner M. France has memories, now he is gently chaffing M. Jean Moreas, whom he imagines as a king in ' le pays latin,' with fifty poets at his heels, ' comme un jeune Homère conduisant les jeunes homérides,' now it is 'Gyp's' last novel, now Madame Bernhardt's 'Cléopâtre.' There is no limit to his impressions, no book or theme in which he cannot find something for his sympathy, and yet, all the time, you feel that everything is seen relatively, all is unconsciously classified. His temperament is a bounteous one, with its greater and lesser needs. These he never confuses. If he does not use them in Matthew Arnold's judicious fashion, he keeps by him great touchstones. All is more or less good, but some is best.

THE poetic drama, as a form, has always had a fascina-

*W. B. Yeats:* tion for Mr. Yeats—his first book contained 'The Countess many dramatic experiments—but one pro-
Kathleen.' blem in the use of it has troubled him as it has others. In much so-called poetic drama the poetry and drama are not one, the poetry is, in fact, unessential; it does not inhere in the conception, but rather cumbers the action with unwieldy ornament. To bring them both into real union, to regard the necessity of brief and simple speech, which is the law of dramatic action, and yet to gain that impression of intensity and distinction which is the soul of poetry—there's the rub. Of course, the difficulty of achieving this is lessened in so far as one's theme naturally belongs to the realm of fancy, and Mr. Yeats had so much in his favour to start with. Yet with what fine artistic austerity he has refused any indulgence from his theme. How resolutely he seems bent on achieving his effects with the fewest possible strokes. In this respect *The Countess Kathleen* is a marked advance on *The Wanderings of Oisin*, in which the poet frankly gave himself up to carousal with his wondrously fecund fancy. The restraint of the drama has evidently been good for Mr. Yeats's muse. All its elemental qualities, its Irish glamour, its deep mysticism, .its dream-like imagination, its alluring beauty, are

preserved, but they are now controlled as well. From whatever point of view we consider it, one is struck with the power with which Mr. Yeats has developed the suggestiveness of his Irish folk-tale.

Yet it was a fine legend to start with, an eerie variant of the Faust motive in an Irish peasant dress. It is curious to notice how still more impressive a fine conception is in a rough material—as the Japanese potters well knew. As types become more universal, though they gain in breadth of appeal, they are apt to lose somewhat in the intensity of it. Mephistopheles is, doubtless, more universal than the two 'goblin merchant men' who came to buy souls in Mr. Yeats's famine-stricken Irish village, but he is hardly so creepy. There seems, too, something more moving about the loss of a peasant soul than that of a philosopher such as Faust. A philosopher does not excite pity. He has his philosophy.

But let us briefly outline Mr. Yeats's drama. It opens in the country inn of one Shemus Rua. The stage direction prepares us for wizardry—so much perhaps he has learnt from M. Maeterlinck—'The Inn of Shemus Rua ; a wood of oak, hazel and quicken trees is seen through the window half hidden in vapour and twilight.' Shemus is out with his cross-bow foraging for food, a heavy famine being on the land and the larder empty. His wife Mary and his son Teig await his coming, oppressed with twilight fears of the supernatural meaning of the drought. The air seems full of portents, Teig has strange things to tell :

'How yon dog bays,
And how the grey hen flutters in the coop.

> Strange things are going up and down the land
> These famine times.   By Tubber-vanach cross-roads
> A woman met a man with ears spread out,
> And they moved up and down like wings of bats.
> . . . By Carric-orus churchyard,
> A herdsman met with one who had no mouth,
> Nor ears, nor eyes—his face a wall of flesh.
> He saw him plainly by the moonlight.'

Mary, a devout simple woman, growing alarmed as Shemus still tarries, bends before a shrine of the Virgin and prays :

> ' Virgin,
> Bring Shemus home from the hateful forest ;
> Save Shemus from the wolves—Shemus is reckless.
> And save him from the demons of the woods
> Deluding dim-eyed souls now newly dead,
> And those alive who have gone crazed with famine.
> Save him, dear Mary.'

Shemus at length returns, and throws a dead wolf upon the floor.   He adds another touch to the hushed waiting horror of the famine :

> ' I searched all day : the mice, and rats, and hedgehogs
> Seem to be dead, and I could hardly hear
> A wind moving in all the famished woods.'

Talking of the famine, he grows reckless.   ' God and God's Mother nod and sleep,' only Satan is awake.   ' He does not nod, nor sleep, nor droop his eyelids.'

> ' I am half-mindful to go pray to him
> To cover all this table with red gold.'

Two horned owls are seen peering through the window, and presently there is a knock at the door, the Virgin's shrine falls from the wall, and two merchants enter, claiming a night's lodging.   They place heavy bags of gold upon the table. They come buying men's souls. Shemus and Teig, fascinated, sell their souls at once, and go and spread the news among the peasants. But Mary resists and curses them in two of Mr. Yeats's finest lines :

> 'You shall at last die like dry leaves, and hang
> Nailed like dead vermin to the doors of God.'

Soon peasants are flocking in to sell. The news comes to the lady of the manor, the Lady Kathleen, a pious woman. She bids her steward give out money to save the peasants. It is now a duel between her and the demons. So long as her money lasts they are thwarted, but breaking into her treasury at night, they have all her gold carried away by the fairies— 'sheogues,' 'sowlths,' and 'tevishies,' spirits of earth and water, in the distinction of which Mr. Yeats gives us some of the most impressive poetry of the kind in English. To call it faery poetry is too suggestive of mere pretty fancy, yet we have no other word. He has heightened the significance of the country side faerie with the spiritual terror of conception evidently caught from his theosophy. Some of his fairies are simple 'good people,' and some terrible larvæ, such as the 'tevishies' :

> 'Lost souls of men, who died
> In drunken sleep, and by each other's hands. . . .
> 　　　　Hither, tevishies,
> Who mourn among the scenery of your sins . . .
> Turning to animal and reptile forms
> —The visages of passions. Hither sowlths ;
> Leave marshes and the reed-encumbered pools,
> You shapeless fires that once were souls of men,
> And are a fading wretchedness.'

The wizardry of this scene, in which, horde after horde, the demons thus invoke their various powers, sets one's hair on end.

Another impressive scene, with an element of Mephistophelean humour in it, represents the merchants at the inn, seated at a table covered with parchments and little piles of gold.  Shemus and Teig stand at the door, encouraging the people to sell.  As each seller comes up to the table, the merchants read aloud from one of the parchments.  A woman steps up:

> ' "What price now will you give for mine?"
>     " Ay, ay,
>   Soft, handsome, and still young,—not much, I think,
>   She has a little jar of new love-letters
>   On a high shelf between the pepper pot
>   And wood-cased hour-glass. . . .
>   She hides them from her husband, who buys horses,
>   And is not much at home, you're almost safe,
>   I give you fifty crowns." '

One cautious man comes to offer half his soul, but in souls there is no retail business.  Then a poet comes—it might have been Mr. Yeats himself:

> ' Alone in the hushed passion of romance
>   His mind ran all on sheogues, and on tales
>   Of Finian labours and the Red-branch kings.'

He asks no price, but begs them to take his soul for nought—he is weary of life.  But they cannot, for he loves the Countess Kathleen, and, therefore, his soul is hers. Presently enters the Countess herself. She has come to sell her soul to buy back those of her people—an offer at which the demons jump, for, after all, there was but small reversionary interest of good in the souls of the others, but her soul were indeed 'a precious jewel for Satan's crown.' Yet as ever, in fairy tales, the devil is cheated of his due. When the Countess dies, and the demons, in the forms of owls, wait for her soul, God, 'who sees the motive and the deed regards not,' sends His angels to

> ' Save her from the demons,
> Who do not know the deed can never bind.'

I must have written enough at least to stimulate the reader's interest, he will have got some hint of Mr. Yeats's cunning development of his symbolism, of the rich concreteness of his expression—likewise his Irish inability to write blank verse—but, of course, I can give him little idea of the fine artistic completeness, of the fantasy of the whole impression, or of the strange 'keening' undertone, as though it were the breath of Ireland's immemorial sadness that is wafted through the whole. Mr. Yeats looks for the day when Ireland shall have a distinctive literature of her own. Maybe he is a ray of its dawn. Anyhow, he may rest content that one of his wishes will be fulfilled, and that he will

> ' Accounted be
> True brother of that company
> Who sang to sweeten Ireland's wrongs.'

Of his shorter poems two or three are perfect, and all have beauty, but most are obscured by that mysticism over which in *The Countess Kathleen* he has more control.

THE Book Beautiful. *Marius the Epicurean* is pre-
*Walter Pater:* eminently that for many of us. Perhaps
'Marius the no book since *Sartor Resartus* has been
Epicurean'—
Third Edition read with such a sense of awakening, and
Revised. indeed it may be said that it has, in some
needed measure, modified the influence of *Sartor*, with
its sublime factory gospel of work. For the imperative
' Do ! ' of Carlyle it substitutes the gentle pleading ' Be ! '
' Be ye perfect ! ' The culture of the individual in a well-
ordered unity, body, soul, and spirit : that is its message.
But not a selfish culture. ' He must satisfy, with a kind
of sacred equity, he must be very cautious not to be
wanting to the claims of others, in their joys and
calamities.' That was one of the earliest axioms Marius
took with him on his progress from the primitive religion of his fathers, through Epicureanism, to that
final mood of his mind in which the careful justice of
such an axiom was being deepened by the warmer
sentiment of a Christian pity. What that mood quite
was we are left a little in doubt—as how else could
it be in regard to a complex being such as Marius?
His experience of life had been too various, too human-
ising, for him to become the bondsman of any mere
dogma ; though in the formulæ of Christianity, the
earlier, unmonastic Christianity, he had, perhaps, come
nearest to finding the formulæ which most expressed
his own gentle individuality—if formula must be !

Some people will have nothing of Mr. Pater. One
has heard them say that he is all manner and no
matter. A strange doctrine, for certainly it seemed to

some of us, when first we read *Marius* with glowing heart, that it was full indeed of burning matters. It seemed that no 'spiritual pastor' had so harmonised the claims of body and soul, so wondrously captured for us those fine elusive moods of which we are hardly aware till we recognise them in another; and that no one had written more movingly of friendship, of good-ness, of beauty, or of death—great matters as we thought. It is true that Mr. Pater's manner is occasion-ally a little too priestlike in its extreme, its maiden-like fastidiousness. But even so, such fastidiousness comes but of his sincerity towards his meaning. It is instruc-tive to remember what he writes of Flavian: 'His dilettantism, his assiduous preoccupation with what might seem but the details of mere form or manner, was, after all, bent upon the function of bringing to the surface, sincerely, and in their integrity, certain strong personal intuitions, certain visions or apprehensions of things as being, with important results, in this way rather than that.' To this sincerity the revisions in the present edition bear almost painful witness. One had looked forward to them with some eagerness, for one might well feel that Mr. Pater could hardly have 'completely revised' his 'golden book' without reveal-ing in the process some new secrets of perfection. I proposed to myself the task of collating the two versions; but that is a task for leisure, and my leisure has not been equal to it, nor, I must add, my austerity. For the task soon began to resemble the numbering of the golden hairs on a beloved head. One kept continually forgetting the collation to luxuriate in the pleasure of mere reading.   So presently I fell to lazily dipping and comparing here and there, at various well-remembered pages.   Besides, devotion even to a master must be kept within bounds, if we are not to make him and ourselves ludicrous ; to register his every trivial change in prosody or punctuation, after the manner of some editors, ' were,' as Polonius wisely said, ' nothing but to waste night, day, and time.'

And so far as I have examined, the majority of Mr. Pater's emendations are merely matters of prosody and punctuation, though such as they are, they are numberless.   We are sometimes sententiously reminded that, though we seem the same person as we did seven years ago, there is actually not a molecule of us which has not been replaced.   Was it not Cowley who ingeniously excused his inconstancy on this Heraclitean principle, though he found it convenient to say five years ?

> ' My *Members*, then, the *Father Members* were,
> From whence *These* take their birth, which now are here,
> If, then, this *Body* love what th' other did,
> 'Twere *Incest*, which by Nature is forbid.'

Such a complete minute change of texture seems to have overtaken Mr. Pater's *Marius* since its first publication in 1885—exactly, you will remark, seven years ago.   Comparing the old text with the present, one is reminded of an ant-hill, the busy units of which are changing every moment, but the total impression to the eye remaining the same.   One recalls, too, that passage in Mr. Pater's exposition of the Heraclitean doctrine of the eternal flux : ' It was as if, recognising perpetual motion as the law of Nature, Marius identified his own way of life cordially with it, throwing himself into the stream, as we say : he, too, must maintain a harmony with that soul of motion in things, by a constantly renewed mobility of character.' Strange dilemma of the artist, that while seeking perfection even his ideal of perfection must be changing.

On every page one finds minute changes in punctuation. Colons replace semi-colons, commas fall out altogether, and Mr. Pater seems to have endeavoured to cure himself of his fondness for the parenthetic dash. With none of his disciples' contempt for the unlearned reader, he has translated one or two Latin quotations which had escaped translation in the other editions— not obviously, as to hurt the susceptibilities of that unlearned reader, but by a graceful repetition, as though merely for emphasis. There is sometimes quite a homely touch in Mr. Pater's writing, very winning ; and one may refer here to his scrupulous care, when possible, to express his thought in simple English. He never uses a word foreign to the language, unless the idea is foreign also. The reader will remember that in one or two instances the chapter headings were simply two or three lines from Pliny, the Vulgate, and in one case a line from Rousseau. These Mr. Pater has now retained as mottoes, but in most cases replaced them as chapter-headings by English titles—not always successful. In one case, at least, he would seem to have carried his complacency towards the merely English reader to a somewhat grotesque result ; for, surely, 'Change of Air' is an oddly undignified, unsuggestive title for the beauti-

ful chapter describing Marius's sojourn at the temple of
Æsculapius among the hills.  How much more fit in every
way was the 'Dilexi decorem domus tuæ'; and few
readers who care to read Mr. Pater at all are so unlearned
as not now and again to appreciate the beauty, the deco-
rative beauty, of a sprig of Latin such as that.  Chap. iv.
of part i. is now described as 'The Tree of Knowledge,'
and chapter vii. appears as 'A Pagan End' instead of
the original and more impressive title of ' Pagan Death.'
In part ii., the journey to Rome (chap. x.) is hardly
distinctly suggested by 'On the Way.'   In part iii.,
there are two changes for the better, chap. xvii. is now
inscribed 'Beata Urbs,' instead of merely bearing the
quotation ' Many Prophets and Kings,' etc., and chap. xix.,
'The Will as Vision.'   In part iv. chap. xxiii., is
now entitled ' Divine Service,' and chap. xxvi., 'The
Martyrs.'   In all the instances except ' Change of Air'
and 'On the Way' the emendations have been im-
provements.   Perhaps they were really too trifling to
record; but, after all, as the old story goes, it is the
trifles that make perfection, and perfection is no trifle.

It is, however, with more anxious expectancy that one
turns to certain passages in the text, passages which to
some of us, coming as that copy of Apuleius came to
the young Flavian, in a 'fortunate' moment, have been
real watchwords of our lives, as many a line in Browning
or Carlyle has been.  Such to me were : 'He must be
very cautious not to be wanting to the claims of others,
in their joys and calamities'; 'not pleasure, but fulness,
completeness of life generally'; 'to be absolutely virgin
towards a direct and concrete experience'; and lastly,

towards the close of the wonderful chapter on the
gladiatorial games : 'Yes ! what was wanting was the
heart that would make it impossible to witness all this ;
and the future would be with the forces that could
beget a heart like that.   His favourite philosophy had
said, Trust the eye : strive to be right always regarding the concrete experience : Never falsify your
impressions.   And its sanction had been at least effective here, in saying, It is what I may not see !   Surely,
evil was a real thing ; and the wise man wanting in the
sense of it, where not to have been, by instinctive
election, on the right side, was to have failed in life.'

One goes to the new edition, prepared to resent any
changes in such passages as these, in the same spirit in
which we resent 'the revised version' of any great
familiar thing.   We feel that any essential change must
be impossible, and all the more resent any merely
vexatious change of phrase, clashing as it does with
our old sacred familiarity.   In every one of the passages
cited, Mr. Pater, in some such vexatious way, offends
against our cherished remembrance of his words.   In
no instance does there seem to have been any real need
of alteration, and except in the case of 'his *favourite*
philosophy,' in the last passage, for 'his *chosen* philosophy' there is nothing characteristic in the changes.
In the first sentence we have for 'not to be wanting to'
'lest he be found wanting to,' and 'not pleasure, but a
general completeness of life' is the new and certainly
closer form of the second aphorism, though one misses
the effect of the word 'fulness.'   But the third, most
helpful, phrase is now rendered unquotable by its being

made to depend on the conclusion of another sentence :
'. . . the impressions of an experience, concrete and
direct, to be absolutely virgin towards such experience
. . .' There is certainly no gain here, but a distinct
loss of force.

If the examples cited may be taken as fairly representative of Mr. Pater's revisions, one may feel comfortable that *Marius* remains much as it was, though
one has all the more reason to fear the possibility of
Mr. Pater's, so to say, being overcome by a grammatical
affection of the nerves, which, if encouraged, will not
allow either him or his readers any peace.  Had changes
been necessary to bring his text nearer to his meaning,
one must have borne them ; but that sentence after
sentence should be pulled about to satisfy,' not the
instinct of expression, but a morbid desire of punctuation, is not bearable.  Yet, after all, however many
septennial changes overtake *Marius*, it cannot well be
robbed of its high beauty, of its deep humanity.  It will
still remain one of the most convincing expressions of
the inherent priesthood of man, whatever be the new
last word of presumptuous biologists, or its mistaken
application by sensualists, who, as of old, take the name
of Epicurus in vain, and who in spite of its central
doctrine, 'not pleasure, but a general completeness of
life,' dare to quote its authority for a life of foolish *in-*
completeness, a mere cultivation of certain detached
appetites.

Mr. Pater has not failed to impress his reader with
that danger of misapplication.  Who can ever forget the
closing passage in 'The Renaissance': 'To burn always

with this hard, gem-like flame, to maintain this ecstasy, is success in life'? But again: 'Only be sure it is passion—that it does yield you this fruit of a quickened, multiplied consciousness.' *Only be sure it is passion!* It is a haunting cry, hard to forget ; and only those who have forgotten it have read Mr. Pater to their undoing.

'PARIS, May, 1892.' Thus Mr. Symons dates his dedication to a lady of his acquaintance.
*Arthur Symons: 'Silhouettes.'* That mere superscription means much. Viewed symbolically there is in it a world of pathos. There is always pathos when any one yearns towards a particular class of life, or centre, as it seems, of 'tone,' with a feeling that there is the ideal state, to be outside of which is to be 'provincial,' *borné*, and other dreadful things. It is the dairymaid's superstition o the 'gentleman,' the parvenu's of the 'upper ten,' the outcast's of 'society.' What 'Budmouth' in Mr. Hardy's *Return of the Native* was to Eustacia Vye, Paris is to Mr. Symons and many young men of the same school. Had Mr. Symons lived earlier he would doubtless have dated his preface from Alexandria. To be 'in the movement' at all costs, in contradistinction to being 'of the centre,' is the aim of these ardent young men. Looking through Mr. Symons's 'contents' his titles prove no less characteristic : 'Pastel,' 'Morbidezza,' 'Maquillage,' 'Nocturne,' 'The Absinthe Drinker,' 'From Paul Verlaine.' But, for all that, he is much simpler

than he supposes, and there are in his book many delicate and beautiful things.  His poems, indeed, look much slighter than they are.  Fragile they seem, and often are, but sometimes it is with the seeming fragility of wrought iron.  They are full of careful observation, and a strenuous art which has measured its form by its matter to a word.  To this more self-conscious art, they sometimes add the unbidden charms of passion and song.  In this poem of 'Emmy' we have also an un-wonted touch of pity :

'Emmy's exquisite youth, and her virginal air,
    Eyes and teeth in the flash of a musical smile,
Come to me out of the past, and I see her there
    As I saw her once for a while.

Emmy's laughter rings in my ears, as bright,
    Fresh, and sweet as the voice of a mountain brook ;
And still I hear her telling us tales that night
    Out of Boccaccio's book.

There, in the midst of the villainous dancing-hal
    Leaning across the table over the beer,
While the music maddened the whirling skirts of the ball,
    As the midnight hour drew near.

There with the women, haggard, painted and old,
    One fresh bud in a garland withered and stale,
She, with her innocent voice and her clear eyes, told
    Tale after shameless tale.

And ever the witching smile, to her face beguiled,
    Paused and broadened, and broke in a ripple of fun,
And the soul of a child looked out of the eyes of a child,
    Or ever the tale was done.

O my child, who wronged you first, and began
    First the dance of death that you dance so well?
Soul for soul : and I think the soul of a man
    Shall answer for yours in hell.'

Let us quote another impression with a fresher atmosphere :

> ' Night, and the down by the sea
>    And the veil of rain on the down :
> And she came through the mist and the rain to me
>    From the safe warm lights of the town.
>
> The rain shone in her hair,
>    And her face gleamed in the rain :
> And only the night and the rain were there
>    As she came to me out of the rain.'

These poems have both strength and charm.    Many
other poems prove that Mr. Symons has a genuine gift
of impressionism.    Mr. Whistler and M. Verlaine are
evidently the dominant influences with him at present,
as Browning, and perhaps Mr. Meredith, were in his
first book.  *Silhouettes* is a marked artistic advance on
*Night and Days*, but Mr. Symons's next volume will
be more crucial.    It will be all the better if he will let
himself go a little more, and not keep so self-conscious
an eye upon his art, which by this time may safely be
trusted to act instinctively.

THE appeal of Mr. Meredith's later poetry is, I fear,
*George* entirely to the faithful.    Coming to a
*Meredith :* new volume of his poems they know
'The Empty
Purse,' etc. exactly what to expect, exactly what not
to expect.    The casual reader frets and fumes.    These
are not poems.    They are simply 'chaos illuminated
by flashes of lightning.'    Exactly.    That is all the

experienced Meredithian expects, and consequently he reads contentedly, picking up what crumbs he may from the master's table.    Doubtless he often sighs for the time when the poet was content with simple beauty, as in *Love in the Valley*, and the comparatively plain but majestic English of *Modern Love* ; but that seems no reason for his rejecting whatever of strength and beauty is still vouchsafed to him.    Like Vivien, he will not throw away his whole apple because of a few pitted specks.    And he, at least, well knows that he has his reward.    He finds it in such a passage as this, which is surely a beautiful description of childhood—the childhood, in this case, of the average young British egoist :

> 'There the young chief of the animals wore
> A likeness to heavenly hosts, unaware
> Of his love of himself ; with the hours that leap.
> In the dingle away from the rutted highroad,
> Around him the earliest throstle and merle,
> Our human smile between milk and sleep,
>     Effervescent of Nature he crowed.
> Fair was that season ; furl over furl
> The banners of blossom ; a dancing floor
> This earth ; very angels the clouds ; and fair
> Thou on the tablets of forehead and breast :
> Careless, a centre of vigilant care.
> Thy mother kisses an infant curl.
> The room of the toys was a boundless nest,
>     A kingdom the field of the games,
>     Till entered the craving for more,
>     And the worshipped small body had aims.'

There is scarcely any sign in this passage of that strange literary disease, a sort of writer's cramp, which has overtaken Mr. Meredith, in a strangely similar form to that in which it also overtook Browning. It is not merely a result of grammatical compression. It is the more compound expression of endless metaphor. Both in Browning, and Mr. Meredith, but especially in Mr. Meredith, the fancy—or should we say the imagination? for the imagery has more of the organic nature of imagination—has passed beyond the control of the writers. It is no longer possible for them to see anything simply as it is, but only in some fantastic image of itself. Almost every word is charged with some such metaphorical allusion, image treads upon image, without the least regard for proportion, and grammatical idiosyncrasies adding to the confusion, what wonder that the casual reader faints by the way? Here is a passage taken at random :

> ' He cancelled the ravaging Plague,
>     With the roll of his fat off the cliff.
> Do thou with thy lean as the weapon of ink,
> Though they call thee an angler who fishes the vague
>     And catches the not too pink,
> Attack one as murderous, knowing thy cause
> Is the cause of community.   Iterate,
> Iterate, iterate, harp on the trite :
> Our preacher to win is the supple in stiff ; . . .'

It is, perhaps, hardly fair to quote such a passage without context, though with context it is but little clearer. It is certainly not worth while to minutely elucidate it, though it will be well for a moment to refer back to the antecedent of the first two lines. Mr. Meredith describes this poem of 'The Empty Purse' as 'A Sermon to our later Prodigal Son,' his central ide being that not till the wealth with which 'grandmotherly laws,' indulge our aristocratic youth

> 'In the days of their hungers impure ;
> To furnish them beak and claws,
> And make them a banquet's lure,'

not till that wealth is spent, and they are brought face to face with the bare facts of life, with 'Earth'—Mr. Meredith's constant lesson—have they any chance of leading sane and useful existences :

> 'Strike Earth,
> Antæus, young giant, whom fortune trips !
> And thou com'st on a saving fact,
> To nourish thy planted worth.'

> 'And think of thy privilege : supple with youth,
> To have sight of the headlong swine,
> Once fouling thee, jumping the dips !
> As the coin of thy purse poured out :
> An animal's holiday past : . . .
> Rubbing shoulder to shoulder, as only the book
> Of the world can be read, by necessity urged.
> For witness, what blinkers are they who look
> From the state of the prince or the millionaire !
> They see but the fish they attract,
> The hungers on them converged. . . .'

The reader will now have some inkling what meaning to attach to 'the roll of his fat off the cliff.' 'The Empty Purse' is briefly a sermon against Mammon— full of Mr. Meredith's radiant radicalism, his belief in brain, his faith in 'Earth,' in expression frequently obscure, but lit up by many a vivid, even lovely line, and, occasionally, passage.  Looking into the future,

Mr. Meredith, with undaunted faith, thus beautifully prophesies :

> 'A morn beyond mornings, beyond all reach
> Of emotional arms at the stretch to enfold :
> A firmament passing our visible blue.
> To those having nought to reflect it, 'tis nought ;
> To those who are misty, 'tis mist on the beach
> From the billow withdrawing ; to those who see
>     Earth, our mother, in thought,
>     Her spirit it is, our key.'

Of the many epigrams of thought and of beauty with which the poem abounds, here are a few taken at random :

> ' He strutted, a cock, he bellowed, a bull,
>     He rolled him, a dog, in dirt.'

> ' There are giants to slay, and they call for their Jack.'

> ' . . . a nursery Past ! '

> ' May brain democratic be king of the host ! '

> ' A Conservative youth ! who the cream-bowl skimmed,
> Desiring affairs to be left as they are.'

> ' Peace,
> Our lullaby word for decay.'

> ' There are those whom we push from the path with respect.
> Bow to that elder . . .
>     In his day he was not all wrong.
> Unto some foundered zenith he strove, and was wrecked.
> He scrambled to shore with a worship of shore.'

> ' 'Tis known how the permanent never is writ
> In blood of the passions.'

> ' I can hear a faint crow
> Of the cock of fresh mornings, far, far, yet distinct.'

> ' Keep the young generations in hail,
> And bequeath them no tumbled house ! '

Surely, if the book contained nothing more than these phrases, it were worth sifting! And there is one more of fine significance which we must not miss —Mr. Meredith's symbolical test of new wisdom:

> '*Is it accepted of Song?*
> Does it sound to the mind through the ear,
> Right sober, pure sane? has it disciplined feet?
>  Thou wilt find it a test severe;
>  Unerring whatever the theme.
> Rings it for Reason a melody clear. . . .'

The more one ponders this test the more suggestive it becomes — by no means is it merely fantastical, though, in the deepest sense, it has a touch of mysticism. There are several other poems in the volume on which I should like to have dwelt—especially the touching ode to 'Youth in Memory,' fuller of 'simple beauty' than any poem in the volume, especially rich in those lovely descriptions of nature in which Mr. Meredith has no rival:

> 'Despite our feeble hold on this green home,
> And the vast outer strangeness void of dome.'

> '. . . the arrowy eagle of the height,
> Becomes the little bird that hops to feed,'

are lines descriptive of age with a very moving pathos. But, of course, Mr. Meredith's philosophy of age is as robust as his philosophy of everything. Accept the conditions, and the compensations are always ready—is his constant lesson. And so to age. Be content to be old, ape no mere mockery of youth, live in your children, and in the thought that you are 'one step above the animal,'—for such is Mr. Meredith's idea of the evolutionary value of living.

ONE opens *The Death of Œnone, Akbar's Dream and*
*Lord Tennyson:* *other Poems* not so much with a feeling
'The Death of curiosity as of reverence. The harvest
of Œnone.' is done and the summer is ended, and
the reaper is gone home. His barns are full, and
these are but gleanings which we shall cherish, be
they rich or scanty. A first glance into this last of
the familiar green books—or the last but one, for unpublished manuscripts, one hears, still remain—tells us
that the poet retained to the end his art of happy
dedication. One has always turned with peculiar ex-
pectation to those familiar little prefatory confidences—
to the reader, it seemed, as well as to the poet's friend
—in which he gave us the fleeting glimpses of a self
at other times so 'occult, withdrawn.' One thinks
especially of that to 'Old Fitz.' Here is the last
we shall read, entitled 'June Bracken and Heather.
To ——':

'There on the top of the down,
    The wild heather round me and over me June's high blue,
    When I look'd at the bracken so bright and the heather so
        brown,
    I thought to myself I would offer this book to you,
    This, and my love together,
    To you that are seventy-seven,
    With a faith as clear as the heights of the June-blue heaven,
    And a fancy as summer-new
    As the green of the bracken amid the gloom of the heather.'

189

'With a faith as clear as the heights of the June-blue heaven'!  How significant is it that our greatest poets, as they have one by one recently taken leave of us, have 'thundered the brave, irresistible message' —Browning, Whitman, and now Tennyson.   By this time everybody knows 'The Silent Voices' by heart, especially those who heard it in the Abbey.   I never expect to experience a thrill more solemn than that which passed through me as the first words broke from the choir :

> ' When the dumb Hour, clothed in black,
>   Brings the Dreams about my bed,
>   Call me not so often back,
>   Silent Voices of the dead,
>   Toward the lowland ways behind me,
>   And the sunlight that is gone !
>   Call me rather, silent voices,
>   Forward to the starry track
>   Glimmering up the heights beyond me
>   On, and always on !'

The secret of Tennyson's powerful charm often seems discoverable, but the simple magic of these few solemn lines eludes one completely.   And it seems to me that fine as is the 'Crossing the Bar,' 'The Silent Voices' must be pronounced still finer.   In one important particular, at least, it is superior.   Its imagery is more universal.  'Crossing the Bar' was just a little marred by conventional symbolism, but there is nothing in 'The Silent Voices' which does not apply alike to 'pagan' and Christian.

Still one other message of faith is to be found in the last poem in the volume,—'God and the Universe':

'Will my tiny spark of being wholly vanish in your deeps and
     heights?
Must my day be dark by reason, O ye Heavens, of your bound-
     less nights,
Rush of Suns, and roll of systems, and your fiery clash of
     meteorites?

"Spirit, nearing yon dark portal at the limit of thy human
     state,
Fear not thou the hidden purpose of that Power which alone
     is great,
Nor the myriad world, His shadow, nor the silent Opener of the
     Gate."'

ONE may regard Mr. Dobson's *Eighteenth Century*
*Vignettes* as prose studies for his *Old*
*World Idylls.*  Therein we gain some
idea of how much reading, how intimate
an acquaintance with fact, is needed before
the poem, the blossom of study, is born.  Mr. Dobson
is the inspired singer of that golden age which is ever
either behind us or elusively ahead.  For some it was
in Greece, for some it existed only in the 'spacious
days,' for Mr. Morris it is 'East of the Sun and West
of the Moon,' for Mr. Dobson it embraces the reigns of
Queen Anne and the earlier Georges.  But before Mr.
Dobson could be the singer of his dream-world, he
had to construct it.  The materials lay all about, but
all unbuilt.  Of these materials his charming volume
of essays gives us many a glimpse.  Some of the
titles will best suggest the contents—'Prior's "Kitty,"'
'Fielding's "Voyage to Lisbon,"' 'A Garret in Gough

*Austin Dobson:*
'Eighteenth
Century
Vignettes.'

Square,' 'An old London Bookseller,' ' Gray's Library,'
'Goldsmith's Library,' 'A Day at Strawberry Hill,'
'Old Vauxhall Gardens.'    On these and many other
suggestive themes Mr. Dobson gossips in his pleasant,
allusive, vivid, and slyly humorous style, in which many
a phrase quaintly recalls the polished age he loves so
well.    What would one not give to know anything so
thoroughly as Mr. Dobson knows the eighteenth century?

PROFESSOR MINTO is evidently of opinion that a good
*William Bell* editor should be seen and not heard.    He
*Scott :* is most parsimonious of himself all through
Minto's
'Life.'    the two fine volumes of *Autobiographical
Notes of the Life of William Bell Scott.*    Only now and
again in the still small voice of a footnote are we aware
of his overruling providence, and in the modest conclud-
ing chapter, narrating those final incidents which it is
given to no autobiographer to record for himself.

In reading such a book of reminiscences one is apt
—a little cruelly, don't you think?—to dwell most on
the relations of the autobiographer with men more
famous or notorious than himself.    We welcome him
for his reflected light, and do not care to see if he
has any attractive light of his own.    In the case of
Bell Scott we are apt to say at once, 'Rossetti, Swinburne, P.R.B.,' to look up in the index all the refer-
ences to such names and matters, and we are perhaps
almost inclined to resent any mere talk about himself
as impertinent.    Meanwhile one can imagine the poor

departed soul hanging over this and that reader hoping for some sympathetic sign that *his* personality, *his* story, has met with that recognition which in its fulness life, maybe, for various reasons denied.  Can you not imagine the thin flame sorrowfully, and, maybe, bitterly, withdrawing itself, finding the reader with no care for *him*?  To have seen Shelley plain is interesting, yet after all, it hardly serves the purpose of a long life.  To be valued only for that is like being read for one's quotations.

However, one perhaps exaggerates the danger in the case of Bell Scott.  At any rate, he was no mere hanger-on to a circle.  One rejoices with him to read that it was the mountain that came to Mohammed in his case. In other words, it was the young, ardent Rossetti who first sought him, having been attracted by certain of his poems.  Dated from 50 Charlotte Street, Portland Place, Rossetti's first letter to him ran :

'A few years ago I met for the first time (in a publication called the *Story Teller*) with your two poems " Rosabell "and " A Dream of Love."  So beautiful, so original did they appear to me, that I assure you I could think of little else for several days, and I became possessed by quite a troublesome anxiety to know what else you had written, and where it was to be found.'

The letter goes on to describe fruitless searches at the British Museum, and ends in an ecstatic strain on having at last discovered Scott through the publication of his mystic poem, 'The Year of the World.'  Soon we find Rossetti sending a little batch of manuscript poems entitled 'Songs of the Art-Catholic,' that significant title covering no less poems than the 'Blessed Damozel,' and 'My Sister's Sleep.'  Thus commenced a friendship which was to continue warm and fast till Rossetti's death.

In reference to the poem of 'Rosabell,' mentioned in Rossetti's letter, I remember seeing in Bell Scott's copy of Mr. Hall Caine's *Recollections of Dante Gabriel Rossetti*, a note against the account of 'Jenny' to this effect : 'Written after reading my "Rosabell."' Scott can hardly have meant more than that the theme of Rossetti's poem had been hinted to him by 'Rosabell'— as it might appear was also his early picture, 'Found' (that in which a country girl is found asleep against a wall in the town by her rustic lover). The only resemblance between the two poems is the general realism of treatment. Scott's contains fine things, and, like all his poetry, has a certain overshadowing of power, but it is too long and too loosely constructed. It has not the dramatic selectiveness, or the vivid closeness of phrase, which characterises 'Jenny'; but, all the same, such a picture as that of Rosabell at the threshold of the tavern standing fascinated by the innocent 'ring-a-roses' songs of a group of children :

> 'She heard them to the end, she stood
> As she were dead while still they sang ;
> Then ran among them with a shriek
> And cursed their innocence.'

Such a picture lives with one, as live such lines as :

> 'And hearts as innocent as hers
> As blindly shall succeed, shall take
> Leap after leap into the dark,
> Blaspheming soul and sense at once,
> And every lamp on every street
> Shall light their wet feet down to death.'

Bell Scott seems to have imputed that touch of artistic frustration one feels in his work to the too dominant influence of Blake, a copy of whose illustrations to Blair's *Grave*, pored over when a child, unduly stimulated all his life that mysticism which was a somewhat disproportionate element of his nature. In an interesting chapter on the curious psychological impressions of his childhood, he has a page on the immoderate cult of Blake, whom, though he himself did much towards his elevation, he feels has been 'by too liberal praise, both as poet and painter, as much over-estimated as he was formerly neglected.'

Common sense, indeed, was evidently one of Bell Scott's precious qualities; for although he entered heart and soul into the vital aspirations of the pre-Raphaelites, he had nothing but ridicule for some of their absurdities, as, for example, when he found Mr. Madox Brown's drawing class sat down to sketch, not from any instructive model, but to copy with minute accuracy a few wood-shavings! He gives an account of a little parley with Mr. Ruskin over a similar point, when that eccentric prophet was insisting that drawings should be made by finishing inch by inch as one went along, all preliminary general sketch being forbidden—palpable nonsense as it seemed to Bell Scott, whom, as a representative of the Government schools, Mr. Ruskin had somewhat loftily ignored.

An incidental chapter of much interest is the account of Thomas Dixon, the Sunderland cork-cutter, to whom Mr. Ruskin wrote his *Time and Tide*. It was through his agency also that Whitman's *Leaves of Grass* first

won an English audience.    No story of the vicissitudes
of books is more curious :

'A travelling bookseller, who had been in America, and been
all through the war with Whitman, had brought over a number of
copies of the first edition, an eccentric man of republican principles and very hard-up.    In America, the book being ignored by
all booksellers, who declined at first even to lay it on their counters,
he had got a quantity of copies and was now trying to sell them
at Sunderland by Dutch auction.    Thomas Dixon, my constant
friend, a perceptive man and a public-spirited, though then only
a working cork-cutter, sent the book to me as a curiosity.
Instantly I perceived the advent of a new poet, a new Americanism,
and a new teacher, and I invested in several copies.    The one I
sent to W. M. R[ossetti] was the cause of his editing the English
edition, which raised Whitman into a celebrity.'

Another incidental chapter of much interest is that on
'The Rising Generation in Poetry,' 1875, giving us a
characteristic glimpse of the precocity of a poet then
known as Mr. 'E. W. Gosse,' glimpses too of O'Shaugh-
nessy and Messrs. Marzials and John Payne, including
too an interesting account of Mr. Nettleship's symbolical
designs, which had evidently much impressed Scott,
but, of course, the amount of piquant latter-day gossip
in Bell Scott's volumes is endless.    These scattered
notes can give little idea of its interest, nor any
fitting idea of the man whose strong and sympathetic
individuality made him a centre of attraction for so
many of the makers of modern art.

THESE Roumanian folk-songs are indeed what 'Carmen
*'The Bard* Sylva' claims for them—'a real treasure
*of the* trove, a valuable addition to the literature
*Dimbovitza':* of the world.' It is as though a phial of
First Series. the world's first precious elixir of poetry,
a draught of 'Aganippe well,' a little pot of the honey of
Hybla, the original earth-sweetness, has been preserved
through the ages, and is suddenly unsealed for us.
From the first page to the last one is overcome with
a fragrant sense of vivid new impressions. Nothing
could be simpler than the symbolism, yet nothing more
original than its various passionate combinations. The
themes are the old, yet ever-resonant, themes of love
and death, on which we are still playing pretty and
subtle variations, but with little hope of striking again
the deep, simple chords. Which of our poets could
pluck out the heart of his theme in lines of such
simplicity as these, the anguished cry of a barren
woman :

'I am she, that hath borne no children ;
  Yet there is no one hath cursed me, I look the same as the
      others.
  But the nests pity me even ;
  The sun, the mother of stars, hath compassion upon me, and
      saith :
  "O childless woman ! what dost thou with all the days I make
      bright ?"
  *Mine ear is full of the murmur of rocking cradles.*
  *" For a single cradle," saith Nature, " I would give every one of*
      *my graves."'*

The italics are mine. Was hopeless longing ever put

into a lovelier line than 'Mine ear is full of the murmur of rocking cradles'?

The tragic note of this poem is mainly the note of the book, a fatalistic melancholy strangely allied to a certain mood of our own time, and strangely in contrast with primitive characteristics taking one back to a time when man had hardly differentiated himself from his surroundings, when trees and mountains were still sentient beings, and, indeed, active partakers in his drama—another characteristic in which the later continental schools of drama and fiction, with their theory of influential environment, are seen once more to touch hands with the primitive.   There is in this volume a wonderful little drama entitled 'Autumn,' in which the gloomy influences of the river and the forest, at a certain moment of tragic reverie, are personified as voices, which prevailingly confirm the man's dark design, not crudely, but with a suggestiveness that makes one think of Maeterlinck.   More benignant personifications are found in such charming lines as these in a song of 'the young Heiduck'—the heroic outlaw of Roumanian tradition :

> 'The Heiduck bore the kiss of his belovèd
> Upon his lips—and first the wind would steal it
> To carry it with autumn leaves away;
> And the wind spake : "Give me the kiss, O comrade,
> And I will make thereof a little flower."
>
> Then the night spake : "Give me the kiss, O comrade,
> And I will make thereof a little star."
> "Nay!" he replied, "the kiss of my belovèd
> Hath mingled with the currents of my blood;
> Here on my lips it lies, and I will give it
> To none, but keep it safe for evermore!"'

And the Heiduck kept it, though he wandered far,

> ' Until he came upon a snow-white meadow,
> White as though turtle-doves had rained their feathers
>                 Thick on the sward.
> And on that meadow the white woman met him,
> Took from his lips the kiss of his belovèd,
> And thrust it in her girdle, like a flower.
> Then down upon the earth the Heiduck laid him,
> Since the white woman on the snow-white meadow
> Took from his lips the kiss of his belovèd.'

The Heiduck had met the Roumanian *belle dame sans merci.*

One other primitive notion is used continually through the poems with dark dramatic effect, that of the dead still, so to say, living in their graves, knowing and being interested in all that goes on among those still living in the sun, being talked to, and even talking ; a conception brought home to us most convincingly, because so simply, in Wordsworth's ' We are Seven.' The idea occurs in many forms in this book : the dead woman who walks abroad in the night, and, for joy of being again above ground, kisses, mortally, any man she meets ; the girl who steals out by moonlight to meet her dead lover, and is followed by her father :

> ' I followed her, one evening,
> My child I followed down into the plain,
> And then I saw how the moon looked on her,
> While she held converse with a dead man there.
> She gently stroked his head, and gave him drink,
> And showed him all the loveliness of earth.
> Between them stood the cross from off his grave.
> I heard the dead man ask her :
> " What dost thou all day long upon the earth ?"
> My child made answer : " I await the night."'

The soldier who cannot sleep peacefully in his grave because he knows not how the battle went :

> ' He sorrowed, that he must go down to it
> Not knowing, and all impotent to ask,
> Which way the fight had gone.
> Into his grave they shut him fast,
> And told him nought of it ;
> And ever since he still doth ask himself
> Which way it went—nor can he sleep in peace.'

The unforgiven woman who goes daily to the grave of her husband, crying ' Hast thou forgiven me ?' to whom always ' Avaunt !' the grave makes answer.

> ' But as she, weeping, turned away and went,
> Behold, the gravestone would uplift itself,
> And the dead man gaze forth,
> Sending a long look after her, that woman
> Who weeping went her way.'

Though primitive in some of their conceptions, conceptions of themes on which man must ever remain ' primitive,' the idea in every case is handled with a fine sense of form, and clothed in brief, vivid, and lovely expression.  For us, with our non-vocal peasantry, it is hard to realise that these poems not only belong to the daily life of the Roumanian rustic, but that many of them are improvisations of reapers and spinning-girls— the theme being passed on from one to another, like a ball.  Many of them, it is true, are the songs of the professional luteplayers, but, whether or no, they have sprung originally from the hearts of the people.  Imagine our peasantry delighting to sing, not to speak of improvising, such poetry !  The songs bear marks of their improvised origin in the little refrains, repeated at beginning and end, not directly bearing upon, but usually striking the keynote of, the theme, such as :

> ‘ Look not upon the sky at eventide,
>     For that makes sorrowful the heart of man ;
>     Look rather here into my heart, and joyful
>         Shalt thou then always be.’

The peasants, very properly, guard these songs as a sacred inheritance, and are very shy of strangers over-hearing them, so much so that Miss Vacaresco, a young Roumanian poet, to whom in the first instance we owe them, although of an old family well known to the peasantry, had to lie eavesdropping in the maize to hear the reapers crooning them.  To hear others she had to affect a passion for spinning that she might join the girls at their spinning parties.

THE second series of Mr. Gale’s *Country Muse* is even
*Norman Gale:* better than its forerunner.  Perhaps the
‘ A Country
   Muse ’—  quality of art is more definitely present
Second Series. in it, or is it only that the selection from
Mr. Gale’s privately printed editions is a stronger one ?

Those two most characteristic love-songs, ‘ Strephon to Chloris,’ and ‘ O to think, O to think, as I see her stand there,’ the omission of which from the former volume I regretted, are now reprinted.  And then there is another similarly daring poem, ‘ The Shaded Pool,’ lovely enough to make the fortune of

any volume : a delicious description of country girls
athing, touched with most reverent, yet roguish, art.

> 'Did ever Love, on hunting bent,
>   Come idly humming through the hay,
> And, to his sudden joyfulness,
>   Find fairer game at close of day?'

Surely Diana herself could hardly object to such an
Actæon as Mr. Gale?  One need scarcely say that the
book from end to end smells of the country as a barn of
hay ; and that the note of faith in life rings through it
sweet and clear as the call of church-bells in a May
morning ; while Mr. Gale's lyrical gift is so exquisitely
fresh that surely he must be more of a throstle than a
man.   Somehow I think of him as that wonderful little
Cupid in ' Daphnis and Chloe,' whom old Philetas found
flitting about among the fruit trees in his garden and
tried in vain to capture, till the young creature, half boy,
half bird, at last, bubbling with laughter, spoke 'in a
voice sweeter than that of the nightingale, the swallow
or the swan.'  Do the inhabitants of Rugby, I wonder,
go out on moonlight nights to hear Mr. Gale singing
among his cherry trees ?—a six-foot-three nightingale.

Mrs. Meynell's Essays, *The Rhythm of Life*, says
*Alice Meynell :* Mr. Patmore, are better than her poems.
Essays and  Prose, not verse, is her more distinctive
Poems.   *métier.*  Perhaps Mr. Patmore is strictly
right.   Volume for volume, the essays strike one as
having more actual achievement than the poems.   But

in comparing them one has to remember that the essays are the recent product of Mrs. Meynell's maturity, the poems the firstfruits of her girlhood. *Preludes*, her first and practically only volume of verse (for the present volume is mainly a re-issue) has long been out of print, and Mr. Patmore commends Mrs. Meynell for recognising her limitations in verse and her implied resolution to abandon its exercise. With this renunciation in mind, let us read this sonnet 'To a Daisy':

'Slight as thou art, thou art enough to hide,
  Like all created things, secrets from me,
  And stand a barrier to eternity.
And I, how can I praise thee well and wide

From where I dwell—upon the hither side?
  Thou little veil for so great mystery,
  When shall I penetrate all things and thee,
And then look back?  For this I must abide,

Till thou shalt grow and fold and be unfurled
Literally between me and the world.
  Then I shall drink from in beneath a spring,

And from a poet's side shall read his book.
O daisy mine, what will it be to look
  From God's side even of such a simple thing?'

Wordsworth is supposed to have copyrighted the daisy; he did indeed, as he himself puts it, sit upon the turf and tease it with whimsical similes, with a lightness of fancy too rare with him; he also moralised and sentimentalised it; but for giving us the daisy itself in its morning innocence he is not to be mentioned with Chaucer. Without any moralising, Chaucer conveys to us the spiritual as well as the physical refreshment of its simplicity. It is magically hidden somewhere

in the simple rapture of his phrase.  Mrs. Meynell's
relation to the flower differs from that of both these
poets, though her aim is allied to Wordsworth's—or
rather her achievement is allied to his somewhat aimless
aim.    Evidently he was trying to interpret the daisy
as a symbol, his several 'shots' at it resulted in several
charming  but  comparatively  superficial  reflections.
Mrs. Meynell, I make bold to say, has been more
successful ; rejecting some subsidiary suggestion, she
has gone to the heart of its mystery—'Thou little veil
for so great mystery.'   Here is the mystic's deep vision
of it, the same transfiguration of the unit by the
absolute as Tennyson's vision of the 'Flower in the
crannied wall,' or Rossetti's of his mistress :

> 'Sometimes thou seemest not as thyself alone,
> But as the meaning of all things that are.'

By confining the mystery within the limits of a humble,
tiny flower, Mrs. Meynell brings it home to us with
the added shock of paradox, and it suddenly flashes
on one that here was the inner meaning of the old
schoolman's question as to how many angels can
dance on the point of a needle.   Who shall expound for
us the law of spiritual gravitation ?   Who knows what
radiant force of mysterious spiritual impulsion goes to
the square inch of matter ?

Mr. Patmore finds Mrs. Meynell's poetical limitation
is that she is not 'classical.'   To be 'classical,' Mr.
Patmore would seem to imply, is beyond the power of
woman.   Man alone can give the stamp of eternity to
his art, for such I conceive to be the interpretation of

'classical'—to say a thing once for all.   That the expression shall be noble follows from that.   If I am right
I cannot well understand how this sonnet on the daisy
fails to fulfil the conditions.    There is one lack, however, in it which I cannot help feeling, and perhaps that
explains Mr. Patmore's dictum : a certain lack of magic,
of rhythmical life.   The syllables have but little of the
moving cadence of song in them.   The words say rather
than sing themselves.   And that I feel is a lack in most
of—Mrs. Meynell's verse.    It rarely flows easily from
the tongue, but drags as though delayed by consonants.
This, however, applies least to Mrs. Meynell's sonnets
(her best poems), where indeed it matters least ; and
'classical' or 'not classical,' I cannot think otherwise
than that 'Renouncement' is a deep, moving expression, simple, poignant, and final, of a tragedy constant
to the human heart.   Though it is the best known of
Mrs. Meynell's poems, it is hardly as well known as
it should be.

When one says that that sonnet equals, if not
surpasses, the finest of the *Sonnets from the Portu-
guese*, one perhaps receives at the same time a hint
why, after all, it is not classical.    It is movingly
passionate, the words flow easily for this once, but,
so to speak, they are not 'crowned'; the poet gives
them no new dignities.   It is the deep cry of a heart
rather in its natural language than in the queenly
speech of the muse.   Their message delivered, the
words stand down and leave us alone with the
emotion.   But then how much is that !   Mr. Patmore
would seem to praise Mrs. Meynell because she

declined to be less than the highest ; but surely such
is perilous praise.  Whatever her place, Mrs. Meynell
as a poet has written a few sonnets which true lovers
of poetry will carry in their hearts side by side with
their most 'heart-remembered' song.  Surely that was
worth doing.

I have left myself but little space to speak of Mrs.
Meynell's essays.  At once, in opening them, one is
aware of the presence of individual style as we are
not in the verses—significant indeed, you say?  But
then remember that style is not, as some foolish people
suppose, born ready-made with any writer.  It grows
more slowly too in verse than prose, perhaps because
prose lies nearer to our natural daily talk.  Mrs. Meynell's
prose is, as I said, recent ; her verse was, for the most
part, written some years ago.  Had she, in the interval,
cultivated it as she has cultivated prose, there is
every reason to think that she would by this time
have been recognised as a poet very definitely herself.
Her poems are, as we have seen in the daisy sonnet,
marked by that rare respect for the unique word which
one apprehends at once to be the marked distinction
of her prose.  I venture to think that she has observed
that respect too self-consciously.  There is too little
joyous life, too much of the literary ascetic, about her
essays.  Style is too much of a hair-shirt with Mrs.
Meynell.  Like the young followers of Mr. Pater, she
always gets the right wording of her thought, but she
sometimes misses its rhythm.  She puts too much
into a sentence.  The words have no room to breathe.
The spacing of one's words is, one need hardly say,

as important as the selection of them. Again, Mrs.
Meynell, cleverly turning about the French dictum, 'The
man is style,' says—and how much one thanks her for
saying it—'I read it as declaring that the whole man,
the very whole of him, is his style.  The literature of
a man of letters worthy the name is rooted in all his
qualities, with little fibres running invisibly into the
smallest qualities he has.  He who is not a man of
letters, simply is not one ; it is not too audacious a
paradox to affirm that doing will not avail him who
fails in being.'  There is nothing that the writer at
all times needs to be taught again and again so much
as that.  Foolish flatterers are all too ready to suffer
him to be anything else so that he be clever.  And
yet there is nothing surer that there is no greatness
not rooted in character, no beauty save the skin-deep
that does not spring from love.  I have quoted Mrs.
Meynell's remarkable statement on style to apply it
to herself.  I regret that 'all her qualities' are not
sufficiently represented in her present essays.  One
has hints occasionally of stores of tenderness and
sympathy which have all too little scope in her volume.
It is largely, I think, the fault of her subjects, which
are mainly of a nature to bring her into collision with
the Philistine, the 'decivilised,' and thus to evoke that
scorn of which she has indeed the poet's full dower.
Consequently a little superiority of tone is too constantly
present in her essays.  She gives herself too few opportunities to be kind.  But her scorn is splendid for all
that.  What could be better than her definition of
'colonialism' as 'only provincialism very articulate,'

and her retort to the colonist's airs of the noble savage
that it was not 'war-paint and feathers' she feared
from him, but that she 'suspected him of nothing
wilder than a second-hand dress coat.'  And how one
cheers as in the essay on 'Penultimate Caricature' she
arraigns the Douglas Jerrold and Charles Keene school
of humour for its monotonous insistence on the gross
bourgeois aspect of humanity: 'indignities of civic
physique, of stupid prosperity, of dress, of bearing,
abject domesticity, ignominies of married life, of middle-
age, of money-making . . . everything that is under-
bred and decivilised.'  Such humourists, she well says,
can hardly escape the charge of vulgarity themselves—
'real apprehension—real apprehensiveness—would not
have insisted upon such things, could not have lived
with them through almost a whole career.'  Mrs.
Meynell finds 'the hint of tenderness' which is always
found in really fine humour, lacking.  At the same
time it must not be forgotten for Keene that where
Mrs. Meynell only sees 'decivilisation,' he saw humanity
as well.  It is but a very small proportion of the world
that remembers its aitches.  Mrs. Meynell would not
surely shut the gates of mercy on the rest.  Shakespeare
didn't.

LATE on a snowy Christmas Eve the poet meets a tot-
tering, white-haired old man, who gasps,
'For God's sake, mortal, let me lean on
thee !' and gives every sign of being our
old acquaintance out of Eugene Sue.
However, he proves to be a diviner personage.  One
began to wonder when by a wave of his hand he stopped
the snow falling.  He is indeed no other than Christ
himself, or rather the weary phantom of himself ; and
he is found thus forlorn in the neighbourhood of Fleet
Street, because Mr. Buchanan has begotten a conception which is at least melodramatically striking.  In a
vision we are taken to Mount Golgotha, and find a
Sinaitic presence sitting there in judgment.  It is the
Spirit of Humanity, and around the mountain are
gathered all the nations of the world to see 'their Christ
this Jew' judged for the second time, the charge against
him being that his scheme of salvation has failed, that
his story of a loving Heavenly Father is a beautiful lie,
that men once more know Death to be lord of all, and
the life everlasting but a fair shadow that robs them of
the real warm life that now is.  The Spirit somewhat
cleverly states the case against him, telling how, finding
'the wild old prophecy of a Christ and king' among his
Jewish fellows, he had 'blasphemously played the Christ
they craved for,' supporting his imposture with 'simple
devices of the wizard's trade,'

> 'And last, presuming on his pride of place
> Profanes the Holy Temple of the race.'

But his crowning offence was in having risen again

after his crucifixion, for from that sprang his tremendous
baneful influence over mankind :

> 'Where this rumour spread,
> All other gentle gods that gladden'd Man
> Faded and fled away ; the priests of Pan,
> That singing by Arcadian rivers rear'd
> Their flowery altars, wept and disappeared ;
> And men forgot the fields and the sweet light,
> Joy, and all wonders of the day and night,
> All splendour of the sense, all happy things,
> Art, and the happy Muses' ministerings.' . . .

Finished his charge, the Spirit summons up from the
ends of the world the various witnesses against him ;
the joyous old gods he has displaced, the sages and men
of science who had been damned and murdered in his
name, the noble army of martyrs slain 'to appease his
lust for life in every land,' Mahomet who had professed
but to be prophet, not arrogantly the son of God ;
Buddha, Confucius, even Prometheus ; then come his
priests to make confession of their sins in his name, and
tribe after tribe of witnesses tramp past the hill—the
crowning touch to the topsy-turvydom of the thing
being the evidence of Judas, who, more than equal to
the occasion, has the audacity to aver that he had be-
trayed his Lord 'because he knew his promise was a
lie.' The book is mainly taken up with these marchings-
past. Meanwhile Christ stands meek as of old, offering
no word to his accusers. The saints then bear witness
in his favour, and he is asked for his defence. With his
answer, Mr. Buchanan's purpose, somewhat ambiguous
all through, becomes quite enigmatical. It really
amounts to a confession of failure—he is old and tired
and would gladly die. As he speaks, he gazes hopelessly

towards heaven, as if no longer sure that God is there. The poem ends with his condemnation to the doom of endless, aimless wandering through time, and the curious prayer, 'God help the Christ, that Christ may help us all !'

Does Mr. Buchanan really mean that Christianity is, so to say, played out ? One would not have expected it from him. His poem can hardly be meant as satire, for it is too serious in style. I confess I am puzzled, and, in any case, dramatic as the conception is—epical indeed the theme is, this dramatising of the death of a great religion—it fails to really impress me because I believe that Mr. Buchanan's news is not true. The influence of Christ in its purest form is stronger to-day than ever ; Secularism is intellectually dead, and everywhere one sees indications of a great spiritual revival.

Whatever may be thought of Mr. Buchanan's theme, it is the best part of the poem ; for it is impossible to praise its treatment. Nearly every new poem of his makes one regret more and more Mr. Buchanan's connection with 'The Adelphi.' It seems to have irreparably coarsened his poetic touch, and made him satisfied with paste where once he gave us something like real diamonds. The verse of 'The Wandering Jew' is perfunctory, destitute of charm, and carrying no conviction. There is not a line that haunts one, an expression that really 'bites.' The whole dramatic treatment, too, lacks dignity. The examination on Golgotha is ludicrously suggestive of the Old Bailey—'What soul art thou ?' 'One Judas, named also Iscariot.' 'Know'st thou the Accused ?'—and, indeed, the whole machinery, especially the supernatural part of it, seems to have been supplied by Messrs. Gatti. *The Wandering Jew* might be described as an Adelphi miracle-play.

The truth is, Mr. Buchanan does not keep his ideas long enough in soak. To have had any success, a poem of such ambitious aim as *The Wandering Jew* should have been let grow as slowly as *Paradise Lost.* But, indeed, busy literary men about town are not the men for such poems. How can they hope to get that still, deep atmosphere wherein alone great poetry is born? Great poetry is not written at a man's club—though it may have been written on club paper. Mr. Buchanan also has too many irons in the fire. As it is, we have at least two unfinished poems of his on hand—'The Earthquake' and 'The Outcast.' Why not work on the latter—a poem distinctly interesting and clever—instead of 'dashing off' epics like *The Wandering Jew*, things begotten between the acts, conceived at the club, and born in a hansom?

'Q.'s' many friends will rejoice in the possession of his verses, *Green Bays, Verses and Parodies.*

*Quiller Couch :*

'Green Bays.'   But they must not, of course, expect to see 'Q.' making a bid at great or even serious poetry. He expressly disavows the attempt, though in a pathetic little confession he avows that the ambition was once his also. But, taking up Keats one day, he discovered that his greatest sonnet was a *réchauffé* of

'Bright Star, would I were constant as thou art.'
Thereupon he drowned all his poetical kittens right
away, and took to parody.　Whether he did well to give
up the game for a reason which might have lost us
nearly every other great poet—for most poets are
'mocking bards' to start with—his volume hardly
supplies us with sufficient data to decide.　But he is
certainly very brilliant in parody.　'I see twenty-two
young men from Foster's watching me, and the trousers
of the twenty-two young men' is irresistible Whit-
manese, and 'The Song of Simple Enumeration' is
as neat a phrase as one could have for Whitman's
catalogues.　And what charming irony in the lay of
the Oxford Fire Brigade is the concluding line, in
the manner of Macaulay, 'Bless all, but most the
lucky chance that no one shouted "Fire!"'　'Q.'s'
whimsical weird humour flickers in its rather creepy
way over one or two of the poems, especially in the love
story of Lady Jane and her gardener, and 'The White
Moth.'　Then there is a charming prologue and epilogue
in mock Old English, one a beautiful dreamy song of
El Dorado ; and the song of 'The Splendid Spur'
should certainly find a place in Mr. Henley's *Lyra
Heroica* :

> 'The scarlet hat, the laurell'd stave
> 　　Are measures, not the springs, of worth ;
> In a wife's lap, as in a grave,
> 　　Man's airy notions mix with earth.
> 　　　　Seek other spur
> 　　　　Bravely to stir
> The dust In this loud world, and tread
> Alp-high among the whisp'ring dead.'

It is to be hoped that the poems 'Q.' sacrificed at the shrine of Keats were not so good as this really stirring song.

ONE might imagine, from their time-honoured reputation as mistresses of allusive gossip, that women would make charming essayists : for is it not the charm of the best essays that they dance their wayward round, unhampered by any responsibility save that of giving pleasure, first to the writer and then to the reader? The necessity of giving pleasure to the writer is paramount, for in no form of literature is it so true that both the sowing and the reaping must be in gladness. This is, of course, true more or less of all writing, but especially true of the essay. The essay-writer must be pleased with himself, his theme, and the world. The moment he loses his *amour propre*, his inspiration flags. 'When in disgrace with fortune and men's eyes,' the poet is often stung to write his finest poems, but not so the essayist. The jug of wine, the loaf of bread, the volume of old verses, a garrulous fire (and, metaphorically speaking, a cheering bundle from Romeike) are the necessary conditions of his art. Vernon Lee, in a preface to her charming little idyll of 'Ottilie,' while admirably characterising the temperament of the essayist, seems to be under a curious misconception of his limitation. 'The essayist,' she says, 'is an amphibious creature, neither fish, flesh, nor fowl; something of the nature of a centaur. For an

*Agnes Repplier:* 'Essays in Miniature.'

essayist possesses, inasmuch as he is an essayist, some
of the instincts of the superior creature called a novelist :
a certain half-imaginative perception of the past, a
certain love of character and incident and description, a
certain tendency to weave fancies about realities ; but
as the centaur has hoofs, so the essayist has peculiarities
which exclude him from the pleasant places of fiction,
which render it proper that he should run along on the
beaten roads of history, and be tied up in the narrow
little stable of fact.'

Obviously, after all, Vernon Lee means something
different from us in using the word Essay. She rather
means 'study,' a useful word which releases the true
essayist from that obligation to fact under which Vernon
Lee groans. Facts to the essayist are indeed but thin
excuses for his covertly talking about himself. Few
essayists have the courage to say outright, like Whitman,
'Myself I sing,' or even with the French critic, 'I propose to talk of myself, *à propos* of Shakespeare, Molière,
Hugo, etc.'; they still keep up the decency of pretending
that they are about to talk of the trivial subject with
which they label each new chapter of 'The Story of my
Heart.'

Miss Agnes Repplier, whose *Essays in Miniature*
have just been delighting me with their short swallow-
flights of criticism, is one of the few people who realise
the authentic charm of the essay. She is, I fancy, one
of the very first of women to realise it, for, despite their
capacity for gossiping essays, women, curiously enough,
have never shown a gift for writing them. Perhaps it is
only my ignorance, but I cannot remember any volume

of essays — real essays, I mean—by a woman; no
volume, for instance, with the familiar sunny charm of
Mr. Curtis's *Prue and I*, not to refer to such great
masters as Lamb and Montaigne.   Perhaps one reason
for this is that the essayist, though he need not be
learned, must have read and generally picked up a good
deal, his mind must be stored with a motley collection
of recollections and associations which, before he makes
magic of them, may well seem the merest rubbish.   His
mind, in fact, is like a boy's pocket, stuffed with dis-
carded treasures of which his elders are not worthy—
string, marbles, peg-tops, strange shells, bits of coloured
pebble, a few old coins of no value at the numismatist's
—treasures strictly personal to himself, a chaos of which,
with glee he knows it, none can make a cosmos but
himself.   Now women bid fair to be more learned than
men, but they have yet to learn the art of wearing their
learning lightly, as a feather in the cap, to play with it,
to chaff it, so to say, as Mr. Lang knows so well how to
do.   For them it is as yet far too much of a solemnity.
The learned woman is still an awful Minerva, she wears
her reading like Amazonian armour, and it clanks and
rattles at every turn of her mind.   It is only a long
familiar association with books, an association in
the blood one might say, that can make an essayist.
For not till it has been realised that in and for itself
learning is merely absurd, and solely valuable, so far as
the writer is concerned, for the artistic use to be made
of it, does the essayist become possible.   In short, the
essayist's great gift, whether playing on the surface like
a merry flame, or operating beneath as an unseen leaven,

is humour.  Humour, more even than religion, will save us from ten thousand snares.

It follows then that the essayist should also, above all men, observe Hamlet's advice to Horatio.  Only at the imminent peril of dulness can he ever be untrue to himself.  Sincerity to his own predilections is the first law of his existence.  He must be ashamed of none of them.  It needs, therefore, you see, as much moral courage to be an essayist as an early Christian.  Miss Repplier touches charmingly on the dangers which beset this sincerity in her first essay on 'Our Friends, the Books.'  How few of us have the courage, she says, to be true to our own taste in our reading !  ' There are people in this world,' she writes, 'who always insist upon others re-modelling their diet on a purely hygienic basis ; who entreat us to avoid sweets or acids, or tea or coffee, or whatever we chance to particularly like ; who tell us pursuasively that cress and dandelions will purify our blood ; that celery is an excellent febrifuge ; that shad-docks should be eaten for the sake of their quinine, and fish for its phosphorus ; that stewed fruit is more whole-some than raw ; that rice is more nutritious than potatoes ; who deprive us, in a word, of that hearty human happiness which should be ours when dining. . . . It is in the same benevolent spirit that kind-hearted critics are good enough to warn us against the books we love, and to prescribe for us the books we ought to read.'  The moment the essayist listens to these confident empirics, he is lost.  Never to be ashamed of his ' Duchess of Newcastle,' never to forsake Mr. Micawber ; that is at once 'his hope and his pyramides.'  If he merely reads with the rest of the world, where is his significance? Let him consider the caddis-worm, how it builds its tiny cabin of whatsoever bit of reed, pebble, or broken glass may take its fancy, and gives no thought to his neighbour : so is the essayist always best dressed in the literary clothes which the rest of the world have agreed long since to cast off.

Miss Repplier, one soon finds, has this courage of her predilections. I fancy her 'Duchess of Newcastle' is Hogg, the Ettrick shepherd. She reset an exquisite passage from him in her former volume of *Points of View* ; and she refers to him in a bright gossip on 'The Humours of Gastronomy.' His shade does not often enjoy the thrill of quotation, so let us hear him :— 'There does not at this blessed moment,' he says, 'breathe on the earth's surface a human being that willna prefer eating and drinking to all ither pleasures o' body or soul.' Is the reader prepared to deny it? However, is it not significant to see a woman, a dainty, cultured woman, enjoying 'The Humours of Gastronomy'? Surely the shade of Byron is troubled. But is it not good to think of? It rings the knell of the bread-and-butter miss, who so long, in the devoted imagination of her lover, 'on honeydew hath fed, and drunk the milk of Paradise.' The era of the Meredith woman, 'relishing well her steak,' as Whitman puts it, is at hand.

But I fear I have made Miss Repplier too much a text for my own garrulity. However, the general principles of essay-writing have not been recalled in vain, as I can thus the more easily point to Miss Repplier as a writer who fulfils them all with easy charm. She is sincere, she has her own definite likes and dislikes and is not ashamed of them, she has read many books and loved more, but she lets fall her apt quotations with the casual grace of culture as opposed to learning ; she has a lively wit, a sunny temper, and that wayward gift of beginning anywhere and taking us nowhere.  One of her best chats is that on 'The Oppression of Notes,' in which with much liveliness she girds at the fussy commentator who, so to say, runs with an ambulance when you have cut your finger, but on a genuine battlefield leaves you to die.  But Miss Repplier has prettier fancies for him. 'He will,' she says, 'build you a bridge over a raindrop, put ladders up a pebble, and encompass you on every side with ingenious alpenstocks and climbing-irons ; yet when, perchance, you stumble and hold out a hand for help, behold, he is never there to grasp it.'   Miss Repplier, has, I believe, a great reputation in America. I hope they don't tease her by taking her too seriously. Has any one called her little Miss Lang ?

THE quest of the qualifying adjective is admittedly a delight under most circumstances.    But there is one thing for which we would seem to seek it quite passionately—another man's success.   Success must never go without its qualifying adjective.   Now everybody was delighted with Mr. Watson's ' Naiad.'  Charming !  Charming !  But soon we heard the still small voice.   If there is no fly in one's

*H. B. Marriott Watson: 'Diogenes of London,' etc.*

honey to start with, somebody is sure to catch one for the express purpose of supplying the deficiency. The one fault with the 'Naiad,' said the fly-catcher, was its archaism. It was written in the style of the eighteenth century. Its world was the world of Watteau. It was implied that on that stage the thing was easier to do. The implication is probably true, but then what concern has the reader with the ease or difficulty of execution? The result is his sole business. 'The Naiad' is a dainty, charming piece of art: what have we to do with the process of its creation?

Moreover, where else could Mr. Watson have set his scene save in some fairyland, such as the eighteenth century has practically become? There was no other way for him to create the illusion so necessary to his, alas, delicious improbability. A young lady is bathing in a river, sans bathing costume. The amorous stream has run off with her clothes, which apparently she had left in a soft bundle on the bank, though too near to the kisses of the river god, his idea apparently being that without her clothes she must willy-nilly remain in his arms. And so indeed she must have done had not a gallant, and, of all people, her suitor, strolled by. But he, as well as the river god, immediately conceives designs. They are far away from any house, and she is practically at his mercy. Her love in exchange for an outfit—that is the bald situation. The outfit is found on the person of a buxom Audrey who also chances to come by, and whom, after no little blandishment, the gallant persuades to disrobe on behalf of the distressed lady. Nothing could be more delicious comedy than the scene

between Audrey on the one side of the hedge and the
gallant on the other, he eloquently pleading, and she
blushingly surrendering one by one the dainty envelopes
of her charms : unless it be the next scene in which he
cautiously doles out one article after, another, on no
easy terms, to the poor Naiad.   It is an irresistible
s tuation, and it is painted with a hand that can never
have marred a butterfly or robbed a peach of its bloom.
*Risqué* is not the word for its theme, and yet the treatment is as innocent as Greek nudity.   There is merry
laughter through it, but it is as we say, 'innocent fun,'
the legitimate laughter of one sex at the other's predica-
ment.   The situation would, doubtless, shock many, the
treatment couldn't.   And this is largely due to the fact
that Mr. Watson has put his people, as I say, in fairyland.   The thing is a charming dream, a fantasy, one of
those beautiful things, as Mr. Wilde says, that are not
and that should be.   But no one knows better than
Mr. Wilde that the moment such things happened they
would cease to lure.   It is because we are always hoping
for them to happen, because we press on and on
breathlessly up the river, believing that in the next
eddy we shall find the pixie combing her wondrous hair
—that we go on living.

And yet, of course, Mr. Watson had not to lay his
scene too far away from everybody.   So it would have
lost its piquancy.   The gallant must tap his boot now
and again with his cane to make believe that it all
happened up the Thames, but the lady, despite her
desire to be clothed, belongs to faerie.   Indeed she is
but a later version of the beautiful widespread legend

of the swan maidens.  The reader will know it from his William Morris.  Sir Edwin Arnold recently adapted a variant of it from Japan.  The fortunate Antaeus has but to seize the bunch of soft feathers while the owner is bathing, and she is in his power.  In Mr. Watson's story the feathers have turned into soft linen and lace, and the shepherd has become a gallant : but at the same time, and that I repeat is its charm, the story remains in fairyland.  It might so easily have been merely nude instead of naked.

That quality, I fear, distinguishes it from the two stories with which Mr. Watson followed it up, and which I think he did wisely in omitting from his very welcome collection, *Diogenes of London and Other Fantasies and Sketches*.  The two stories referred to were witty and undoubtedly amusing, but they just missed that saving touch.  It was not so much that there was a superfluity of naughtiness about them, but that they gave one the impression of being made, not born, of being written to a demand rather than spontaneously dreamed.

Turning to his volume as a whole, one does, I fear, feel that, however successful in occasional stories, his eighteenth century manner is a convention that he overworks.  It grows monotonous, and too frequently lapses into a spiritless euphuism.  ' Costume pieces ' are pleasant now and again, but a run of them makes one yawn for Pinero and evening-dress.  *Diogenes of London* and *The Sword of the Kadi* especially prove that Mr. Watson has a pretty gift of allegory, and the irony of the latter is exceedingly fine.  If anything, he allegorises too easily.  We frequently spy the moral

too soon.   Then Mr. Watson indulges, as he is far too
good an artist to be allowed to do, in the 'feeble-
forcible.'   If I remember aright there is a scene in the
*Naulakha* where the hero is brought into exciting
proximity to a monkey.   Mr. Kipling impressively tells
us that his hero at that moment was actually aware of
the smell of the monkey—what delicacy of the olfactory
nerves !—and I remember how a certain reviewer came
down with his fist—'By heaven, but that is genius !'
Certain reviewers cannot resist a smell.   It convinces
them at once.   'The Mark of the Beast' was another
instance.   However, what I want to say is, that we
smell the monkey just a little too often in Mr. Marriott
Watson's stories.   He still tries to 'bogey' us with
calling a corpse 'a thing'—'the thing in the copse'—
and he expects us to curdle when he tells us that 'the
body sank in a heap at Derracott's feet.   He watched
it huddle limply among the damp and yellow leaves !'
This is a quotation from the worst story in the book,
'The Stroke of One.'   'The House of Dishonour' is
another story in which Mr. Watson piles on the agony
for all he is worth ; but he hasn't given us another
'House of Usher.'   Then, too, we get an occasional
touch of *National Observer* cynicism which is not Mr.
Watson.   He is far too good-natured and chivalrous at
heart for such airs.   Nor is Mr. Watson quite himself in the essays which make the latter part of his
volume.   He has not been able to shake off his gods,
Mr. Stevenson and Mr. Henley.   Though they contain occasional fine things, these essays, as indeed one
or two of the stories, give one the impression of too

hurried composition.   The sentences gasp for breath.
There is no rhythm, no rise and fall, in the writing—
save here and there as in 'The Facility of Life,' which is
perhaps the best.   But the faults are the faults of haste,
I fancy, and Mr. Watson's merits are unmistakable and
irresistible.   If you object to his eighteenth-century
style, don't forget that it marks a preference, an idiosyn-
crasy.   His method is his own, whether it is improvable
or not.   His volume is not one more collection of
the machine-made American *conte*, so clever and so
characterless.   It has a personality.   It makes us aware
of a man, and a man of high spirits, who carries us
along with him like a generous wind, of simple open-air
passions, with inexhaustible relish for life, a roguish
blade of a fellow, who kisses his hand to every pleasure,
who laughs at constancy but is constant all the time,
most gallant and tender of wooers, the very pick of boon
companions—here, surely, are plenty of excellencies to
be going on with.

IT is curious how some authors contrive to impress their
*Walter Pater :* individuality upon the externals of their
'Plato and   books, and by some subtle influence create
Platonism.'   a harmony between type, paper, and binding and the spirit which they clothe.   One can even
tell our best-loved books by their feel, and certain it is
that our Swinburnes, our Morrises, our Stevensons, and
perhaps, most of all, our Paters, have all characteristic
physiognomies familiar as the faces of dear friends.

There is no more curious witness to the power of personality, for fonts of type, one would have said, are unimpressionable things, not readily responsive to the delicate influence of the spirit.  Yet even in cases where men use the same font, there will something steal into the page, it may be in the 'leading,' or in the arrangement of the paragraphs, in the length of sentences, the preference for Latin or Saxon words, that will give each of their books a distinctive complexion.  Some writers hold that the reader loses much by not being able to read them in manuscript.  M. Mallarmé, for instance, was at one time so careful of his 'moi' that he had his poems published in lithograph from his original manuscript.  We are not all so sensitive as that, but one does not need to be hyper-sensitive to feel the Paterian aura about all Mr. Pater's books.

That gracious union of the austere and the sensuous so characteristic of Mr. Pater's writing, the temperate beauty, 'the dry beauty' beloved of Plato, and advocated with such winning charm in this 'series of lectures,' *Plato and Platonism: a Series of Lectures*, find expression, too, in the sweet and stately volume itself, with its smooth night-blue binding, its rose-leaf yellow pages, its soft and yet grave type.  So distinguished and yet so far removed from the eccentric !  To merely hold one of Mr. Pater's books in the hand and turn over its pages, is a counsel in style.  As the Greek women during conception would look often and long upon the statue of Apollo, so the dreamer of beautiful books should often handle such books as these of Mr. Pater.  They will refine even the sense of touch.

How little does he know of books who deems them only to be read!

But I dally too long in the portal. And yet, how can I presume in the short space at my disposal here to glibly 'review' so beautiful a gift as these new essays of Mr. Pater? It is true that by this time I have read them through; but, once reading! What is it? and not the reading of the happy scholar, fellow of his college, who in cloistered peace gives his whole heart for full untroubled hours to the book of his love—but the hasty, worried reading of the distracted journalist, who must snatch his spiritual meals now and then as best he can. I can but, like the divining rod, point here and there where the gold is hid, and leave you to find it for yourself.

Mr. Pater, with nice artistic sense, has not striven, like most other writers, to disguise the fact that these essays were first lectures, but here and there he has preserved little hortatory phrases, which remind one that he is addressing himself to a little band of youthful students of philosophy. Doubtless he has felt that the mere knowledge of the papers having to be thus addressed to an audience would, in however slight a degree, modify them from the essay proper, and that to attempt to disguise such modifications would be a delicate loss in sincerity of appeal. Thus a favourite exhortation, frequent in his other writings, is here more frequent than ever, constantly reminding us of the lecture room, or rather, we would say, the Academe. 'Well!...' The reader knows the charming cadence. 'Well! Life was like that.' There is something curiously seductive about

this very characteristic interjection, something that puts
the reader in instant *rapport* with the writer.   It conveys
the very sound of his voice into the sentence.   I do not
know any recent writer, except, perhaps, Mr. Stevenson,
who has this intimate accent.   Another charm of Mr.
Pater's attitude towards his reader is his urbane' indifference to the amount of his learning.   He does not
affect the assumption that the reader knows everything,
but, when he occasionally implies his possible non-
acquaintance with certain masters, he does it in a way
that seems to say that, no doubt, the reader knows many
other things of which he is ignorant.   Thus he doesn't
even take it for granted that his students should know
Wordsworth's great ode.   Literature is so vast, life so
short, that they may well have not come up to it yet.
But when they do. . . .

Verily, these are but the crumbs that fall from the
master's table, but they are indicative of the feast.   The
chapter which charms me most of all is the first.   It
deals with the Heraclitean doctrine of the eternal flux
in things—

> '. . . all flits away
> Light and life together.'

as the old Anglo-Saxon scop sang.   Mr. Pater never
writes so beautifully as when on this theme.   You
will remember the pages upon it in *Marius*.   In this
first and the two subsequent chapters, he criticises
the usual conception of Plato as an absolute pioneer
of philosophy, and traces his several obligations to
Heraclitus, Parmenides, Zeno, Pythagoras, and Socrates.

And in doing so it is wonderful what a sense of vista his imagination is able to throw for us behind a world that one rather thinks of as but just beginning. I cannot make a more characteristic or more beautiful quotation than a few passages from this opening chapter :

'Plato's achievement may well seem an absolutely fresh thing in the morning of the mind's history. Yet in truth the world Plato had entered into was already almost weary of philosophical debate, bewildered by the opposition of sects, the claims of rival schools. Language and the processes of thought were already become sophisticated, the very air he breathed sickly with off-cast speculative atoms . . . Some of the results of patient earlier thinkers, even then dead and gone, are of the structure of his philosophy. They are everywhere in it, not as the stray carved corner of some older edifice, to be found here or there amid the new, but rather like minute relics of earlier organic life in the very stone he builds with. . . . It is hardly an exaggeration to say that in Plato, in spite of his wonderful savour of literary freshness, there is nothing absolutely new : or rather, as in many other very original products of human genius, the seemingly new is old also, a palimpsest, a tapestry of which the actual threads have served before, or like the animal frame itself, every particle of which has already lived and died many times over. Nothing but the life-giving principle of cohesion is new ; the new perspective, the resultant complexion, the expressiveness which familiar thoughts attain by novel juxtaposition. In other words, the *form* is new. But then, in the creation of philosophical literature, as in all other products of art, *form*, in the full signification of that word, is everything, and the mere matter is nothing.'

Much of Mr. Pater's book is taken up with suggestive exposition of what one might call Plato's æsthetic apprehension of ideas—the power his sensuous instincts gave him of realising for himself and his readers abstract ideas as though they were visible appearances. For, austerely regulated as it was, Mr. Pater reminds us that Plato's nature was a richly sensuous one, the temperament of 'the lover.' 'He is a lover, a great lover, somewhat after the manner of Dante.' And even more suggestively does Mr. Pater show us that the apparently paradoxical banishment of the arts from Plato's republic was not because he condemned them, but because he feared that the citizens must love them too well.

'Art, as such, as Plato knows, has no purpose but itself, its own perfection. The proper art of the Perfect City is in fact the art of discipline. Music [in the broad Platonic sense], all the various forms of fine art, will be but the instruments of its one over-mastering social or political purpose, irresistibly conforming its so imitative subject units to type : they will be neither more nor less than so many variations, so to speak, of the trumpet-call.'

Of Lacedæmon, the city that seemed to Plato nearest to his august ideal, Mr. Pater in his eighth chapter gives us a wonderful 'imaginary portrait,' one of the most beautiful passages of his beautiful book.

IN what does decadence consist? In a self-conscious *John Gray:* arrangement of 'coloured' vowels, in a 'Silver- fastidious distribution of accents, result-points.' ing in new and subtler harmonies of verse —say some. In the choice for themes of disease and forbidden things generally—say others. For my part, while I see that both characteristics mark the modern decadent school, I do not think that either is the starting-point of that school. In regard to the first,

are we to say that in proportion as language becomes
more and more the perfected instrument of expression,
the more it develops literary means to literary ends,
it is decadent?  Surely such a perfection is in the
direction of growth, not decadence.  On such a definition Virgil and Tennyson were decadents, and, moreover, it implies that the great old poets sang like a
bird on bough, without a thought of style.  But did
they?  Chaucer, so 'frank and hale,' certainly did not,
for one.  The second definition would make decadents
of Rabelais and Swift.  The real core of decadence
is to be found in its isolated interests.  Its effects are
gained by regarding life as of but one or two dimen-
sions.  Its recent development almost entirely confines
its outlook on life to the colour-sense.  It puts men and
dead game on the same basis—of colour.  As I have remarked elsewhere, M. Huysmans is taken with the effects
of colour on a tippler's nose, Gautier with the same effects
in a beggar's rags, but each ignores the humanity of both.
Shakespeare could jest about Falstaff's nose, but he
gave us the rest of him as well—how much !  Decadence, therefore, it seems to me, comes of the decadent
regarding his theme *in vacuo*, isolated from its various
relations—of morality, of pity, of humour, of religion.
Judged from this standpoint, Mr. Gray's poems
are not so decadent as he would have us suppose.
They are luxurious to the last degree, they are subtly
cadenced as the song the sirens sang, they will
dwell over-unctuously on many forbidden themes —
'many whisper things I dare not tell'—they are each
separately dedicated to every more or less decadent

poet of Mr. Gray's acquaintance, and their *format*, an adaptation of the Aldine italic books, is of a far-sought deliciousness. But in spite of his neo-Catholicism and his hot-house erotics, Mr. Gray cannot accomplish that gloating abstraction from the larger life of humanity which marks the decadent.

Maybe he will accomplish it in time, but such a picture as this, a picture of trawling at night, entitled 'Wings in the Dark,' makes one hope he will not. I have not space for the whole poem :

> ' Full-winged and stealthy like a bird of prey,
> All tense the muscles of her seemly flanks ;
> She, the coy creature that the idle day
> Sees idly riding in the idle ranks.
>
> Backward and forth, over the chosen ground,
> Like a young horse, she drags the heavy trawl,
> Tireless ; or speeds her rapturous course unbound,
> And passing fishers through the darkness call
>
> Deep greeting, in the jargon of the sea.
> Haul upon haul, flounders and soles and dabs,
> And phosphorescent animalculæ,
> Sand, seadrift, weeds, thousands of worthless crabs.
>
> Low on the mud the darkling fishes grope,
> Cautious to stir, staring with jewel eyes ;
> Dogs of the sea, the savage congers mope,
> Winding their sulky march Meander-wise.
>
> Suddenly all is light and life and flight,
> Upon the sandy bottom, agate strewn.
> The fishers mumble, waiting till the night
> Urge on the clouds, and cover up the moon.'

The reader will not fail to note here the simplicity of the means and the richness of the impression ; he will notice, too, such cunning effects as the repetition 'idle' in the first verse, and the curious predominance of the letter 'r' throughout.

Though frankly a disciple of modern French poets, Mr. Gray's verses remind one more, in their quaint deliciousness, of certain old English poets, of Crashaw especially; and a certain affinity to the work of Mr. Bridges corroborates this.   The wind of Provence also blows sweetly through his verses.   But to whatever school he may now, or eventually, belong, he has a gift of epithet, of dainty colour and subtle rhythm, such as distinguish his *Silverpoints* from any recent English poetry.   He has a very great deal in common with the typical decadent, his book is full of affectation, but it is strongly marked by genuine individuality as well.   Here is another fascinating verse taken at random :

> ' The shadows lie mauven beneath the trees,
> And purple stains, where the finches pass,
> Leap in the stalks of the deep, rank grass.
> Flutter of wing, and the buzz of bees,
> Deepen the silence, and sweeten ease.'

And in illustration of what I have said of that hopeful sign of Mr. Gray's not being quite able to isolate himself from human interests, here is one verse more :

> ' In every kiss I call you mine,
> Tell me, my dear, how pure, how brave
> Our child will be !   What velvet eyne,
> What bonny hair our child will have !'

Is not this absurdly domestic in a decadent?   Really Mr. Gray must check these natural impulses.

M. ANATOLE FRANCE tells us in one of his charming
*J. A. Symonds:* 'contes de lettres,' as he prettily describes
'In the Key of his causeries, that, having just finished an
 Blue.' eager perusal of one of M. Paul Bourget's
novels, he immediately turns to his *Imitation of Christ*,
and reads 'à la page où elle s'ouvre toute seule,' as
a kind of corrective, or, at any rate, contrast; and
he paradoxically heads the resultant causerie with
the saintly phrases. Thomas à Kempis, Paul Bourget,
and all between! That might be no bad definition of
culture, and certainly it is typical of the catholicity
which is M. France's great charm. Whatever his
subject may be, he is always able to put himself at the
sympathetic point of view. Just the same charm
characterises, in even fuller measure, the writings of
Mr. John Addington Symonds. There is no corner of
history on which the human spirit has left its impress
that is not eloquent to him, and to which he is without
some answering sympathy. His is the insatiable
curiosity to experience the best that has been thought
and done in the world, but the artist's rather than
the scholar's: the passionate inquisitiveness of the
Renaissance, when the mere acquisition of learning
was tinged with romance. And, consequently, whatever subject he writes upon, we feel a confidence that
he treats it with a full knowledge of all its relations,
its antecedents, and all its various conditions. Culture
has done its perfect work, and endowed him with its
greatest gift—the sense of proportion. There are some

for whom the sense of proportion means merely the sense of the littleness of mortal concerns.

> 'To learn that man
> Is small, and not forget that man is great,'

as a recent poet (Mr. Arthur Benson) finely puts it, is perhaps not given to many : what one might term a sense of graduated proportion, which not only measures one's particular interests against the fixed stars, but also puts them in proper relation to each other. The best paper in a book of many interests is one which deals with this very property of culture :

> 'A man of moderate ability who cannot see beyond the world of beetles, beyond the painter's studio, beyond the church or chapel, beyond the concert room, beyond the grammar of an extinct language, or some one period of history, is apt to be intolerable. Culture teaches him his modest place in the whole scheme. Culture is, therefore, absolutely essential to the mental well-being of persons confined by their craft or profession to a narrow range of intellectual interests.'

This is well put ; and one or two of the examples strike one as particularly piquant. Who does not know of one or two university professors who are learned indeed in their 'grammar of an extinct language' or in 'some one period of history'? How would they stare if we were to tell them that they lacked the very primary element of culture ! Yet the world will probably go on confounding Middle-English with culture for no little time to come. That a man can be cultured and yet know no language but his own needs culture to understand. The superstition of learning is the longest a-dying of all.

> 'The world's an orange—thou hast suck'd its juice;
>   But wherefore all this pomp and pride and puffing?
> Somehow a goose is none the less a goose
>   Though moon and stars be minced to yield it stuffing.'

I must quote two or three more passages from this wise essay. In answering the question, How are we to achieve culture? Mr. Symonds well says that

' In the case of rare and specially gifted natures, there is no need to ask this question. They attain culture, and more than it can give, by an act of instinct. They leap to their work impulsively, discover it inevitably. . . . In dealing with culture, then, we have to regard the needs of talent rather than the necessities of genius: intellectual faculties of good quality, rather than minds of an exceptional, unique distinction.'

And in speaking of genius, Mr. Symonds evidently does not refer to merely creative genius, but also to the genius for character. Who does not know of many among his friends possessed of such undemonstrative genius, men and women whose names fame may never consecrate or vulgarise, but who, for the circle in which they move, are a radiating centre of sweet and noble influence? Culture, says Mr. Symonds again,

' makes a man to be something; it does not teach him to create anything. It has no power to stand in the place of Nature, and to endow a human being with new faculties. It prepares him to exert his innate faculties in a chosen line of work, with a certain spirit of freedom, with a certain breadth of understanding.'

And once more :

'I must repeat that culture is not an end in itself.   It prepares a man for life, for work, for action, for the reception and emission of ideas.   Life itself is larger than literature, than art, than science.   Life does not exist for them, but they for life.   This does not imply that it is better to be a man of no culture than a man of culture.   The man of culture is obviously capable of living to more purpose, of getting a larger amount out of life, than the man of no culture.   He can also judge more fairly in all cases of comparative criticism.   Still, I am unable to perceive that the refinements of the intellect on any line of its development involve an ennobling or a strengthening of the human being.   Given individuals of equal calibre, as many wise men may be found among the artisans and peasants as among reputed *savants*.   Household proverbs are not unfrequently a safer guide to conduct than the aphorisms of professors. . . .  The life of no great nation lies either in humanism or in science.   The arts and literature of Italy in the sixteenth century did not make her powerful or virtuous.   The so-called progress to which she is now sacrificing the monuments of her past, a progress dominated by scientific notions, has substituted ugliness and vulgarity for beauty and distinction, without adding an iota to her strength or general intelligence.   We ought not to despise culture.   The object of this article is to demonstrate its value.   But the nearer a man has come to possessing it, the less will he over-estimate acquirements or accumulations of knowledge, the more importance will he attach to character, to personality, to energy, to independence.'

How good it is to hear a man who is one of the supreme types of culture saying these things, striking a blow at that arrogant supremacy of intellect— 'intellect,' too, which is frequently but the wrong label for merely phonographic memory—vindicating the simpler, and therefore deeper, wisdom of 'simple, natural persons.'  As the meek inherit the earth, so do the simple inherit the mysteries.  The 'foolish wise man' misses them in a cloud of formulæ, which are, after all, but so many names for all the matters of which he is ignorant.  Yet it needs a learned man to fight this battle against learning, for with him can be no suspicion of sour grapes.

The paper next in suggestiveness is a masterly review of M. Zola's *La Bête Humaine*, containing a theory of idealism in literature which I have noticed several smart people eagerly appropriating, and which is indeed very ingenious and plausible. ' It is one of the *mauvaises plaisanteries* of the epoch,' says Mr. Symonds, ' to call M. Zola a realist. Actually, he is an idealist of the purest water.' Why? Because while all his details are studied from the life, the synthesis which he makes of them is incompatible with experience. This certainly proves that M. Zola is not a realist in the most inclusive meaning of the term ; but to disprove him a realist does not necessarily prove him an idealist. I will let Mr. Symonds speak for himself :

' Zola's realism consists, then, in his careful attention to details, in the naturalness of his connecting motives, and his frank acceptance of all things human which present themselves to his observing brain. The idealism which I have been insisting on, which justifies us in calling *La Bête Humaine* a poem, has to be sought in the method whereby these separate parcels of the plot are woven together, and also in the dominating conception contained in the title which gives unity to the whole work. We are not in the real region of reality, but in the region of the constructive imagination from the first to the last line of the novel. If that be not the essence of idealism—this working of the artist's brain not in but on the subject-matter of the external world and human nature—I do not know what meaning to give to the term.'

But does the mere working of the constructive imagination among a mass of materials, irrespective of the end to which it works, constitute idealism? I am aware that such is not the original meaning of the word; but the sense in which men have long agreed to use the verb 'idealise,' and such general sense must be regarded if our vocabulary is to be of any service to us, is—to make more beautiful than reality, to touch to finer issues. M. Zola makes life even more ugly than reality. Have we not here an antithesis rather than a correspondence? It is true that both ends are attained by the same selective exercise of the imagination. But then what different ends! For the common process by which the ends are reached it would be well to have a word in common—but surely that word is not idealism. For the end reached by M. Zola it would be useful to have a word. One might, perhaps, term it 'inverted' idealism, but one must, at the same time, describe vice as inverted virtue. The Black Venus is the muse such inverted idealists serve, a goddess fascinating in abnormal moods and for a few people.

Beauty is doubtless in a large measure a relative quality, but there are, all the same, certain axioms arrived at by the general feeling of mankind, to disregard which must mean endless confusion: one is that the Venus of Milo is beautiful, the other that the Black Venus is ugly. One does not forget that eternal change is constantly transforming our conceptions, and that words and the things they stand for are all constantly changing together; but we cannot afford to dwell on that principle too minutely—else description or definition becomes impossible. We have, or we seem to have, certain pauses in the flux, where we can stand and say 'that is' and 'that is not.' It seems so, at any rate; and unless we accept the fiction, life and literature are alike impossible. What we regard as beauty to-day may be ugliness a hundred years hence—but what is to become of us if beauty and ugliness are to be regarded as synonymous terms? We know that the matrimonial sentiment is a matter of geography; but to keep a harem in England is to imperil domestic unity, for all that.

In the essay which gives the title to the volume, Mr. Symonds draws attention to the limitation of language in regard to colour:

'It is easy,' he says, 'to talk of green, blue, yellow, red. But when we seek to distinguish the tints of these hues, and to accentuate the special *timbre* of each, we are practically left to suggestions founded upon metaphor and analogy. We select some object in nature—a gem, a flower, an aspect of the sky or sea—which possesses the particular quality we wish to indicate. We talk of grass-green, apple-green, olive-green, emerald-green, sage-green, jade-green; of sapphire, forget-me-not, turquoise, gentian, ultramarine, sky-blue; of topaz, gold, orange, citron; of rose and cherry, ruby and almandine, blood and flame. Or else we use the names of substances from which the pigments are compounded: as yellow-ochre, burnt-sienna, cadmium, lamp-black, verdigris, vermilion, madder, cinnabar. To indicate very subtle gradations, the jargon of commerce supplies us liberally with terms like mauve, magenta, eau-de-Nile, peacock, merdad'oca, Prussian-blue, crushed strawberry, Venetian-red, gris-de-perle, and so forth to infinity. It is obvious that for purely literary purposes these designations have a very unequal value. Some of them are inadmissible in serious composition. The most precise often fail by interpreting what is absent from the reader's mental eye through what is unknown to his intelligence. Not everybody is familiar with jade, cadmium, almandine, Nile-water.   What the writer wants would be a variety of broad terms to express the species (tints) of each genus (hue).'

This paucity of terms, however, is not, Mr. Symonds remarks, wholly against the artist.   'It forces him to exercise both fancy and imagination in the effort to bring some special tint before the mental vision of the reader.'   In fact, it provides for him, like the necessities of rhyme, an artistic gymnastic.   Mr. Symonds makes no attempt to increase our colour vocabulary; but, accepting the conditions, he assays, in the spirit of a literary gymnast, to show what may be done even with so restricted means.   The result is a series of studies of the 'colouring' of a gondolier, whose blue blouse in its environment of gloom struck Mr. Symonds one evening in Venice.   Here is the first study:

> 'A symphony of black and blue—
> Venice asleep, vast night, and you.
> The skies were blurred with vapours dank:
> The long canal stretched inky-blank,
> With lights on heaving water shed
> From lamps that trembled overhead.
> Pitch-dark! you were the one thing blue;
> Four tints of pure celestial hue:
> The larkspur blouse by tones degraded
> Through silken sash of sapphire faded,
> The faintly floating violet tie,
> The hose of lapis-lazuli.
> How blue you were amid that black,
> Lighting the wave, the ebon wrack!
> The ivory pallor of your face
> Gleamed from those glowing azures back
> Against the golden gaslight; grapes
> Of dusky curls your brows embrace,
> And round you all the vast night gapes.'

Mr. Symonds makes several studies of Augusto in various settings. Though ingenious, one cannot profess that they are inspiring ; perhaps they would appeal more to one if Augusto were anything but a man. Humanity resents his being made a mere 'clothes-horse' of. So complete an isolation of the colour-sense strikes one as unnatural, though, after all, it is no more unnatural than the isolation of the sense of form in drawing from the life : but even so, form means more, includes more, than colour, nor have we yet quite got over our feeling that there is indignity towards the human creature in the life-class. Mr. Symonds evidently feels this as he closes :

> 'Come back, my Muse, come back to him
> Who warmed the cold hue, bright or dim.
> Those ivory brows, those lustrous eyes,
> Those grape-like curls, those brief replies ;
> These are thy themes—the man, the life—
> Not tints in symphony at strife.'

The essay has a secondary interest as being an intermezzo in prose and verse, an interest it shares with 'Clifton and a Lad's Love,' an idyll of friendship : but neither appear to me to indicate the possibilities of the intermezzo form—the verse in each case being merely set amid the prose, and not blossoming out of it, by irresistible impulse, as though one talking should suddenly break out into song. In passing, one may refer to a curious form of prose and verse intermezzo, recently given us by Mr. Wilfrid Blunt, in his translation of a part of the great Arabian epic of Abu Zeyd—'The Stealing of the Mare.' In that epic, the narrator, first of all, sketches out an episode, at a fair length, in prose, and proceeds to re-tell the whole, with constant amplification, in verse ; like a painter first making his study, and then painting his complete picture.

The remaining contents include essays on 'The Dantesque and Platonic Ideals of Love,' which will be read with curiosity by those interested in Mr. Symonds's views on the same theme in his *Life of Michelangelo* ; an especially welcome and generously appreciative paper on a poet unjustly inglorious, Edward Cracroft Lefroy ; 'Mediæval Norman Songs,' dealing with the Vaux de Vire ; 'Notes of a Somersetshire Home,' Sutton Court, the home of the Stracheys ; and three admirable papers on Elizabethan dramatic and lyric poetry—'Some Notes on Fletcher's Valentinian,' 'The Lyricism of the Romantic Drama,' 'Lyrics from Elizabethan Song-Books.' The second paper, insisting on the essentially lyrical character of much of the so-called dramatic writing of the Elizabethans, is specially suggestive.   Of 'Romeo and Juliet,' Mr. Symonds says :

'The whole play is a *Chant d'Amour*—an exhalation of human love, in poetry assuming the dramatic mantle.   All the incidents of action fall away and sink into their place before the simple fact that Romeo loves Juliet, and Juliet loves Romeo.   This play is the lyric cry converted into drama.'

Referring to Dryden, in the same paper, Mr. Symonds makes a discovery which will be of much interest to students of literary origins, no less than the original model of Mr. Swinburne's haunting 'Garden of Proserpine' stanza. Mr. Symonds quotes the following verse from 'The Spanish Friar' :

> 'Farewell, ungrateful traitor,
>     Farewell, my perjured swain !
> Let never injured creature
>     Believe a man again.
> The pleasure of possessing
> Surpasses all expressing :
> But 'tis too short a blessing,
>     And love too long a pain.'

Mr. Symonds tells us in his preface that he has endeavoured to make the present collection of essays representative of the different kinds of work in which he has been engaged. This makes the volume somewhat multifarious in character ; but what a diversity of interests, and all so richly assimilated !

THOUGH Mr. Crackanthorpe simply records certain phases of modern life as he sees them, entirely without comment, it is inevitable in his method that the mere telling includes much painful, and some pleasurable, irony. Occasional cynicism was hardly to be avoided, but Mr. Crackanthorpe never goes out of his way to be cynical. If his method, rapid without being jerky, invites one, his *dramatis personæ* cannot be described as inviting. The prostitute, whom, I think, he has treated more fearlessly than any one yet in English fiction, the drunken wife, the

*Hubert Crackanthorpe: 'Wreckage.'*

card-sharper, of such are his human 'wreckage.' If his
stories have any moral, it is that dreary modern moral of
the irresistible force of circumstance.   The poor woman
who has just left her drunken husband hugging a prostitute at the public-house, will, for a little while, resist the
temptation that offers her starving baby a little food, but
in the end she will give in to the little man who tempts
her as she stands looking over the bridge into the river ;
the drunken wife has her moments of remorseful love,
but she will go on drinking ; the successful sharper's wife
may despise him in her heart, but when he comes home
with six hundred odd pounds she must go on 'loving'
him.   '"Six hundred and thirty-four pounds !" she repeated, half to herself.   "How much is that in francs?"
"Nearly sixteen thousand."   "And my pearl isn't angry
any more?"   "Je t'aime," she murmured in reply.   Their
lips met.'   The best story in the book, that in which the
irony is nearer humour than cynicism, is entitled 'A
Dead Woman.'   A country inn-keeper, Richard Rushout,
sorrows for a dead wife, who had been the beauty of the
countryside.   It is joy to dwell on her memory, and he
sits in the bar at nights, and talks with his old farmer
friend Jonathan Hays.   Presently he discovers that
Jonathan has a reason for his sympathy.   His wife had
not been all he thought her.   The world is not large
enough for Jonathan and he.   They are to meet at a
cross road at midnight.   Nearing the rendezvous
Rushout has a stroke, and is ill for some time.   During
his illness, Jonathan inquires about him, and when he is
well again, instead of the old jealousy reviving, the two
men find themselves drawn together, because they had

each loved the dead woman. 'Each was conscious of a craving to talk about her, to hear the other mention her name. "Richard, she was a grand woman." "That she was—sich splendid hair." "Nay, but 'twas her eyes that were the finest." " Black—jet black."

'"D'ye mind how wild she was the day I was for lettin' young Will Dykes drive the mare?" "That I do." "Were ye sweet on her then?" He put the question in hesitating timidity. "'Twas the first occasion I had a kiss from her," answered Jonathan defiantly. "When was that?" "Whilst ye were fetchin' the new skin rug."' So, calling for another glass, they continue their naïve converse, and if any one thinks Rushout loved his wife any the less for his complacency, surely he is the cynic, and not Mr. Crackanthorpe. There is a humanity about this story which promises more than all the rest. They are perhaps clever pastiches after little masters. 'A Dead Woman' is more like Mr. Crackanthorpe's own, or at least it suggests greater masters.

MESSRS. ELLIS and YEATS have at length completed *William Blake.* their great task, and their vindication of Edited by Ellis Blake has for some weeks been exercising and Yeats. the minds of all Blake students, desultory and laborious. Its three tremendous volumes are divided between 'The System,' 'The Meaning,' and 'The Books.' The first volume contains an admirably written memoir, and the third, in addition to the better

known works of Blake, the hitherto unpublished *Vala*.
This volume contains many lithographic reproductions,
in which one cannot but miss the colour of the originals.
It were quite idle and presumptuous in any critic to
pronounce offhand as to the value of Messrs. Ellis and
Yeats's labours.   Yet it does not need any very long
study of them to see that they have certainly reduced
the chaos to a considerable degree of order, and that
whether or not they have succeeded in elucidating the
whole myth, important sections of it are now comparatively clear.   To this end Messrs. Ellis and Yeats
have had the advantage of a long study of mysticism
generally, and have thus been able to view Blake's
mysticism in relation to those other systems from which
it sprang.   Obviously, editors with merely artistic and
literary standards are out of court in regard to Blake,
whom it suffices them to dub a 'mystic' and pass on.
This familiarity with mysticism makes Messrs. Ellis and
Yeats occasionally forget that it is an esoteric study,
and that its terminology is often obscure even to the
cultivated reader.   Still, on the whole, having regard
to the extreme difficulty of the subject, they are very
successful in making themselves clear ; and the first
chapter of *The Symbolic System*, that on 'The Necessity
of Symbolism,' is a most suggestive exposition of the
mystic point of view.   Nothing could well be more
illuminating or better calculated to put the non-mystic
reader *en rapport* with their unfamiliar moods of thought.

'The necessity of symbolism' is the materialism
of man.   Shut up within his five senses, he refuses
credence to anything which they cannot comprehend,

and 'having denied the existence of that for which his
bodily life exists'—the soul, for which properly his senses
are but ministers of experience—'man begins an un-
ceasing preoccupation with his own bodily life, neglect-
ing to regard it as a symbol.' 'The mind or imagination
or consciousness of man may be said to have two poles,
the personal and impersonal, or, as Blake preferred to
call them, the limit of contraction and the unlimited
expansion. When we act from the personal we tend to
bind our consciousness down to a fiery centre. When,
on the other hand, we allow our imagination to expand
away from this egoistic mood, we become vehicles for
the universal thought and merge in the universal mood.
Thus a reaction of God against man and man against
God.' Originally the whole of nature existed but as one
of the thoughts of God, without conscious knowledge of
itself, but this consciousness gradually dawning, desire
of separate corporeal existence awoke within it and thus
came the Fall—'the fall into division'—and the wider
and wider severance of nature and man from God.
Therein is the significance of the religious aspiration to
be 'made one with God,' or, as Blake expresses it, the
'resurrection into Unity.'

It is the aim of mysticism to keep man awake to this
divine origin and significance of life, by the use of
impressive symbols of its operations and issues. This,
it will be said, is also the proper aim of poetry and all
the arts. It is, of course, but Messrs. Ellis and Yeats
suggestively explain, 'the chief difference between the
metaphors of poetry and the symbols of mysticism is
that the latter are woven together into a complete

system.' Illustrating this by a line in *King Lear*, they continue, 'the "vexed sea" would not be merely a detached comparison, but, with the fish it contains, would be related to the land and air, the winds and shadowing clouds, and all in their totality compared to the mind in its totality.' A complete mystic system then would be, so to say, not an epic of one people or time, but an epic of the universe. As such a system would include the *Iliad*, so mysticism includes poetry.

To all who are not slaves of their five senses this must seem a reasonable enough statement of the mystic's aims. To the merely artistic mind the stupendous majesty of design, to which Michael Angelo's imaginations were as the span of a child's hand, must impressively appeal.

But has any mystic given us such a colossal epic of the universe? Have these complicated systems really impressed the imagination of man more than the noble fragments of symbolism given to us by the great poets? One power all mystics more or less seem to lack is that very touch of universality which is the common property of great poets. They nullify their great imaginations by wedding them to a narrow, sectarian, or provincial terminology. This, Messrs. Ellis and Yeats admit, is the drawback with Swedenborg and Bœhmen. With all their mighty dreams, they remain sectaries for sectaries. They have no wide or permanent appeal. Blake, however, his editors claim, is not hampered in this way. He speaks directly to the pure poetic genius in man, without any intermediate theological terminology. But, though this be true in some degree,

surely Blake's system has none the less a more serious
limitation. The terms of theology have a certain, comparatively wide, currency, but the terms in which Blake
often wrote were absolutely of his own coinage, and had
merely a personal significance. For instance, Lambeth
happened to mean much in his personal history, and so
he uses it as a symbol—but to whom but himself does
Lambeth thus appeal? And so all through. All the
events and circumstances of his own temporary life are
made to do duty for his eternal meanings. Of course,
every accident of our lives may be symbolic for us, but
such accidents are not necessarily competent as symbols
for all men. Thus, it seems to me, that Blake's mystical
system is limited in appeal as dialect poetry is limited,
and for the same reason. He expressed the eternal
meanings too often in the dialect of his own everyday
history, instead of in such universal world-language as
the world alone can understand. To my mind it seems
that one of his single mystic sayings is more valuable,
even as mysticism, than the vast amorphous body of any
one of his complete myths. Such a saying as that, often
quoted by the editors, which declares that 'our digestion
also is managed by angels.' Not only our thought-
processes, but the very humblest offices of the body are
mysteries. Who can explain the transformation of food
into flesh? No profounder criticism on materialism
can be imagined.

But, some one is impatient to ask, Wasn't Blake mad
as well? Personally, I think he was—in regard to relatively unimportant matters. It seems madness in him
to attribute the idea of his etching process to the direct

inspiration of his dead brother, because the discovery of such processes belongs to the normal operation of the human mind—though it must at the same time be admitted that we don't rightly know how that normal operation comes about, and that, for all we know, sudden ideas, 'inspirations' as we call them, may be whispered to us by 'angels.' Blake's conversations with Crabb Robinson seem especially to point to derangement, and I think the editors make a mistake in not frankly admitting the possibility of a strain of madness in Blake, instead of trying to prove him sane on every point. For suppose Blake did make odd mistakes in regard to the lesser matters of everyday life, a curious unreasonable use of human facts and methods, he made no mistake about those profound matters of which human life is but symbolic. He was sane enough on 'the great things.' Comparing great with small, he was, in everyday life, like an illiterate poet, whose dream is whole and sound, but who, in endeavouring to express it, makes ludicrous havoc with grammar and strange bewildering use of all the conventional methods of expression. He strikes one as an angel, half-mortal by mistake, to whom the use of mortal language and standards is bewildering. Blake will seem sane enough in heaven. Therefore, why trouble to vindicate his merely mental sanity? We overrate merely mental sanity, as much as we underrate spiritual sanity. A man may have the most perverted ideas of right and wrong, he may be wilfully sensual, and all that is morally and spiritually depraved, and we say nothing about his sanity; but if he happens to get a fixed idea that there are only six days in the week, and obstinately holds that the moon is green cheese—really quite unimportant misconceptions—we shut him up and appoint administrators of his estate. If a few more of us were mad after Blake's fashion, it would be no bad thing for the world. And, of course, quite apart from Blake's madness on mysticism, we have the undisputed treasures of his lark-throated lyrics, and his wonderful harmonies of line and colour. These all of us can enjoy, and in these at any rate, apart from their artistic appeal, Blake's mystic lesson is articulate for all to hear and understand.

MR. MALLOCK is scarcely a poet. For him ''tis too late to be ambitious' in that kind. Curious

*W. H. Mallock: 'Verses.'*

is this yearning in man for 'the loved Apollian leaves.' The laurel of prose never seems to bring content. As middle-age glooms, the distinguished proseman is eager to give it all, for one leaf of the true Parnassian evergreen. The little treasured screed of boyish verse is brought out from its hiding-place, and the old boyish hopes raise their flutes once more. Even the dusty historian, witness Mr. Lecky, must sooner or later unlock his heart. But the poor song-bird has been neglected too long. It may, indeed, be served up as a dead nightingale, and make us a scanty meal in one edition, but 'le pigeon ne chantait plus.' Mr. Mallock has been too long a mocker to turn poet at the eleventh hour. Perhaps he was a poet to begin with, but he

was a mocker at an equally early age. Even his Newdigate, 'The Isthmus of Suez,' in 1871, breathes the
spirit of despair :

> ' What power or knowledge is there to unite
> The never-mingled seas of faith and sight ?'

he cries. To infuse 'modern doubt' into a Newdigate
is not given to all men. When *The New Republic* was
published, the charming verse-parodies of Matthew
Arnold, Rossetti, and others which it contained, were so
like real poems, that curiosity was aroused as to whether
Mr. Mallock shouldn't actually leave off jesting, and
write poetry in earnest. Mr. Mallock answered this
interest by a volume of early verses—'written between
my seventeenth and my twentieth year'—disappointing,
derivative, neo-Pagan, neo-Catholic, things. However,
as Mr. Mallock was scrupulous to record the exact day
and hour of inspiration to his verses, they were at least
interesting as autobiographical revelations. One smiled
to find the cynic in bud writing thus at sixteen :

> ' I did not offer thee up mine heart,
>    Nor did I ask, thou know'st, for thine.
> I only said, " Until we part
>    Lend it, and I will lend thee mine." '

But even then Mr. Mallock had a poetical past of at
least eight years behind him. For does he not record
how, at the tender age of eight, he sat on his swing and
composed these lines on Celia :

> ' The breezes are sighing
> About me, above me !
>    Oh, I should be happy,
> If Celia would love me !

> But without Celia's love
> The breezes may blow ;
> And, for all that I care,
> To the devil may go !'

Certainly it was good lisping in numbers—even if the babe had read his Suckling.

This little Mallock on the swing must have much resembled the 'Child' to whom one of Mr. Mallock's new poems is addressed. No one beats Mr. Mallock at finding the canker, or rather the mere eggs of the canker, in the fresh young bud. Even in the eyes of a child he is able to discern the world-weariness :

> 'O sad as death, and soft as love,
>   What 's this that I in you behold?
> All life seems gazing from the eyes—
>   The eyes of eight years old. . . .
>
> Between your eyelids swims the look
>   That says, "My faith in prayer is o'er."
> Your mouth seems quivering to the lost,
>   "Kiss me that kiss once more !" '

For witty, cynical verse, somewhat after the manner of the late Lord Lytton, Mr. Mallock has certainly a very brilliant talent. We have had nothing for a long time more irresistibly clever than those verses in *The New Republic*, addressed by 'A Philosophic Lover' to 'The Wife of an old Schoolfellow.' Mr. Mallock reprints them, and as they are the best in his new volume, I cannot do better than recall them to the reader :

> 'Let others seek for wisdom's way
>   In modern science, modern wit,—
> I turn to love, for all that these,
>   These two can teach, is taught by it.

Yes, all.   In that first hour we met
  And smiled and spoke so soft and long, love,
Did wisdom dawn ; and I began
  To disbelieve in right and wrong, love.

Then, as love's gospel clearer grew,
  And I each day your doorstep trod, love,
I learned that love was all in all,
  And rose to disbelieve in God, love.

Yes, wisdom's book ! you taught me this,
  And ere I half had read you through, love,
I learned a deeper wisdom yet—
  I learned to disbelieve in you, love.

So now, fair teacher, I am wise,
  And free : 'tis truth that makes us free, love.
But you—you 're pale ! grow wise as I,
  And learn to disbelieve in me, love.'

There is the true Mephistopheles laugh.   The two poems that approach serious poetical beauty are both from *The New Republic*—'Pulveris Exigui Munus,' the imitation of Matthew Arnold — and that 'New Francesca,' sung by the wicked, witty Mrs. Sinclair, who so shocked Dr. Jenkinson by her naïve query as to Greek love-poetry.   'They were a little obscure, perhaps—much Greek is—or ——' hesitated the doctor. 'Corrupt?' suggested Mrs. Sinclair innocently.   There are no new ones to match their mood, which, though it feigned to be mockery, was much more nearly true passion.   The new things are mainly epigrams of despair, such as this on 'Will'—bitterly, almost impiously, headed, 'O living will, that shalt endure' :

'We strive to will the right ; but what 's our will ?
A die whose casts we nickname good or ill,

Loaded by fate—a tendency, a taint,
Which fate has dealt us.　This with all her skill
　Does Science prove : and this is man's complaint :
"Sinning, an idiot conscience stabs me still,
　Which yet has no one blessing for restraint."'

One of the cleverest things in the book is a parody of
Mr. Swinburne, entitled 'A Song after Moonrise' :—

' I bowed my laurell'd head
　Above my lyre, and said :
" What new song shall I sing across the strings?
　Madden'd for whose new sake
　What new noise shall I make?"

And I answer'd : " Lo, I will sing of no new things ;
　I will turn to her once more
　I have sung so oft before—
Freedom—and worship her, and curse some kings. . . .
By the seas that link us and the lands that sever,
　By the foes upon our weather-side and lee—
By all these things and all other things whatever,
　We call and howl and squeak and shriek to thee,
　　Calling thee early and late,
　　Wild, inarticulate,
Calling and bawling that thou set something free."'

Which reminds me that I am the happy possessor of
the rare squib, *Every man his own Poet* ; or, *The
Inspired Singer's Recipe Book,* by a Newdigate Prize-
man, which Mr. Mallock published at Oxford in 1872.
It is a wonderful little pamphlet.　The thing, of course,
has often been done, but never more brilliantly.　I
am too true an admirer of Mr. Swinburne to reproduce
the recipe 'How to write a Patriotic Poem like Mr.
Swinburne,' but the recipe 'How to Make an Ordinary
Love Poem' will hurt no one's susceptibilities, and is
perhaps the cleverest of all : 'Take two large and

tender human hearts, which match one another perfectly. Arrange these close together, but preserve them from actual contact by placing between them some cruel barrier.   Wound them both in several places, and insert through the openings thus made, a fine stuffing of wild yearnings, hopeless tenderness, and a general admiration for stars.   Then completely cover up one heart with a sufficient quantity of chill churchyard mould, which may be garnished according to taste with dank waving weeds or tender violets : and promptly break over it the other heart.'

Yes, the child is father to the man—if Mr. Mallock ever was a child.   The child in Mr. Mallock was born mocking, and the man must now go on mocking till the end.   And yet Mr. Mallock might have been—what ?

THE fate of Basse is perhaps one of the most pathetic,
*William Basse:* paradoxically speaking, in the history of
**Edited by** oblivion.   Forgotten poets, or rather poets
**Warwick Bond.** remembered by a very few, are plentiful. The number of quite forgotten poets it is obviously impossible to estimate.   Evidently Basse does not belong to those, else we should not be speaking of him.   But he is as near to them as a man may well be.   A breath nearer and he had tumbled over into the pitchy darkness.   His singularity is this, that whereas the nearly forgotten poet was usually somewhat of a figure in his own day, and had at least the pleasure of seeing his name on a title-page, Basse, though occasionally referred

to by his contemporaries, and evidently of some account amongst them, was certainly not a figure, and his best work, that which he had so carefully filed and polished, has lain in manuscript for two hundred and forty years. So had they gone on lying had it not occurred to Messrs. Ellis and Elvey, who possess the manuscripts, to ask Mr. Warwick Bond to edit them, and to publish them in the sumptuous volume before me. It was a sweet, charitable act. Poor Basse! if he could only know. How would he exclaim, with Herrick (whom he probably lived long enough to read), 'Like to a bride come forth my book at last!' Of course, his publishers will have sent him a copy!

Few figures are so completely lost in shade as Basse. With all Mr. Bond's learned pains, his history is still all mays and mights. He was probably born about 1583, probably born and schooled at Northampton, probably a page to Lady Wenman, of Thame Park, and certainly a retainer of the family, probably at Oxford, probably a friend (as certainly a disciple) of Spenser, probably a musician as well as a poet, almost certainly married, burying 'Helinor ye wife of Willia Basse,' 23rd Sept., 1637, and probably died at Thame some time during 1653. 1653 was the very year he had hoped to publish his long-hoarded *Pastorals*, hoped to burst out into sudden flame, old man as he must have been. He had his manuscript all carefully prepared down to the title page, which it is pathetic to see facsimiled in Mr. Bond's edition.

Two associations, however, have served to keep his memory in the minds of lovers of books; the reference to him in *The Complete Angler*, and his epitaph on Shakespeare—especially the former. From what Walton says, Basse had evidently some note as a song-writer, probably as a composer of the words, not the music. 'I'll promise you,' says Piscator, in chapter v. part i., 'I'll sing a song that was lately made, at my request, by Mr. William Basse, one that hath made the choice songs of the "Hunter in his Career," and of "Tom of Bedlam," and many others of note; and this that I will sing is in praise of Angling.' The reader will remember the song beginning 'As inward love breeds outward talk.' Verses four and five have most merit, the fifth being especially characteristic of Basse's moralising vein :

'And when the timorous trout I wait
  To take, and he devours my bait,
  How poor a thing, I sometimes find,
  Will captivate a greedy mind ;
    And when none bite, I praise the wise
    Whom vain allurements ne'er surprise.'

His epitaph on Shakespeare has a verve to which he rarely attains, and, as it cannot be said to be well known, I will quote it :

'Renowned Spencer, lye a thought more nye
  To learned Chaucer, and rare Beaumond lye
  A little neerer Spenser, to make roome
  For Shakespeare in your threefold, fowerfold Tombe.
  To lodge all fowre in one bed make a shift
  Untill Doomesdaye, for hardly will a fift
  Betwixt this day and that by Fate be slayne,
  For whom your Curtaines may be drawn againe.
  If your precedency in death doth barre
  A fourth place in your sacred sepulcher,
  Under this carved marble of thine owne,
  Sleepe, rare Tragœdian, Shakespeare, sleepe alone

> Thy unmolested peace, unshared Cave,
> Possesse as Lord, not Tenant, of thy Grave,
> That unto us and others it may be
> Honor hereafter to be layde by thee.'

These lines had evidently struck Ben Jonson, for he obviously alludes to them in his verses prefixed to the first folio :

> ' My Shakespeare, rise ; I will not lodge thee by
> Chaucer, or Spenser, or bid Beaumont lye
> A little further, to make thee a roome, . . .'

incorporates indeed their striking openings for which, with the majority of readers, he probably gets the credit.

Basse's *Pastorals* are based on Spenser's *Shepherd's Calendar*, the fashionable form of his day.  They have, as became a disciple of Spenser, a moral intent, being confessedly '9 Eclogues in Honor of 9 Vertues'; their *dramatis personæ* and their themes are the conventional figures and themes of Elizabethan pastoral, and each ends with an 'Emblem' in the approved fashion— 'Jesper's Emblem,' 'Cuddy's Emblem.'  Mr. Bond does not claim for them that they reach a high level of poetry.  They are never impassioned, seldom contain any of those striking beauties 'that into glory peep,' but pretty pastoral bits abound, and there is diffused through the whole a genuine sense of poetry, as the sweet-brier diffuses a meadow, and yet defies us to say, 'it is here,' or 'it is there.'

MR. T. E. BROWN has won a well-deserved reputation as the poet of Manx humour and pathos. His new volume contains a small section of studies in the same *genre*, entitled *In the Coach*—a miniature Manx Canterbury Pilgrimage.   The old fisherman's story is the most successful, entitled 'Jus' the Shy.'   He relates how a fleet of them, returning home from the North Sea fishing, were driven southward by a gale, and were obliged to put into a strange bay.   There was a castle at the top of the bay, and to their surprise they find emblazoned over one of its doors the Legs of Man.   It appears that the lady of the castle had once lived in Manxland, and loved its people ; and hearing of the fishermen in the harbour, she sent an invitation for them all to go to dine up at the castle.   The men accepted, but when the time came they never turned up, simply because the strong rough fellows were— too shy !

*T. E. Brown : 'Old John ; and other Poems.'*

> ' To have dinner with her, aye ! dinner, think of that now !
> A hundred-and-sixty of us—what ? aw, I 'll sweer.
> Dinner though ; so promised sure enough ; and the day come,
> And there wasn a sowl of us went, not a sowl, by gum !
> No ! and the pipers blawin,
> And the curks drawin,
> And the preparations they 'd be havin, so I 'm toul',
> And there wasn a sowl, no, not a sowl.
>
> *And what for was that ?*  What for ? just the shy, the shy,
> That 's the what for, and that 's the why,
> And that 's the way with the Manx ; aw, it is though, aw,
>     they are, they are,
> Mos' despard shy . . .'

Not discouraged, the great lady asks them 'to tay,' with a slightly better result. Sixteen plucked up courage and went,

> '*But the res*' *?* you're wondrin.　Chut!
> Jus' the shy, and nothin *but*
> The shy.　Aw, no use o' talkin,
> The shy it's shawkin.
> No *raison*, says you : not a bit.
> *Amazin*, says you.　Well, that's all you'll get,
> That is the raison, and the for and the why—
> Jus' the shy.'

Surely this is charming humour, the true humour, with those kindly tears somewhere about it which distinguished it from the new.

Another humorous, but less sympathetic, sketch is that of the incensed husband :

> 'Conjergal rights! conjergal rights!
> I don't care for the jink of her and I don't care for the jaw of her,
> But I'll have the law of her.'

What a finely ironical comment on the working of the marriage laws !

In the majority of the verses, however, which make up his new volume, Mr. Brown makes a bid for consideration as a poet of other themes than these Manx humours. And a good bid, too, on the whole. He succeeds in impressing us as a man with a strong individual hold on life. He sees with no one's eyes but his own, and what he sees and feels moves him with a strong manly emotion, a quality which he is able to get into his verse, and which atones for many of its defects. Those defects he seems to owe to

Browning.   He is often crabbed and impatient, and
writes verses such as this :

> ' Else were our life both frivolous and final,
>    A mere skiomachy,
> Not succulent of growth, not officinal
>    To what shall after be,
>    But Fortune's devilry
> Of Harlequin with smirk theatro-columbinal.'

He has yet to realise the truth of form ; and, instead
of compressing his ideas, he often expands them in
long shambling anyhow metres.   Thus he is rather a
poet of occasional fine lines and verses than of complete poems.   He is seldom so completely satisfactory
as in :

> ' A garden is a lovesome thing, God wot !
> Rose plot,
>    Fringed pool,
> Ferned grot—
>    The veriest school
>    Of peace ; and yet the fool
> Contends that God is not—
> Not God ! in gardens ! when the eve is cool?
>    Nay, but I have a sign ;
>    'Tis very sure God walks in mine.'

Such verse as this has roots, and for such authentic
throb of humanity as beats in Mr. Brown's poems,
such sturdy faith in life, for the fresh air and sunshine all about his book, and the gleaming beauty
that occasionally flashes through his obscurities, we
cannot be too thankful.   It is merely gratitude, therefore, to insist that more care for form would make
Mr. Brown considerably more effective as a poet.   He
should not quote Greek in English verse.   Certainly

one has more chance with Greek than with Sir Edwin Arnold's Hindustani, but it is no less bad as art. He needs, too, to guard against an allusiveness that leaves too much to the reader. Though the title-poem *Old John* contains a few fine lines and verses, it is too much of a personal colloquy between Mr. Brown and his old Covenanter servant, and it is only near the end that the eavesdropping reader begins at all to realise the 'Dear, brave, old Scotchman.' And what meaning does the title 'Lime Street' convey to anyone who does not know Liverpool. Greek, big 'out-of-colour' words, diffuseness, obscurity—let Mr. Brown avoid these and he will write us many more poems as good as one on 'Poets and Poets'—of which I quote the opening verse :

> 'He fishes in the night of deep sea pools
>    For him the nets hang long and low,
> Cork-buoyed and strong ; the silver-gleaming schools
>    Come with the ebb and flow
> Of universal tides, and all the channels glow.'

If Mr. Brown was thinking of himself, he was not far wrong.

WORDSWORTH'S 'violet by a mossy stone, half hidden from the eye,' is, perhaps, not the most appropriate quotation one could find for the more recent modern poet. Diffidence and unpracticality are no longer typical of the poetic temperament, and future humour founded upon those supposed characteristics

*Lord de Tabley : 'Poems, Dramatic and Lyrical.'*

will be mere anachronism.   A well-known publisher
tells me that the keenest business men of his acquaintance are his poets.   Evidently the struggle for existence has at last developed in the poet those qualities
of which he was most in need, and modesty and absence
of mind will no more handicap him in the race of life.
At a time, therefore, when poets are not so much born
as boomed, it is a matter of curious interest to encounter
a poet who for the last twenty-five years has indulged
that

> '. . . delight in singing, though none hear
> Beside the singer,'

content, like the Greek sculptor, to leave his work to
the all-seeing eyes of the gods.

Not that Lord de Tabley has quite fulfilled Thomas
Ashe's pathetic description of himself as 'the singer
no man listens to.'   It is, perhaps, mainly his own
fault that he has not taken the place in modern letters
to which his work entitles him, and which twenty years
ago the critics were well disposed to offer him.   After
seven years of fruitful poetic effort he suddenly ceased
singing, or sang under his breath ; and thus there are
those who know him well as an authority on the comparatively frivolous subject of book plates, who know
nothing of *Philoctetes* and other studies from the
antique, which place him second only to Mr. Swinburne as a follower of the Greek tragic poets.

Let us indulge ourselves in a date or two.   In 1863
Lord de Tabley made simultaneously his *début* as
numismatist and poet.   His essays 'On Greek Federal
Coinage' and 'On some Coins of Lycia under the

Rhodian Domination and of the Lycian League' may
be found by the curious in the *Transactions of the
Numismatic Society* for that year.    Our present concern is with the little volume of poems, the title of
which anticipated Mr. Ruskin's better known work,
' *Praeterita*, by William Lancaster.'   The first verse of
a young man is usually more retrospective than that
of his elders.    We know that ' Pope was sexagenary
at sixteen,' and how those innocent dreaming lads the
'Two Brothers' wrote of 'Memory! dear Enchanter!'
in their Lincolnshire garden.    But in so naming his
poems, 'William Lancaster' did not merely follow the
law 'that nearly all young poets should write old,' but
thus indeed divulged at once one of the permanent
characteristics of his muse.    The melancholy of the
Greek poets had already entered into his soul, and
that sad wind which blows out of the past into the
present was to make an undertone in all his verses.
*Praeterita* also bore more open witness to the bent
of its writer's mind in the short blank verse studies
*Minos, Semele*, and *Philoctetes*.    It is significant of
the maturing laborious artist that Lord de Tabley made
no use of the latter in his later drama.    A study of
Saul indicated too the writer's interest in the dramatic
possibilities of Hebrew history, which was afterwards
to express itself in his tremendous figures of Nimrod
and Jael.    Though the dramatic element of Lord de
Tabley's talent was thus foreshadowed, the main
achievement of this first book was lyrical.    The influence of Tennyson was observable here and there,
perhaps most in the deliberate exactness of the charm-

ing nature sketches, and but little in the cadence of
the verse.   That was marked by a sweetness more
austere than Tennyson's, a winter rather than a summer
sweetness, the sweetness of 'winter's sometime smiles.'
A particularly happy use of stanzas with unrhymed tails
was characteristic of the lyrics :

> 'Light of love and cold of brain,
>   Shall I trust thy tears,
> Linking hand on hand again?
>   In untutored years,
>     Ah, but this was sweet.'

and again :

> 'Kiss and touch my hand, and part :
> Sighs are farewell of the heart.
> Dream a moment in thy joy,
>   Wake a world of years.'

And over and above particular qualities there was
a strongly marked general firmness of style.   There
was nothing glib or merely facile about the verse.   The
words, so to say, were not carried off their feet by the
rhythm, but moved to it with a sure tread.   The poet
was evidently a scholar as well as thinker, dreamer, and
lover.   This sureness of touch was evident in all the
operations of his talent.   He clearly possessed, or was
far on the way towards possessing, a firm hold of his
faculties.   There was no timidity in his writing, no
uncertainty in his vision, or obscurity in his thought.
He knew exactly what he had to say and how he wished
to say it.   This is, perhaps, the cardinal virtue of Lord
de Tabley's poetry.

   I have dwelt at some length on *Praeterita*, because of
its illustrating potentially, and to some extent actually,

its writer's principal characteristics.   It will suffice, with one exception, just to name the volumes which have succeeded it : *Eclogues and Monodramas*, 1864; *Studies in Verse*, 1865 ; *Philoctetes*, 1866 ; *Orestes*, 1867 ; *Rehearsals*, 1870 ; *Searching the Net*, 1873 ; *The Soldier of Fortune*, 1876.   In addition to these poems and dramas Lord de Tabley had written two novels : *A Screw Loose*, 1868 ; *Ropes of Sand*, 1869 ; the latter a title which one notices, as a coincidence, has been recently employed by Mr. Francillon.   In 1880 he also published his well-known *Guide to the Study of Book Plates*. All these books were published either under the pseudonym of 'William Lancaster,' or 'William P. Lancaster, M.A.,' or as 'by the Hon. John Leicester Warren.'   The beautiful, admirably representative, volume of selections, with some new poems, just issued, completes Lord de Tabley's bibliography.

With this volume before us it is only necessary to turn back for a few moments to *Philoctetes*, which remains Lord de Tabley's most ambitious achievement.

However one may regard the imitation of the Greek drama, one cannot but feel a certain admiration for the artistic heroism which prompts a modern poet to make so tremendous an essay.   To fail in great endeavours or to succeed in lesser ones, which is the better?   For my part I am with Phaethon.   It is something, after all, to have tried to drive the chariot of Phœbus.   The skill of the decorator is charming, but the courage of the architect is noble—and ever rarer.   And to compete against Sophocles !   Surely it is an essay worth failing in.   To compare Lord de Tabley's *Philoctetes* with that of Sophocles might not be all unprofitable, had one the necessary space ; for it is surprising with what inventive force the modern poet strikes out a new grouping of the old figures, and, indeed, an appreciably original characterisation of his hero, making him somewhat less of a whiner and touching him with something of the impersonal sublimity of a Prometheus. It is more proportionate to compare it with the classical work of Mr. Swinburne and Matthew Arnold. Set against *Merope*, there can be little question of its superior vitality. It lives all through, as *Merope* scarcely breathes. Comparing it with *Atalanta* as poetry, one feels at once Mr. Swinburne's marked pre-eminence ; but as drama I am inclined to think that the advantage is with Lord de Tabley. There are noble choruses in *Philoctetes*, but it would be idle to claim for them the pomp and magic of those in *Atalanta*. On the other hand, *Philoctetes*, as drama, has, I think, more of the statuesque severity of the antique than *Atalanta*.

I wish I might pause here to make an extract from it, the narrative of the death of Heracles as related by Philoctetes, an episode which Lord de Tabley reprinted separately in one of his later volumes, but which I am disappointed to find that he has omitted from his new selections. A more strenuous piece of naked narrative, tense and clean as a racer's muscles, one could hardly find in any modern poet. The reader may seek it either in its place in *Philoctetes* or extracted in the volume *Rehearsals*.

I will here quote instead a portion of the 'Zeus' chorus from *Orestes*—a drama which, I think, surpasses

*Philoctetes* as poetry, though it falls much beneath it as drama—which I am glad to find in the new volume :

> ' Let us go up and look him in the face—
> We are but as he made us ; the disgrace
> Of this, our imperfection, is his own—
> And unabashed in that fierce glare and blaze
> Front him and say,
> " We come not to atone,
> To cringe and moan :
> God, vindicate thy way.
> Erase the staining sorrow we have known,
> Thou, whom ill things obey ;
> And give our clay
> Some master bliss imperial as thine own :
> Or wipe us quite away,
> Far from the ray of thine eternal throne.
> Dream not we love this sorrow of our breath,
> Hope not we wince or palpitate at death ;
> Slay us, for thine is nature and thy slave :
> Draw down her clouds to be our sacrifice,
> And heap unmeasured mountain for our grave,
> With peaks of fire and ice.
> Flicker one cord of lightning, north to south,
> And mix in awful glories wood and cloud ;
> We shall have rest, and find
> Illimitable darkness for our shroud ;
> We shall have peace, then, surely, when thy mouth
> Breathes us away into the darkness blind,
> Then only kind." '

Here is the true iron in the voice, the genuine bass which cannot be imitated, and comes naturally or not at all. Strength without strain is, then, the characteristic of Lord de Tabley's poetry which arrests us first. He has authority. He is an architect. Along with his strength we soon find the sweetness and fecundity of strength. He is austere, not from poverty of nature, but from control of his wealth. He can, when he

chooses, delight us with efflorescence, charm us with
variety of curious ornament, and pour out his fancies
like a prodigal.  He is strikingly rich in invention—a
rare gift nowadays.  As a contrast to the stern beauty
of the passage just quoted, let the reader find that
voluptuous, wizard description of Circe's chamber, sur-
charged with colour and perfume, and stiff like a
tapestry with brilliant pre-Raphaelitism of detail.  If
not precisely pre-Raphaelitism, a striking exactness of
detail and rare firmness of realisation are characteristic
of all Lord de Tabley's work.  It is especially noticeable
in the charming nature pictures to which I have
referred, and in these verses from his most important
new poem, a finely sustained 'Hymn to Astarte':

> 'What foreland fledged with myrrh,
>    Vocal with myriad bees,
> What pine-sequestered spur,
>    What lone declivities,
>       Will draw thee to descend,
>       Creation's cradle-friend?
>
> The sun feeds at thy smiles,
>    The wan moon glows thereby.
> The dædal ocean isles
>    Terraced in rosemary,
>       The brushwood in the bed
>       Of the dry torrent head,
>
> The rolling river brink
>    With plumy sedges grey,
> The ford where foxes drink,
>    The creek where otters play—
>       Yearn upwards—all of them—
>       To grasp thy raiment's hem.'

Lord de Tabley has evidently been no less minute an

observer of nature than Lord Tennyson or Mr. George Meredith.

In his dramatic studies the same absolute vision impresses us. His imaginative hold upon his theme in such a poem as ' Jael,' for example, is almost grim. We seem to be looking right into the tragic eyes of the strong melancholy woman. We seem to see as clearly as in a picture that one drop of pallid blood steal 'out of his forehead underneath the nail.'

Quotation, short of complete poems, would convey but an imperfect idea of Lord de Tabley's finest work —the beauty and tragic strength of ' Phaethon,' the moonlike glamour of ' Daphne,' the stern passion of ' Nimrod,' the rich earthiness of the ' Ode to Pan.' It would be like bringing an inch of marble as a sample of the beauty of some Greek statue.

THE vengeance of his enemies would seem to have
*Ben Jonson :* pursued Ben Jonson even beyond the
Dr. Grosart's grave. There is, perhaps, no other in-
' Selections.' stance in literature of so great a poet so
shabbily treated by posterity. It is true that *Every Man in His Humour* held the stage till well into the present century (being revived by Dickens in 1845), but, of course, the stage is no real test of poetical fame, and the fact that Jonson is so little read is of more signifi-cance. The legend would still seem to hold that his

works are a mass of classical adaptations and allusions, stiff in movement, devoid of natural magic; that his characters are mere types of 'humours,' lacking the warm blood of humanity; that his lyrics are merely stiff-jointed elaborations of art, ingenuities of mechanism such as those hollow earthenware birds which warble when filled with water, rather than the real birds of the wood.

Of course, there is a certain measure of truth in these objections, though it is equally undeniable that in no few of Jonson's lyrics did he snatch a grace beyond the reach of art, and that his figures often live with the true inspiration of humanity. Besides, of the vast fertility of invention shown in the plots alone of so large a body of plays, of the inexhaustibility of fancy displayed in his masques, of the almost Balzacian observation of the manners of the time—we hear nothing of all these and other qualities which make those nine volumes of Gifford's edition one of the richest mines in the whole of our literature. It has, indeed, been a mine which has done no little to enrich the treasure of other poets. Milton surely owed much to Ben Jonson, and Herrick might be said to be a rib taken out of his side. He certainly represents the lyrical side of Ben Jonson's gift carried to more unfailing perfection; he might be almost accurately regarded as the reincarnation of Ben Jonson's lyrical faculty. Whatever learning Herrick had was mainly derived from Jonson, and his serious themes were Jonson's frivolities, his 'underwoods' as he would call them. It is perhaps not very generally known how much one of Herrick's most exquisite and famous lyrics owes to Jonson; that ' Nightpiece to Julia,' beginning

> ' Her eyes the glow-worm lend thee,
> The shooting stars attend thee ;
>     And the elves also,
>     Whose little eyes glow,
> Like the sparks of fire, befriend thee.'

In a masque entitled 'The Gipsies Metamorphosed,' Ben Jonson has the following :

> 'The faery beam upon you,
> The stars to glisten on you ;
>     A moon of light,
>     In the noon of night,
> Till the fire-drake hath o'er-gone you !
> The wheel of fortune guide you,
> The boy with the bow beside you ;
>     Run aye in the way,
>     Till the bird of day,
> And the luckier lot betide you.'

One of the first charms of Herrick's poem is the delightful metre, and that we see is not to his credit but to Ben Jonson's. In actual beauty of fancy Jonson's is little inferior to Herrick's, the first four lines at least are equal to Herrick's, and it is really only in that allusion to the ' fire-drake,' one of those characteristic clumsinesses of a learning not always assimilated by his genius, that his touch is at fault.

To the frequent nobility of Jonson's blank verse, this fine panegyric of poetry from the original version of *Every Man in His Humour* will bear witness :

> ' Indeed if you will look on poesy
> As she appears to many, poor and lame,
> Patched up in remnants and old worn-out rags,
> Half-starved for want of her peculiar food,

> Sacred invention ; then I must confirm
> Both your conceit and censure of her merit ;
> But view her in her glorious ornaments,
> Attired in the majesty of art,
> Set high in spirit with the precious taste
> Of sweet philosophy ; and which is most,
> Crowned with the rich tradition of a soul,
> That hates to have her dignity profaned
> With any relish of an earthly thought,
> O, then, how proud a presence doth she bear ! '

As we read such lines as these we realise that Jonson did not receive that epithet 'rare' for nothing. 'O Rare Ben Jonson !'—the reader will remember is his only epitaph in the Abbey. How he came by it is a pretty story. 'His friends,' said Gifford, 'designed to raise a noble monument to his memory, by subscription, and till this was ready nothing more was required than to cover his ashes decently with the stone which had been removed. While this was doing, Aubrey tells us, Sir John Young, of Great Milton, Oxfordshire, whom he familiarly calls Jack Young, chanced to pass through the Abbey, and, not enduring that the remains of so great a man should lie at all without a memorial, gave one of the workmen eighteenpence to cut the words in question. The subscription was fully successful ; but the troubles which were hourly becoming more serious and which long after broke out into open rebellion, prevented the execution of the monument, and the money was returned to the subscribers.'

Thus that charming impromptu of a country gentleman remained his only epitaph, and indeed for those who love him no man's fame sounds more sweetly in four words than Jonson's in that simple—'O Rare Ben Jonson !'

There was, of course, another monument to his fame in a volume of elegies composed by thirty or forty of his poet friends, that *Jonsonus Virbius* which should be one of the best answers to his detractors, one of the most generous tributes to a dead poet ever made. We have in our own day seen such another tribute in *Le Tombeau de Théophile Gautier*, in which Mr. Swinburne mourned in several languages. Among the many fine panegyrics in the *Jonsonus Virbius* these lines of Cleveland, one of Jonson's most promising and best loved 'sons,' may themselves be said to be famous :

> ' The Muses' fairest light in no dark time ;
> The wonder of a learned age ; the line
> Which none can pass ; the most proportion'd wit,
> To nature, the best judge of what was fit ;
> The deepest, plainest, highest, clearest pen
> The voice most echo'd by consenting men ;
> The soul which answer'd best to all well said
> By others, and which most requital made.'

There could be no finer answer to those who carp at Jonson's indebtedness, or that of any other great poet, to other writers, than those last two lines.

DOUBTLESS, I am far from being the only one of Mr.

*Rudyard Kipling : ' Many Inventions*

Kipling's readers who, with every new collection of his stories, makes first for the little chapter-heads of vivid, tantalising verse. They are not infrequently better than the stories they preface, and, doubtless, if Mr. Kipling were called upon, like Rousseau, to face the judgment-seat with one of his books in his hand, he would be well advised to choose the *Barrack-room Ballads*. In *Many Inventions* he treats us to two whole poems by way of prologue and epilogue—a hint he perhaps first learned from Mr. Buchanan. The first is one of those almost religious celebrations of the art of the story-teller which are apt to ring a little melodramatic, though in the case of 'Soldiers Three' there was a piquancy in the apparent contrast between the artist's material, his 'clay figures,' as he termed them, and his exalted religious way of regarding them. Mr. Kipling thus drawing back from his clay statuettes, with all the solemnity of the Creator resting on the seventh day, was a lesson in artistic seriousness. His prologue to *Many Inventions*, a kind of prayer to the spirit of *True Romance*, is hardly so convincing. The poem belongs to the same order of cheap mystical verse as that memorable prologue to *The Barrack-room Ballads*, originally written, the reader may remember, as a satire on the injunction against the Rabelais pictures, and afterwards lovingly adapted to the memory of Mr. Kipling's dear friend, Mr. Balestier. For Romance to be addressed in capitals like the Deity is at least confusing.

More to one's taste is the vigorous sea-ballad with which Mr. Kipling concludes his volume. It is far too technical. Whole verses are thus incomprehensible; but one 'puts up' with that for the catching rhythm and some of those almost brutally forcible imaginative phrases, which were perhaps more conspicuous in 'The Ballad of the Bolivar' than in any other of Mr. Kipling's

poems. The first verse illustrates both the faults and
the charm of Mr. Kipling's method :

'Heh! Walk her round. Heave, ah, heave her short again!
  Over, snatch her over, there, and hold her on the pawl.
  Loose all sail, and brace your yards aback and full—
  Ready jib to pay her off and heave short all!
Well, ah, fare you well; we can stay no more with you, my
    love—
Down, set down your liquor and your girl from off your
    knee;
  For the wind has come to say :
  " You must take me while you may,
If you'd go to Mother Carey where she feeds her chicks at
    sea!"

Here is another fine version of the chorus :

'Well, ah, fare you well, for the Channel wind's took hold
    of us,
  Choking down our voices as we snatch the gaskets free.
      And it's blowing up for night,
      And she's dropping Light on Light,
  And she's snorting under bonnets for a breath of open sea.'

And I am afraid I cannot resist quoting the whole of
the last verse :

'Wheel, full and by; but she'll smell her road alone to-night.
  Sick she is and harbour-sick—O sick to clear the land!
  Roll down to Brest with the old Red Ensign over us—
  Carry on and thrash her out with all she'll stand!
Well, ah, fare you well, and it's Ushant gives the door to us,
Whirling like a windmill on the dirty sand to lea :
    Till the last, last flicker goes
    From the tumbling water-rows,
And we're off to Mother Carey
(Walk her down to Mother Carey!)
Oh, we're bound for Mother Carey where she feeds her chicks
    at sea!'

It would seem that Mr. Kipling has it in his power to be laureate of Jack Tar as well as 'T. A.' Naturally all strong vivid life appeals to him. It is to be hoped he will some day give us a volume of 'Fo'c's'le Ballads.' It is curious that among all the talk concerning the laureateship a little while ago, Mr. Kipling was so seldom mentioned. Yet he has struck the most manfully national note of any recent poet. Though many have essayed to be Tyrtaeus, their eye was so manifestly on the wreath that they failed to convince us of their sincerity. There is more of the true fire of patriotism in one line of Mr. Kipling than in all their frigid complimentary odes to the British Lion.

But I am saying nothing of the stories. Most, if not all, of them are already known to the readers of the magazines. 'Badalia Herodsfoot' meets us again ; also that unhappy 'Brugglesmith,' the kind of thing a clever young man writes when he thinks he has the public under his thumb — a dangerous plan. 'The Finest Story in the World'—a description which unfortunately does not apply to Mr. Kipling's story — turns up once more. There is, too, a story, or rather, an allegory, entitled 'The Children of the Zodiac,' an exercise in that cheap mysticism above referred to, in *genre* somewhat between Miss Olive Schreiner's *Dreams* and a 'fantasia' by a new humourist—though not unrelieved by touches of imagination, whenever Mr. Kipling approaches the concrete. 'Judson and the Empire' is an attempt at extravaganza which hardly comes off. The best story in the book, to my thinking, is 'The Disturber of Traffic.' Mr. Kipling would seem to

think well of it himself, as he opens his book with it.
It is the story of a lighthouse man on a lonely station
in the Southern seas, who gradually goes mad with
having nothing to look at day by day but the wavy
lines of the sea in front of him, no one to speak to
but an amphibious creature, half man and half seal,
'an Orang-Lant, what they call a sea gipsy,' with skin
in little flakes and cracks all over from living so much
in the salt water, and 'webby-foot' hands—not 'a com-
panionable man, like you and me might have been
to Dowse,' adds the narrator.  Oppressed with the
eternal wavy lines of the sea, Dowse gets it into his
poor head that it is the ships passing through the
strait that makes the water so 'streaky.'  So he sets
to work on a brilliant idea to stop the inconvenience,
throwing a line of wreck-buoys across the neck of the
strait.  This, for a time, frightens the troublesome ships
away, but presently comes a man-of-war on survey, not
to be frightened.  'You leave me alone and I'll leave
you alone,' cries Dowse to the boat's crew, come ashore
to make inquiries.  'Go round by the Ombay Passage,
and don't cut up my water.  You're making it streaky.'
He is persuaded to go off and see the captain.  On
the way he addresses the sailors as 'white mice with
chains about their necks,' and speaks to the captain
in nursery rhymes.  Going forward, he catches a reflection of himself in the binnacle brasses, 'and he saw
that he was standing there and talking mother-naked
in front of all them sailors, and he ran into the fo'c's'le
howling most grievous.'  This climax is very skilfully introduced, coming, as it does with a similar shock

upon the reader as upon poor Dowse himself. 'The Story of the Beast,' in its uncanny power, reminds one of 'The Mark of the Beast.' It is hardly less creepy, but less disagreeable. There are two or three fine Mulvaney and Ortheris stories, 'My Lord the Elephant,' 'His Private Honour,' and 'Love o' Women,' each of which is worthy of the prestige of those heroes. 'Love o' Women' is marked by Mr. Kipling's rare touches of tenderness. One must not forget to mention 'A Conference of the Powers,' that dialogue in which the point of view of the despised dainty-handed civilian—in the person of a supposed distinguished novelist—is skilfully contrasted with that of the man of battle—represented by three young soldiers just back from active service in Burma. 'You! Have you shot a man?' asks the half-affrighted novelist of one of the beardless boys, 'and have *you*, too?' 'Think so,' said Nevin sweetly. Before the night is out the crestfallen novelist begins to suspect that his own trade, as Michael Angelo said of oil-painting, is only fit for women and boys. That is apparently Mr. Kipling's own point of view, though, with the inconsistency of all chanters of the sword, he still sticks to the pen—and he always manages to make his readers feel like that novelist, that we peaceable stay-at-homes are poor milk-and-water creatures, and that there is nothing in the world worth doing save slicing and 'potting' your fellow-creatures. His blood-thirstiness is an affectation which still clings to him, and his memory for technicalities, to which he owes much of his force, is in danger of overgrowing his art. But, all deductions made, the new volume is quite worthy of its famous forerunners.   The tremendous verve, the grasp and fertility of Mr. Kipling's gift, is as wonderful as ever

THERE could hardly be a greater shock of contrast
*Henry James:* than to pass from Mr. Kipling to Mr.
'The Private Henry James.   It is like passing from
Life.'   a swarming world of tropical sunshine
into some dim-lighted Hades, peopled with low-voiced
aristocratic shades.   It takes us some time to realise
that we are still dealing with flesh and blood.   And
I confess that Mr. James's *dramatis personæ* grow
too shadowy for me, their drama too imperceptibly
refined, and the real pleasure I find in Mr. James's
more recent books is that of the style—when it also
is not too pedantically wire-drawn.   Some of the char-
acterisations in *The Private Life* and other stories are
very happy.   A lady in perpetual mourning had been
described as 'the queen of night,' and Mr. James adds,
'the term was descriptive if you understood that the
night was cloudy.'   She was also 'rather submissively
sad.   She was like a woman with a painless malady.

END OF VOL. I.

Printed by T. and A. Constable, Printers to Her Majesty
at the Edinburgh University Press